SAVAGES

INFANTRY CULTURE IN THE GLOBAL WAR ON TERROR

ST BLACKWELL

SAVAGES

Infantry Culture in the Global War on Terror

Copyright © 2023 by ST Blackwell

First Edition

Cover design by Cindy Caulfield

Published by Tactical 16 Publishing

Colorado Springs, Colorado

www.Tactical16.com

ISBN: 978-1-943226-85-6 (paperback)

Praise for SAVAGES

"Fast-paced read about the hardships and lessons learned about becoming a Marine, and life on and off the battlefield."

–Gerry Fredo, Personal Coach

"Savages is a rare, raw, and unapologetic window into the ethos of an enlisted Marine infantryman serving in the height of the Global War on Terror. As the largest conflict in over 75 years rages on the European continent and tensions mount in the Taiwan Strait, we are reminded that the age of conventional, large-scale, ground combat between peer nations is far from over."

–Business Leader, former Marine Infantry Officer and Instructor

Contents

Introduction

Whether you picked this book up in a store, ordered it online, or just happened to stumble across it, thank you for your interest. There are a plethora of veteran written accounts concerning the War on Terror, so what makes this one any different? Why should you devote your time- the one thing we can never get back- to this?

This book is the product of seven years' labor towards something that can provide a fresh perspective on America's most recent wars. It pointedly states our legacy as fighting men in the Global War on Terror and shows the unique culture that we built during that time. That culture was established on the values of discipline, toughness, selflessness, lethality, proficiency, and example. The pages that follow are littered with examples of each.

It is that set of core values that I turned to, after my time in uniform, to continue developing and that is a very important aspect of who we are. Ultimately, we will be remembered not only for the conduct and result of the war, but also for our contribution to society in its aftermath.

Previous generations didn't have the means to affect how they were remembered as quickly as we do. Veterans of past campaigns were limited by technology whereas we are propelled by it. Today anyone can post online in a matter of seconds, what would've taken years to produce half a century ago. We have the means and opportunity to tell the stories that impact how we are remembered with immediacy. And I would argue that we have a responsibility to do so.

Since I started writing this, Russia shocked the world with its invasion of Ukraine and China has grown increasingly aggressive towards Taiwan. The need for capable warriors has never been greater and understanding what it takes to make them is in these pages.

I believe in this work and what it represents. I have endeavored to portray my experiences, as a Marine infantryman, in the most emotionally vulnerable and visceral manner possible. Contrary to much of what it is currently on the shelves, it will challenge you to view the campaigns as more than failed efforts to spread democracy, protect civilians, or nation build. For us, the War on Terror was our opportunity to pursue another way of life. It served as the arena for us to prove our mettle in and define ourselves as a small portion of our generation who wanted more out of life and fought for it.

From 2007 until 2016, this experience showed me that there *is* good that comes from war and the preparation for it. The personal development that occurs in the profession of arms is unmatched due to the urgency that comes with an environment dominated by mortal consequence. And as painful as many of the experiences were, they shaped me into a better man, husband, and father.

This journey, that transformed me from a young, idealistic man into a veteran, fully immerses you in the culture that made all of it possible. It identifies inaccurate assumptions of the armed forces and challenges the view that all servicemembers are the same in ability, capacity, and contribution to the War on Terror. In essence, the cultural state of the services more closely resembles a conglomeration of tribes instead of one large group.

This book is not meant to degrade the commitment, bravery, or performance of others. It is not meant to destroy reputations or angrily place blame and it is not a chronicle of personal achievement meant to garner glory or attention. Rather, it examines this culture through my perspective, focusing on the great men that animated it and altered my trajectory as a human being.

As strong as the bond is between Grunts across time and space, experiences still vary to a degree, and I do not have the right to chain every infantryman to my personal views.

I have replaced every name of those that I served with and fought alongside, excluding myself and our Fallen, with a pseudonym to respect their privacy. Other names such as elected officials, senior military personnel, and various authors have remained for the sake of accuracy. Collective terms such as *we* and *us* are in specific reference to men that I served with who share the same views.

The story begins in 2016, after my time in uniform. A critical self-examination of that stage of my life prompts the reflection of my service and leads us to where I am now, writing the next chapter of my life. I had to dig into the past in order to come full circle and move forward.

I am fortunate enough to have been a part of something much greater than myself. It is my sincere hope that this book can present an accurate picture of the infantry and clearly identify what our legacy should be. We are not protectors or liberators but warriors. And I hope that much is clear after you complete this journey with me.

Chapter 1

Disconnect

I sat in a small, crowded training room on the second floor of a corporate office building staring at a whiteboard. There was a middle-aged human resources employee next to it that alternated between barely legible scribbles on the surface and regurgitating information from a nearby laptop to pass us the required material. As she droned on, I shifted my sight to the other participants that were seated around the same wooden table as I was, most of whom were listening intently. Constantly adjusting my focus kept me from falling asleep.

Company-mandated training always seemed to have a numbing effect. Having spent the previous near decade in the Infantry, I found no value in it. I felt like I was being desensitized to a much softer way of thinking.

I had been with the company for a year and sessions like this were quite regular and predictable. There was no study of leadership qualities, tactics, or communication; no critical information concerning a capable enemy that I could harness and use to my advantage. It was bland and tasteless. The little knowledge and experience I had gained over the previous year with the company already invalidated much of what was being peddled. Occasionally, I felt a spark of anger at this dull material, which consisted of listing out random concepts such as loyalty, leadership, vision, and the like that had no connection to one another in this environment. My pessimism reminded me that, on the bright side, I hadn't been completely assimilated yet.

As I sat there, scanning the white walls and the other faces for signs of similar frustration, I couldn't help but wonder what I was doing with my life and how I had ended up here.

I was a wanderer of sorts, a stranger in the strange land that was "home," after having spent years of my life in the sand and mud, freezing and sweating in countries all over the globe and experiencing life in a way that no one sitting in this room could relate to. Those experiences shaped the way that I viewed everything so drastically that I could not understand the people around me, and I didn't want to accept a mentality that wasn't shaped by those trials.

The separation was undeniable, and it seemed that connecting to anyone without similar significant life experiences was impossible.

Most days, these emotions would spike and converge in a mental maelstrom of searing rage, ultimately ending in the disappointing realization that this was my life now. The pattern was an extreme internal ebb and flow.

I snapped back to the present as the training session mercifully progressed to its closing moments.

Usually, I gathered my things and sought the nearest exit as quickly as possible. The last thing I wanted was to get caught in a worthless with someone who couldn't or didn't care to understand who I was.

Today, however, was a little different. The group was a hodgepodge of employees from different shifts and locations. For the last three agonizing hours I had been sitting across the dark wooden conference table from two Human Resources workers who appeared to be addicted to the company Kool-Aid. The same seemed to be true for the fresh crop of newly hired managers who were hearing all of this for the first time.

The dark sense of humor I had developed in the infantry produced a mental playlist of visuals like Buffalo Bill from *Silence of the Lambs* screaming his mantra, "It puts the lotion in the basket! It does what it's told!" It was my subconscious reminder to simply do my job, not rock the boat, and just earn my pay quietly.

But I just couldn't resist the opportunity that lay in front of me. I decided to break away from my self-imposed isolation and ask a question.

I flagged down one of the HR women and asked, "Why do employees actually quit this job?" I asked.

"Typically, it's because of their leadership." she replied.

I stood there for a moment, hoping she would elaborate, and then stepped away to get my fourth cup of free coffee which was the only good thing about the small gatherings. *"Leadership? It's bull shit that that term is even used here,"* I thought.

I turned back to the woman and asked, "And what about managers, why do we usually quit?"

"I don't know. That's a good question." She hesitated and turned to her peer for the assist.

"They usually quit because they think there's something better out there," came the answer. "But they usually come back once they realize that there isn't."

I gave a small nod of understanding and stirred ridiculous amounts of sugar and non-dairy creamer into my small Styrofoam cup. Then she asked, "Are you going to quit?"

"Absolutely." I said, "The second that my kids go to school and my wife can find a career, I'm moving on."

"But why?!" they both asked, shocked.

I went on to explain in a very well-practiced and watered-down manner that I don't think that my personality and attributes were suited for this type of environment. Their looks of pity evolved to a sympathetic expression that conveyed mild discomfort. Another employee a few seats down to my left chimed in. "Are you military?"

I replied positively and observed the shift in their body language. Coupled with their facial expressions, they portrayed the general attitude of having heard the conversation before and I had to remind myself to hold my disgust inside.

I hated, absolutely hated, being generalized like this. Last year had shown me that the term "military" was the common standard of blanket classification. To everyone else, we were all the same. The concept of how the services were organized or the differences in function, occupational specialty, and culture weren't even an afterthought, it seemed.

Briefly, I debated if this was the right moment to shatter that stereotype and ran through the conversation in my head, completely drowning out my coworkers' dialogue.

Think of it like this: if you stood at twentieth floor window overlooking a busy, rain drenched city avenue during the morning rush hours, what would catch your eye? More than likely, you would see the sea of umbrellas bobbing and swaying as they shield their carriers on the way to their destinations. But what about what's underneath? Would you notice specific individuals under those umbrellas? Would it be accurate to assume that every one is the exact same as the person next to them? Of course, not. They wear different clothing. They carry different objects. They go to very different workplaces. But the view, twenty floors up, shields those differences.

I subconsciously nodded to shield my detachment as continued my internal monologue.

It was 2017 and America had been fighting the War on Terror for the better part of two decades. One would think that meant a lot of combat veterans returning to the States but that's just not how this war had turned out. People knew so little about who was fighting because so few of us went in the first place.

On the one hand I understood. Generalizing was simple and didn't require deep thought. On the other hand, it was simply unfathomable that any war could go on for this long without most Americans gaining a deeper understanding us and the war.

I pulled myself back into the moment and exchanged the typical pleasantries before we all went our separate ways.

Over the next few months, I tested the waters with my peers and supervisors, intently trying to understand the collective mentality. It showed me that people weren't narrow-minded, loathsome, or condescending. They were just preoccupied with living their own lives.

Most combat veterans hadn't come forward with their stories, which only contributed to the growing divide. I was one of them. Most people subconsciously shaped their view on us and the war around Hollywood war films, or worse, the good word of politicians and service heads.

Six months after my conversation with the HR people, I left the company. And they were right. I did think that there was something better out there. My search for that took me back overseas to Afghanistan as a contractor and I couldn't help but laugh at the irony of ending up here, again, of all places.

I had committed myself to writing something that would help shape our legacy as a fighting generation and I threw myself into it, full force. If that was the goal, then I knew I would have to start at the beginning and explain just how different it was during our era of war.

Chapter 2

The Pursuit Of Purpose

True and meaningful purpose is what drives everyone. To one person it could be the pursuit of wealth or a career that pushes them to excel. To another that purpose could be found in raising a family. For many of us who chose the infantry, it was the aspiration to something life altering that attracted us to a world filled with adventure, danger, and privation; something outside the norm that could be worthy of remembrance. Consider the reason why a normal, sane, healthy individual would willingly sign a contract that carries with it the potential to die or be permanently maimed. Without the promise of something more than the mundane and typical existence, they wouldn't.

There are other factors that attracted us to such a life, factors like a sense of idealism, patriotism, and legacy. There are some young eighteen-year-olds who show up at a recruiting station on their birthday, ready to sign and leave on the next bus, that have a mind teeming with notions of nobility and the possibility of humble and great achievement. Others simply have no idea what to do once they get out on their own.

The patriot has a deep-seated moral obligation to serve his nation that has been ingrained in his character from a young age. The legacy has grown up observing the effects of such a life on parents or siblings and feels a responsibility to live up to the example of those prominent figures. But purpose, and the journey to discover one's purpose, is the "why" that brought us to the table.

The actual realization of this goal isn't something that comes overnight. There is no grand revelation that jumps out of nowhere and hits you like a kick in the nuts or jars you from sleep one random night. It is a gradual and evolving realization that comes through self-examination. Purpose—once recognized—will result in commitment, not motivation which is a temporary emotional response to overcome a specific obstacle. Commitment lasts a lifetime.

I could've been classified as all the above. My grandfather had served in the Navy during the Korean War and my parents had instilled a deep sense of patriotism in me and my siblings as far back as I can remember.

In middle school, I watched my older brother, Phillip, build himself into a one-man wrecking crew on a varsity football team. I spent days after class waiting in the weight room for him to finish his workouts before we went home. After his team won two state championships, those days served as a reminder to me that hard work was the key to achieving success.

Our parents worked faithfully and diligently to provide us with an amazing living. Our grandparents provided that for them. I've never had to look hard to find an example of strong work ethic in my life.

After my brother graduated, I started getting into trouble at school. It was a private institution with a hefty tuition fee that naturally attracted wealthy families from the surrounding cities. My classmates never hesitated to point out how out of place our family was because our parents had to work hard to keep us in the school. I thought the best way to respond was to hit them, which got me removed quickly.

I bounced from one school to another until I found a healthy outlet for my aggression in my freshman year of high school: wrestling. I lived for it. Our coach was an old Army vet that didn't divulge much about his service but carried himself in a markedly different manner and required us to do the same.

Having observed my older brother, before he went on to play college football, I took advantage of every opportunity to put in additional work. We remained close after he graduated, despite our separation. Yet regardless of how hard I pushed and how diligently I worked, my efforts never translated to success in competition. In hindsight, wrestling was a necessary and socially acceptable emotional outlet for me.

During my sophomore year, my brother cut his football career short and enlisted in the U.S. Marine Corps Reserves. While I loved watching him play ball and was fascinated with his journey of success, it became very clear that this was the right decision for him. Three months later, he had become a Marine and our parents took me to Parris Island, South Carolina to see his graduation ceremony. I was awed by nearly everything I saw, from the ceremony itself to the barely adequate facilities and the no nonsense drill instructors.

The greatest part of it was seeing the monumental change that had occurred in Phillip. Once the die-hard college athlete, the man I saw on "the island" was a disciplined professional. It was as if they had reached into his core and pulled out the very best part of him. Observing his bearing and discipline as we walked the grounds together, he showed me that there was a way to continue the pursuit of greatness after high school; that I could make myself into something more through hard work and sacrifice. That experience occurred at a pivotal time in my life when I was grappling with my athletic frustrations and beginning to wonder what I was going to do with my life. It planted the seed that would grow into my decision to enlist.

As my senior year rolled around, I visited a few colleges with my wrestling buddies and weighed my options. The collegiate scene just didn't appeal to me the way it had in years past, even with the possibility of continuing to wrestle. I wanted that something more that I had seen in Phillip.

On top of that, combat was nearly guaranteed if I signed up with the infantry. My brother had explained to me that there was a massive difference between the infantry and everyone else. All the other jobs that the Corps offered were meant solely to support the grunt on the ground. He explained that grunts carried themselves differently because they had a different culture that amplified the Marine Corp's tenets and added to them. It was more than just earning a title at one of the recruit depots. It was a lifestyle that valued toughness, selflessness, and collective hardship in the pursuit of strengthening the whole. In a way he was preparing me for the reality that while becoming a Marine is a truly great achievement, for the infantry the real journey begins after that. And it only gets harder.

So, if I signed up as a supply bubba or an administrative type and passed recruit training, I'd be a Marine, but I wouldn't be in that inner circle that lived on the edge. I wanted to be in the action, not just on the outside of it or to miss it all together. The "action" at this point in the War on Terror, meant either Iraq or Afghanistan and the Marines had seen heavy combat in both theaters.

The prospect of going to war played a huge part in my decision to enlist. Our parents had raised us to revere combat veterans and understand that while we cannot relate to their experiences, we must respect the hardships they endured. As the decision confronted me, I viewed it through a competitive lens. Fighting in the war would serve as validation for the training and I wanted that test. I craved that moment when I could look back on my life and realize that I had struggled so mightily for something and succeeded. On top of that, the opportunity to fight in a war may only come once in a lifetime. If I passed on it, I'd regret not accepting the challenge. Would a star athlete train and work tirelessly day in and day out only to sit on the sidelines during the championship game? Absolutely not. So why would I do this if I wasn't going to go full speed ahead?

I wasn't going to hold anything back. It was all or nothing. I was going to find out who I really was and what I was truly capable of or fail spectacularly in the process. So, I made my decision to sign the contract with Uncle Sam and the Marine Corps.

Not wanting to let my older brother outdo me, who was with me throughout the entire recruiting process, I went all in for four years of active duty in the infantry. It worked out nicely because Phillip would receive points towards a promotion for helping recruit me and I would get the opportunity I had been searching for. I felt that I had a decent idea of what I was getting myself into.

My brother hadn't held anything back about his time at Parris Island, so I understood more than most about the training and discipline that were waiting for me there. He told me that the best thing to do was not quit and pass everything the first time. If I failed anything it would be harder to pass the second time around. On top of that, the Marines didn't become one of the most feared and respected forces by just letting anybody through. They kicked recruits out that couldn't pass any training requirement. If I failed, I'd be right back here, and I knew I'd never be able to look him in the eye if I didn't earn the title of Marine.

After we left the recruiter's office, Phillip and I parted ways with our father, who was beaming with pride, and went back to his apartment to celebrate with his roommate who was also a Marine. When we arrived, he tossed us each a beer and wryly told Phillip that he had a special place in hell reserved for profiting from my inevitable misery.

In July of 2007, I came back to Parris Island, this time as a recruit. For the past two months, since I had signed the contract, I had been expecting a first-person rendition of Stanley Kubrick's *Full Metal Jacket* and wasn't entirely disappointed. The squad bays we were housed in were just as I remembered them: long concrete hallways divided into three sections. The middle third was denoted by black paint running the length of the bay, known as the highway. It was flanked on both sides by a row of evenly spaced pillars. Perfectly aligned with the outward edge of these were rows of old metal bunk beds, followed a small gap in between them and the outer walls that framed a few small windows.

Every recruit in our eighty-man platoon was lined up facing the highway with our heels touching the black line as our drill instructors were introduced. Mayhem ensued as soon as the commanding officer left, and the door shut behind him. I found myself dumping all the items that I had been issued in the previous twenty-four hours onto the concrete floor as our instructors screamed for us to find specific items.

As I rifled through the scattered contents, other recruits were sent flying into the metal bed frames or doubled over from hits to the ribs. The tone was set- if you don't move fast enough or fail to fulfill an order in any way, corrections would be immediate and painful.

The drill instructors never spoke. They screamed with a shrill and harsh tone that sounded like banshee and sent chills up the spine. With every order they gave, they began counting down from a random number faster than any human being is supposed to be able to count-always at maximum volume. If you weren't where you were supposed to be with the gear you were ordered to have standing in the exact position expected, discipline followed immediately. And didn't stop for the entire time we were there.

Everything was regulated, from the way we stood at attention to the volume and intensity of our voices and the words we used to reply to a command. There were consequences for every single infraction, regardless of how small or seemingly arbitrary. For example, when standing at attention, if your hands were not closed with the length of the thumb pressed precisely against the seam of your trousers, a drill instructor would drive his knuckles into your metacarpals until it was fixed. Once or twice was enough to send the message to the entire outfit.

"Pain retains" was the motto screamed at us by our series gunnery sergeant, who handled a higher level of responsibility than our drill instructors. He seemed to appear out of nowhere and carried himself with more confidence than they did, which didn't seem possible until we saw it with our own eyes. Every other day, he led physical conditioning for the entire series, which consisted of our platoon and several others. He appeared at the time to be ten feet tall and three hundred pounds of solid muscle, but he moved like a man half his age. I didn't scare easily but this man was intimidating to put it lightly.

The clock laughed at us for the next three months as we neared graduation and more and more, we began to see nearly every time we got fucked up it was because we weren't working as a team. In this type of environment, with nowhere to hide, we figured out almost instantly who the weak links were—and there was no sympathy for them at all.

The preferred punishment was being sent to the quarter deck, which was a small square at the front of the bay reserved for recruits to be physically thrashed through a series of non-stop exercises with up to three or four drill instructors in their face the whole time. There were days where it was always occupied by some unfortunate recruit that couldn't move fast enough or respond to a command with enough intensity.

If we were moving around the base enroute to a classroom lecture or training event, the island had sand pits strategically placed that served as alternate venues for correction. They were far worse because of the fleas that infested them and latched on to you for hours after the activity. Scratching and swatting at the Island's infinite infestation was grounds to be sent to the quarter deck or thrown back into a sand pit.

There was no limit to how many times this could happen. Some days a recruit would get done paying the price of an infraction only to not run quickly enough from the quarter deck or sand pit and be sent straight back. Over time, the drill instructors started punishing other recruits for the mistakes of the ones who just weren't getting it which led to a few scrums that were immediately shut down.

We progressed through the various training events, such as the obstacle course, swim and rifle qualification, physical fitness test, and even written tests. The events had a remarkable way of thinning the ranks. Somebody always failed something and before we knew it, we were down to about sixty recruits in the platoon, with one final event left: the Crucible.

The Crucible was a four-day evolution away from the squad bays and classrooms. We had been out in the wilderness plenty before but only for a day at a time. This was designed to push us beyond everything we had experienced before. The end was so close that I could almost taste it. If I could just pass this last test, then it would be over, and I could go home with the pride of accomplishment. I would be a Marine. The only thing that stood in my way was the Crucible.

After nearly three months of training and being constantly tested, most of us relished the challenge. We had all been through too much to quit now. Most of the problem recruits had gotten their act together and visits to the quarter deck or sand pit were much fewer than in the previous months. We had a swagger about us in close order drill and carriage that was unique to us. It was that rare confidence that can only come from being tested repeatedly and succeeding under the most arduous of circumstances. I didn't know it yet, but my entire career would be characterized by this.

For the administrative clerk, the aircraft mechanic, or the supply Marine, challenge and suffering wouldn't be infused into daily life like it was now. Things would tone down for them a bit. But for us who aspired to be infantrymen, it was only the beginning.

The next day we marched out before sunrise, with everything we would need on our backs. The entire series moved together in formation. I was smoked by the time we stopped, having no idea how many miles we had covered. Over the next seventy-two hours, we completed every training requirement all over again with a few new ones mixed in. The drill instructors were in overdrive, ramping up their corrections and moving us from one event to the next on minimal sleep and nutrition.

We moved simulated casualties across the landscape, worked in small groups to negotiate obstacles spanning several miles, and beat the hell out of each other in boxing matches. We were lucky to bed down for an hour or two a night. When the abrupt wakeup call came, always all too soon, we were moving rapidly to our next training station within three minutes. There was no time to warm up or ease into it.

One second, we were fast asleep, enjoying the bare minimum rest required by the body to keep functioning, the next we were powering through the obstacle course, or negotiating the shakily built confidence course- which was a series of high walls, platforms, ziplines, and cargo nets suspended thirty feet in the air.

I hated the confidence course. It was different than the last time we ran it as a platoon. It took an entire day and there were only a few recruits allowed on the obstacles at a time. The rest of us were at the mercy of a drill instructor off to the side receiving additional instruction or being thrashed.

One of the best parts about recruit training was that it exposed us to parts of ourselves we were previously unaware of. We learned a little bit more about our fears and capabilities. The confidence course showed me that I am absolutely terrified of heights. I moved so slowly and cautiously through each hindrance that our drill instructors nearly had aneurysms from "encouraging" me. It took every ounce of effort I had to focus on moving slowly and surely until I was safely on the ground, where people belonged.

I understood why they called it the confidence course. I hated it because it brought me face to face with my new fear. But I understood it. I knew that I could do it again if I had to.

This time around, during the Crucible, was different. It wasn't the heights that bothered me, or so I told myself, or the threatening rain. It was facing the same fears under more adverse conditions.

I was so exhausted that all I could tell myself was, "don't slip." As

I snapped my head from side to side searching for the next hand hold of a cargo net or a way across a gap between the shaky platforms and ragged swinging ropes, I was more worried about staying awake. It would be a miracle if I could make it through this without losing my grip and ending up like a splattered tomato on the ground.

I just kept inching forward. The light drizzle that had started brought a welcome reprieve from the oppressive humidity. Before I had time to really enjoy it, I had finished the dreaded course and the group was moving again. It was on to the next exercise and the next after that until it was done.

We were tired, dirty, and ragged when the time came to march back. The tone and carriage of our drill instructors changed as we powered through the movement. The sun was up and the loud, viscous "encouragement" we were used to was replaced by marching cadences led by every Marine in our chain of command. It felt like a celebratory victory march instead of a death drive.

The march passed by in a flash and we settled into perfect formation on a large concrete slab the size of several football fields known as the parade deck. Sweating, heaving, and struggling to stay standing, we held as still as we could.

The drill instructors that had exemplified what it meant to be a Marine for the past three months started at the front and moved to each of us in a precise yet reverent manner. This was the moment that had brought me to the island.

As one stepped in front of me, I held out my left hand and in it was placed a small black emblem of eagle, globe, and anchor. He looked me straight in the eyes as if he was peering into my soul and, shaking my other hand, said, "You earned this, Marine."

That was the first time I had ever been called "Marine." I can't remember what I said in response or what was happening around me. The pride that burned within drowned everything out and I finally understood the shift in their demeanor. It was respect. They honored us for truly earning the title. And no force in heaven or on earth could take it away.

Graduation day came soon enough, and everyone seemed proud and happy to leave "the land that God forgot." Our final days were spent preparing for the graduation ceremony, which was little more than a recruiting tool. It was more for everyone else than us. The one that mattered to us, that had actually meant the start of our lives as Marines, had taken place days before, tired, dirty, and permanently stained by the sand and dirt of Parris Island. My parents had told me in their last letter that they would be here to see it, but that Phillip was training with his unit.

As we marched across the parade deck in service Charlie uniforms, it seemed so different being a participant instead of a spectator. I understood what everything here meant. I was motivated, confident, and ready to leave. I wanted to see my old world through the different lens that I earned at this place.

I could feel the pride and happiness radiating from my parents after the ceremony. They were so happy to know that I had accomplished what I set out to do. The challenges here had shown me how lucky I was to have them. They laid a foundation for my siblings and I to build on that we couldn't understand until we faced life's obstacles on our own.

As we drove away from the Island, heading back towards Tennessee, I felt so out of place riding in a civilian vehicle and wearing normal clothes. I had ten days of leave before I had to report to the School of Infantry at Camp Geiger in North Carolina.

I took a minute to reflect on what the last three months meant. I had earned the uniform and title of Marine for life. All the athletic struggles I had faced before seemed so small now. They paled in comparison to what I had just been through.

Perhaps the most important thing that I kept from Parris Island was that I had irrefutable proof that I wasn't a quitter, and I was capable of more. And that was priceless to me. It's what makes us different that everyone else on the planet. And I liked being different. I didn't know what all the Corps had in store for me, but I knew that this was what purposeful living was. Struggle is what amplifies the enjoyment of life.

From Parris Island, we all scattered to the winds. Those of us with Infantry contracts went to the School of Infantry (SOI) East, Infantry Training Battalion at Camp Geiger, North Carolina, for the next two months. Everyone else went to Marine Combat Training (MCT) which was roughly three weeks long, before attending their occupational schools. This marked the point in which we, as grunts, separated from other Marines. Interaction between us would be limited for the remainder of my tenure.

It was obvious that Camp Geiger was different. It wasn't the aesthetics. The neatly aligned squad bay buildings, small mess hall, and post exchange were quite similar to Parris Island. But the nature of what we were doing wasn't. The importance of parade ground drill movements became a thing of the past and the emphasis was on learning actual fighting skills. The physical aspects of the training were vastly more intense.

We hiked everywhere at a four-mile-an-hour pace, carrying our seventy pounds of weapons, pack, and armor with us. Rain or shine-it didn't matter.

I didn't know it at the time, but SOI wasn't under as much of a political microscope as the recruit depots. That gave our instructors the opportunity to train us in a more realistic fashion. For the first few weeks, our fifty-man class attended all classroom instruction and a field exercise, together.

Afterwards, we were divided into different specialties within the infantry, and we didn't get to choose which one. I was just fine being a rifleman. Some of the guys in my platoon wished they had been chosen to become machine gunners or assault men, but nobody wanted to be a mortar man. Regardless, the Corps needed them. So, the Corps got them.

Our training followed a carefully laid out plan. The first day or two of each phase we learned about a different skill in a classroom or around the squad bays. The rest of the time, we were out in the field. Each part culminated in a conditioning hike that was incrementally longer than the one before. We started with a 5-kilometer movement and moved on to a ten, then fifteen, and finished with a twenty. The pattern was classroom, practical exercises, field time, then hike.

Weekend liberty was authorized for those who earned it. We had men fall behind on hikes, leave their rifle laying on the ground, or get caught using tobacco or a cell phone frequently. An infraction such as this kept them on base while the rest of us got to enjoy all the adventures that Jacksonville had to offer.

Our combat instructors were crafty. There was a stark difference between them and the drill instructors we had seen on the island. I never saw one in his service or dress uniform. Their camouflaged utilities were worn, with small patches here and there sewn on to conceal holes and rips. They sported the uniform with a quiet sort of pride that stoked my curiosity. They were markedly different than the clean-cut Marine leaders of Parris Island.

One of the most important aspects of SOI is that it removes some false notions a new Marine conceives before and during recruit training. Our drill instructors had preached and screamed about motivation our entire time on the island. They helped us believe that it could pull us through any adversity we would ever face.

After the first week at SOI, I noticed that nearly half of the Marines in my class didn't seem to care about what we were doing. That motivation had vanished. The priority shift from the manual of arms and close order drill formations to patrolling in the rain and hiking until skin peeled off our feet took a different toll. Save for a few, everyone still did what they had to do to pass the evaluations and make it through the rough hikes and long field operations. None of us enjoyed it, but we were determined to do our duty.

Two students claimed to have suicidal thoughts and were placed under constant watch, which took time away from our already limited nights and weekends. One of them had been meritoriously promoted before we left Parris Island, a month ago. A form of merit-based recognition, Meritorious promotions recognized Marines that performed better than their peers. And yet, here he was, content to sit around all day, playing on a cell phone or reading instead of training with us. Many of us suspected they just wanted to go home.

I wondered why they suddenly decided to quit. It was as if both had gone home on leave and enjoyed looking pretty in their uniforms, then decided that they had checked the military box, so it didn't matter anymore.

The other guy had failed training and been recycled twice. If he didn't pull through with us, he would be gone; sent back home as a civilian as if he was never here. The pressure was clearly wearing on him.

Most of us wanted nothing to do with them. They were regarded with a sort of passive dismissal. But a few Marines went out of their way to try and offer support, which was their decision, but mostly we wanted them to go get the help they needed as quickly as possible before their mentality spread.

Our instructors reported them, separated them, and ensured that they couldn't be hurt. They existed to teach us critical skills, not comfort us. We were preparing for environments where concepts like equality and compassion don't exist. Because of that, we defined self-worth and value differently than society. The focus is on preparation for war and hardening the mind and body to endure the inevitable rigors of those environments.

One of the reasons why everything was so difficult was to identify these people before combat. It's better to find out now than it would be down range in the middle of a firefight. It may seem heartless and cruel but immediately moving them away from the platoon is what should have happened. Training could not come to a halt to accommodate two men's emotional state.

Standing in the open squad bay one night on "suicide watch," as we called it, something dawned on me. I realized that just because someone wears a uniform, it doesn't make them a good or capable person. That came as a shock to me because I was raised to respect everyone in the armed forces.

Of the two, one went away and the other stayed with us, struggling through every aspect of training. It was great that he didn't seem suicidal anymore but that was yesterday's news. He still couldn't keep up on hikes or runs or follow simple instructions, and we singled him out for it.

It was understood by all that struggle was inevitable. It was expected because of the nature of the infantry lifestyle and the fact that we knew we were headed for war. If you pushed through pain and discomfort, and never quit- nobody cared. We all suffered together.

If a Marine let those outside factors shut them down mentally, we treated them very differently. It became very clear to me then and would be constantly reinforced throughout the entirety of my career that infantrymen eat our own. The veteran instructors reminded us constantly that mistakes made in our profession have far-reaching and permanent consequences. Only the best should be put in situations where that kind of risk is taken.

It would take many years for me to see that there was a better way of dealing with these types of situations, but for now, that was it. We turned our focus back to the top priority of training for the Global War on Terror.

Above all else, SOI introduced us to the highly physical nature of what we had signed up for. The amount of time dedicated to morning workouts, tactical training, and hiking far surpassed every other allotment. Outside of the classroom, nearly everything was performed in full kit with weapons always within arm's reach. The morning physical training sessions grew more and more strenuous, and hikes were longer with heavier packs. Our feet bled and our backs felt like solid knots of frozen flesh. I remember returning home for a ninety-six-hour liberty to celebrate Thanksgiving that year and seeing my mother's appalled expression when I removed a palm sized sheet of skin along with my socks.

Hiking is an incredibly challenging test of will and endurance, which came as a shock to many of us who competed in sports. Traditional athleticism, endurance, and strength aren't the same as long distance load bearing capability, especially over significant distance in rough terrain and against the elements. We had to teach our bodies how to perform basic movement patterns under new constraints. Weight adds a new dimension to training which is why those of us that had grown up playing football, wrestling, or running track and cross country still struggled. Grunts have a saying that, "Ounces equal pounds and pounds equal pain." So, if any item, down to an extra pack of cigarettes or extra warm clothes, wasn't necessary for survival- it didn't get packed. Comfort be damned.

By the end of my time at SOI, my feet would feel like hardened leather. Of all the movements that we conducted the longest was twenty kilometers, but it was the easiest one because we had gradually progressed to that level. Adapting to this standard of constant physical stress showed us what the human body is capable of, especially when a man won't quit.

The day after we completed the second hike of ten kilometers, one of our instructors escorted us to chow, as was customary. He must have noticed that many of us were limping and falling out of step or doing whatever we could to avoid the discomfort of marching on twisted ankles and blistered feet.

We lined up slowly, shuffled our way through the entrance and down the line to devour a simple meal before leaving to accomplish the rest of the day's tasks.

After, instead of marching off without a word, he pulled the entire platoon onto a small patch of grass and trees away from the chow hall and told us to step on our blisters and keep the discomfort inside. The man was a veteran of the Fallujah fight and could easily hike circles around all of us. With that kind of experience and example, we all took him seriously.

He was a gaudy looking man, with high cheek bones, a square jaw, and eyes that seemed to pop out of his skull. Despite his slightly creepy facial features, he moved effortlessly under a hiking load and possessed an unsettlingly calm demeanor.

He explained to us that Marines outside the infantry, or POGs (Persons other than grunts), were always looking for a reason to say that we weren't any tougher than they are. This was that fierce competition that Phillip had told me about. At Parris Island, we were told that your occupational specialty didn't matter; that the title of Marine superseded all. We understood that wasn't the case, now. Life was going to get easier for all of them after their little twenty-one-day field operation. We had combat veteran infantrymen waiting on us in the Fleet Marine Force, where the training would ramp up before we deployed.

As he spoke to us then, beneath the trees and overcast sky, I understood what I had been feeling since we finished that hike. It was like a phantom silently watching me ever since. When the instructor gave voice to the matter, it became clear that this was a new sense of added responsibility. We had just done something that none of us ever had before and that most Americans would ever do in their whole lives.

The conditioned inclination of most Americans is to kick back and enjoy a nice long rest after anything that causes strain. The expectation within the infantry is to be capable of performing at this level consistently without displaying the natural discomfort that comes with it. It's just another day in the life of a Marine grunt.

We formed up and went on about our business as directed and the lesson stuck. We began to take pride in our pain, not out of masochism, but because of the result. Feeling that pride became far more important than the comfort of failing. The temporary discomfort of a long hike, a vicious storm, or many nights without sleep didn't seem to compare to the knowledge that I was facing challenges most people never would—and succeeding.

As our time in SOI ended, I took stock of what I had learned about the Corps, the infantry, and myself. Everything that I saw or read about on the news painted us as these big hearted "nation builders." I had seen and heard speeches from politicians and generals assuring the world that we were in Afghanistan to help the people build a strong, independent country- not conquer and destroy. That didn't sound at all like what I was being trained for and it definitely wasn't what I wanted to be when I enlisted. As I discussed it with the other Marines in my class, they made it clear that they didn't want to be tactical project managers either.

The mission of the Marine rifle squad is *to locate, close with, and destroy the enemy through fire and maneuver and to repel the enemy assault through fire and close combat.* We had recited it so many times that it became etched in our minds. We were constantly reminded by our instructors that very soon it wouldn't be training anymore and not all of us would return home. It was just a fact. Rounds would be breaking the sound barrier on a collision course with our bodies and all that mattered at that point were the skills we had acquired, the dedication to those on our right and left, and the will to win at any cost. The fight didn't have to be pretty, or make people back home happy, but it did have to result in victory.

If the American people or the politicians wanted to view us as these stoic guardians of peace and justice, that was their right even if it wasn't an accurate picture of who we are.

SOI was my introduction to a culture that was different than the rest of the Corps. It was one founded on discipline, toughness, and proficiency. And because it is so vastly different from American society, we had to have those tenets trained into us. It wasn't enough to simply be told what is acceptable. Our instructors were men of iron and honor because they had to exemplify these traits by showing us how to conduct ourselves.

The drill instructors from the island and combat instructors here had five months to overwrite nineteen years of cultural differences and send Marines to their units as works in progress to be completed by the veterans there. A near impossible task but one that they took seriously and excelled at. Because of that time constraint, the training had to be brutal.

By constantly facing adversity and temporary defeat, each man was confronted by some difficult truths. I had grown used to being told that I could never do things good enough. That there was always a way to get better and progress as a Marine and an infantryman. Simple tasks had to be executed with more precision and always to perfection. Every skill that we were taught was perishable. It was understood that we would be required to sharpen them constantly if we win when it counted. And winning the fight overpowered everything else.

Under this constant scrutiny, I learned that failure is a far more effective teacher than success. So many politicians, and even some parents, see parts of our lifestyle and condemn it for its cruelty and brutality. They focus on the punishment instead of the lesson. The loud and harsh ass-chewing from an instructor, hours of manual labor, or deprivation of time off and creature comforts like cell phones and nicotine privileges, or the ability to refuse to train without consequence. They just see kids being beat down and don't bother to look deeper and notice the internal development and the positive results that are only visible after the fact.

These instances build discipline, confidence, and accountability. They highlight the importance of the team over self and helps turn boys into men—not just warriors— but capable, confident men who can pass this knowledge onto the next generation in any walk of life.

The second lesson I learned is the capability of the human body. Socrates said, "No man has the right to be an amateur in the matter of physical training. It is a shame for a man to grow old without seeing the beauty and strength of which his body is capable." For many of us, the physical aspects of life remain the gateway to our mental faculties. Physical challenge focuses the mind and increases the drive to accomplish great things. More importantly, it helps us achieve balance between being fathers, husbands, and warriors. In other words, we are living proof of the philosopher's words. Being good at one aspect makes us better at the others.

Physical pain, challenge, failure, and the self-awareness that results from them are not only expected in the infantry- but essential. The willingness to seek them out is viewed within the community as a defining trait of character and dedication to something greater than self. At the end of the day, it is not only your life in the balance, but also every other man's in the formation. The thought of failing them because you lack the will to put in more time to learn the trade or work through pain and ignore discomfort is unbearable to any Grunt worth his salt. The infantry is a culture built on the foundation of team before self.

In early December of 2007, I graduated from SOI and reported to 2nd Battalion, 6th Marine Regiment (2/6) where I was assigned to Echo Company. After the small ceremony that paled in comparison to the one on Parris Island, we gathered our personal effects and loaded onto waiting buses bound for Camp Lejeune. There were no more than twenty of us assigned to 2/6.

The commute through Jacksonville was short and not more than a half hour later, we pulled through the front gate of our new home. I was so nervous that it was difficult to focus on anything other than what lay ahead.

We had all heard stories from our instructors about the battle-hardened Grunts that awaited us in our first unit. The rumor mill among green Marines in a schoolhouse knows no limits and from day one, horrifically hilarious stories were spread around about the hazing we would endure. Extreme exaggeration is arguably the most impressive ability that a group of grunts possesses.

It started with warnings from our instructors when correcting a mistake. Something simple like, "If you leave your rifle laying around in the Fleet, your team leader is going to fuck you up." Before long the underground rumor mill had circulated stories of new Marines being force fed ungodly amounts of liquor and told to streak naked through the streets of Jacksonville.

As we exited Highway 24, one part of me sincerely hoped I wasn't speeding straight towards an ass beating. The other part was terrified of not living up to the expectations of the seasoned veterans I was about meet. They had recently returned from the city of Fallujah in Iraq, and I half expected them to be ten feet tall with superpowers.

It was dark by the time we arrived. A Sergeant representative escorted the four of us that were assigned to Echo company across a football sized patch of grass enclosed by four identical three-story brick buildings that resembled a cheap hotel in a horror movie town. A few Marines could be seen on the balconies that ran the length of the barracks drinking and carrying on only to stop and rejoice at the sight of fresh meat arriving. My stomach turned as one of them announced it as loud he could.

The Sergeant that had escorted us across the quad, took each of us to our assigned rooms. Luckily, it was a Friday night and most of the company was out in town, which afforded me the opportunity to drop my gear in my new quarters and take a deep breath.

The walls were an odd sort of off-white color and a grey rug concealed most of the pale tile beneath. A small nook in the back left housed a sink and two wall lockers and a door to the right led to a bathroom that was shared with the Marines staying in the next room over. It was nice to be out of a squad bay and have some semblance of privacy again. I never thought that I would miss something so basic until now.

There were two sets of furniture and a bunk bed. I set about unloading the contents of the green seabag I had brought with me, which was all I had to my name. The combination locks on one of the wall lockers and two of the other cabinets in the small ten-by-twelve room told me that I wouldn't be living alone.

A few minutes into my organizational endeavor, a knock on the door sent a jolt of lightning through my body and I shot across the room to open it. I instinctively snapped to parade rest, my feet shoulder width apart at a forty-five-degree angle and hands right over left against the small of my back.

The man of average height and build with tan complexion standing at the entrance to my humble abode introduced himself as Lance Corporal (LCpl.) Jolo, my fire team leader. He told me to grab a notebook and follow him.

My pulse quickened as I walked behind him on the balcony. I peered in the rooms as we passed by to see some of the other new arrivals doing pushups or wall sits, covered in sweat. They were swarmed by the senior Marines of the company, like the one I followed now, who were pushing them to go faster and harder, trying to discover their physical and mental limits. As we passed them, I wondered what the hell was about to happen to me.

He brought me down to ground level and we stopped on a small patch of grass next to the concrete stairwell. He didn't want anyone else around for our first meeting, which would turn out to be one of the most important of my life.

To my surprise, LCpl Jolo spoke confidently and calmly. There was no anger or condescension in his tone or demeanor. He was a straightforward kind of cat and laid out what was expected of me clearly. Pointedly, he stated that I was bring every matter to him before anyone else in the chain of command. It didn't matter what time it was or how great or small the question or situation, he expected to be informed of everything first.

He explained that schoolhouses designed their training to be easily understood. It was more about efficiency and graduation quotas. That meant much of what I was taught at SOI was outdated and had to be trained out me. My focus needed to be on learning everything that I could from him and his veteran peers, fresh off a combat deployment. This is the part that worried me. It was the first explanation of what I would be doing at my new unit, general though it was, and as he spoke, again I wondered if I would have what it took to succeed. In that moment, I was reminded of the fact that I had chosen a life that was going to be constantly challenging.

Every standard of military bearing and courtesy, such as uniform appearance and addressing senior personnel by rank and last name, was to be adhered to without fail. I knew that I could do that, at least.

The last two points he presented in our opening conversation would stick with me for the rest of my life. He told me never to fall behind on any movement, whether it was a hike or run. And lastly, he looked me square in the eyes and said, "Don't mistake my kindness for weakness."

Over a year later, 2/6 returned from the 26th Marine Expeditionary Unit in the spring of 2009. A MEU was commonly referred to as a "booze cruise" because instead of going to war, like we all wanted, each company within the battalion embarked on separate Navy ships to sail around and serve as a sort of quick reaction force to any crisis in a certain part of the world. The name "booze cruise" comes from the drunken shenanigans that occur in various ports. Letting a bunch of grunts loose in a foreign country that have been cooped up on a ship, deprived of female companionship with several paychecks to spend is just asking for trouble.

Just before the deployment, I was transferred to LCpl. Badams' team. It stung a bit because I had grown accustomed to the way Jolo did things and his expectations. True to his words in our first encounter, Jolo drove me to learn everything I could about being an infantryman. He refined the skills that I had been shown in SOI and injected lessons they had learned from Fallujah. Patrolling no longer meant walking in a certain part of a formation and looking in an assigned direction. It meant moving in a manner that made me hard to kill and constantly analyzing my surroundings. In an urban area, every window could house shooter; every small alleyway and intersection could be a kill zone for an enemy ambush. He taught me how to make myself a hard target: where to move, how to get there, and why. The same nuance was applied to every basic skill from land navigation with map and compass to weapons manipulations and room clearing.

When I was moved to Badams' team, I had progressed from the greener-than-grass Boot that Jolo received from SOI. But I still had a long way to go.

The term "Boot" is involuntarily bestowed on all grunts that haven't deployed. It served as a reminder to the newer Marines, like me, that we hadn't accomplished anything of note, which kept us from slacking off after SOI.

The entire training cycle and deployment was characterized by fighting. At any point in time, our seniors would herd us into a room or onto an open patch of grass or even the concrete floor of an open squad bay. Once all of us were assembled and kneeling in a circle, the seniors called out two random names, and we would let loose.

Several of them were always present to keep things from getting out of hand or major injuries from occurring. It was an outlet for aggression and gave us a chance to demonstrate our prowess.

The veterans would move around and occasionally rotate in. While the circle of Boots marked the boundaries of the action, they'd scream at us as loud as they could, challenging us to fight harder, to push, and to display the maximum amount of violence necessary to win. They wanted us to make the other man quit.

The point wasn't to be cruel or to pick on the new guys. It was to harden the mind and body to pain and to remind us to always be ready for a fight. Over time and after completing countless bouts, we developed a comfort and respect for interpersonal violence with the full knowledge that one day, perhaps sooner than we thought, it would be for real.

I didn't realize it at the time, but it also allowed our team leaders to see what we were made of and observe the intangible qualities that we possessed. They were able to see how we would act in a stressful situation and learn about our character. It was a window into each man's internal works and our intangible makeup.

Violent interactions, such as this, would remain consistent throughout my entire career. Rank meant nothing once the gloves were taped on, all that mattered was how well the fight went. Every match was an opportunity to find out a little bit more of what I was capable of. It fostered respect between us because we were able to see, in the most visceral manner possible, if the man across from you would back down or roll over and take a beating without fighting back.

We also settled disputes in a similar manner. Less people were involved because the larger Marine Corps frowned on fighting unless it was approved martial arts training, which is what we passed it off as when a curious officer observed.

As Boots, we performed every working party, stood all hours of watch while in the field, and served barracks duty alongside a Non-Commissioned Officer. Separating Boots from the "seniors" who had deployed, gave us a target to aim for in our development. It reinforced the fact that we value experience- especially combat experience. We would remain designated as Boots until we completed our first deployment and the best of us would be selected as team leaders to replace ours as they left the Corps or moved on.

Badams was a different character. Not a lesser man or leader but went about things in a different manner. His expectation of bearing and professional courtesy was the same as Jolo's. He had been the radio operator (RTO) for his squad in Fallujah whereas Jolo was the point man for his. Radios in the service work about as well as two tin cans joined by string, so the RTO must be intimately familiar with several different types and prepared to be constantly fixing them. The environment plays a huge part in the effectiveness of the radio and a quick a look at history confirms that grunts never operate in places with sunshine and rainbows.

This wonder of modern communicatory capability is both loved and hated. Any extra weight, but particularly a radio and extra batteries, is no joke. Add on the fact that rain, snow, dense vegetation, or any form of atmospheric interference make the damn things crap out all the time and it's easy to understand why the RTO is one of the angriest guys in any squad.

As poorly designed as they may be, radios are the lifeline of any unit. If the squad needs anything external such as mortars, air support, resupply or medical evacuation, the only way to get it is the radio.

Badams was like a big, athletic, frustrated older brother. He hated the bureaucracy of the Corps, just like Jolo and the other team leaders, but he was committed to making myself and the other Boots successful. Having been to combat before, none of them wanted to get a phone call in the future after their service ended, telling them one of us had been killed because we weren't trained properly.

He was smart, observant, and damn near invincible. There was no hiding any infraction from him. Every morning before physical training he was up early to inspect my room and uniform. Before every field op, he checked my gear and after he inspected my weapon. If anything was missing or out of place, I had to do the whole process of presentation or cleaning all over again, not just the parts that were wrong. Everything had to be done right every single time.

On runs or hikes, he never seemed to break a sweat. It was as if he was impervious to pain. I was not. So, when I struggled, it was to the tune of Badams forcefully reminding me that other men's lives depended on me being able to pull my weight and theirs.

He had a reputation for being able to hit people very hard and the last thing I wanted to do was experience it.

While on liberty, whether at home or abroad, infantrymen operate off what we call "big boy rules." Meaning that causing a scene or acting like a drunken jackass isn't acceptable. When it does happen, it is your buddy's responsibility to put a stop to it, whatever it takes. Badams would just knock somebody out that couldn't handle their drink. He didn't care if it was in Jacksonville or places like France and Greece, where we had port visits on the MEU we had just returned from.

I had more than enough motivation to not fall out of a hike and learn my new job.

Badams entrusted me with the SAW. The M249 squad automatic weapon was a light machine gun that we had been introduced to in SOI. Given the nature of schoolhouses, we only had a few that were passed around during foot movements, mainly to aid the conditioning process.

Now, it was my personal weapon, and it came with higher responsibility. I had to know everything about it: the ranges at which it was effective, how to carry it, load it , unload it, move with it, and how to keep it running in humidity versus rain, snow, or heat.

Our team leaders chose who would carry it based on our physical toughness and future potential. The additional weight and responsibility helped build character and shape us into future team leaders. It was a point of pride among the boots to be chosen as a SAW gunner.

The weapon itself weighs an additional nine pounds compared to the M16 and requires the gunner to carry a minimum of six hundred rounds, compared to the two hundred and ten of a normal rifleman. Much like the radios, the SAW required constant attention to operate properly, and it absolutely had to at- being the team's chief means of gaining and maintaining fire superiority.

From day one, Badams and the other team leaders taught us that our survivability in a firefight hinged on the SAW gunner's proficiency. Odds were in our favor if I could pour rounds into the enemy and either kill them all or at least suppress them as we closed the distance. If not, we all had a good chance of getting killed.

Nearly all our team leaders, like Jolo, who had been deployed to Fallujah and had trained us were nearing the end of their contracts and looking forward to civilian life. That left a huge vacuum we had to fill. We had a few squad leaders remaining and one or two coming in from other units for the next deployment cycle.

The rumor was that we were headed to Afghanistan this time. Given the turnover Echo Company was about to experience, most of us would see combat for the first time as team leaders if the scuttlebutt turned out to be true.

At this point in my career, having just returned from my first deployment- and no longer a Boot, I reflected on the past year and half of my life. We had just returned to Camp Lejeune after lengthy leave block, which gave me time to spend with my family and see Tennessee again.

The only negative aspect of my experience, thus far, was the fact that I hadn't gone to combat. Collectively, our entire company saw the MEU as a lesser deployment. We had seen more of the world than most ever would, which none of us really appreciated. We visited France, Greece, and Turkey on liberty and trained in Kuwait and Saudi Arabia, but it hadn't been what we had signed up for. We wanted war.

Still, it hadn't been a waste of time. We had seven months to train under the direct supervision of experienced seniors and hone our skills. As we neared the end of the deployment, they started putting us in their role as team leaders, just so we weren't lost when we got our own Boots to train. The process of breaking our bad habits from SOI, refining our skills, and hardening our mentality made more sense when the shift began. I understood why they were so hard on us and corrected every small infraction from wearing chipped chevrons to missing a small piece of grime when cleaning a weapon.

Badams helped evolve my understanding of discipline. Not the type of discipline that entails starched uniforms and pretty, shining rifles being twirled for a recruiting commercial, but the type that sustains a man in the hurricane of external factors that naturally exist in infantry operations.

Discipline, to an infantryman, refers to the habits of thought and action that form consistently acceptable performance throughout training and deployment. Actions like not sleeping on post, cleaning your rifle constantly, properly camouflaging, routinely checking gear and equipment, anticipating and planning for tactical setbacks, studying the trade during the weekend, and working out without being made to do so are all just a few simple examples.

I was in love with this culture, embracing the constant challenge to become something more than an average man. The thought of wasting my life in the typical civilian cycle of working, spending money, and working more seemed so fruitless. The anger and overly competitive nature that I exhibited in high school had been harnessed into something that was not only acceptable but encouraged. I didn't have to change who I was to earn respect. All I had to do was work hard, learn, and grow.

We treated each other fairly and based off a well-established expectation. Men that worked themselves into the dirt to master the infantry trade earned the respect of everyone around them. Those that didn't were ostracized. The effectiveness of the team mattered more than the feelings of any one individual.

Dishonesty and disputes were handled between men without involving higher authority. If a simple conversation didn't resolve the matter, then fighting would. We expected each other to air grievances and work them out, then move on as a team without harboring resentment. We expected the pursuit of perfection from one another, and we bled and worked for it together. Nothing builds a dedicated team like shared hardship and adversity. And I had found my team in the infantry. Where toughness, loyalty, a fighting spirit, and selflessness were celebrated.

Chapter 3

Zach

As is normal after returning from a deployment, units undergo a sort of shake up. Infantry Battalions, like 2/6, are divided into three companies, headed up by a company commander and company first sergeant. Each company has a gunnery sergeant, affectionately known as Gunny or Guns, and an executive officer to assist them. Companies are further divided into three platoons, with a platoon commander and platoon sergeant, who command three squads. Three fire teams, each headed by a team leader, make up a squad.

Typically, the officers and senior staff switch companies and some of the squad leaders move to other Platoons. With all the team leaders getting out plus the normal command personnel changes, 2/6 was going to look very different. Damn near everyone that was going to be in a leadership position would be new at it or from somewhere else.

Rather than wait for each short timer to reach their end of active service date, the new chain of command moved those with less than six months left on their contract into their own platoon, allowing us to slide into the billets earlier and gain more experience.

Infantry units are highly competitive organisms. Each platoon competes against the others and squads within battle one another for supremacy. So, on days like today, in late Spring of 2009, that competitiveness adds an element of anxiety. Nobody wanted to get moved to another Platoon.

Having just returned from our post deployment leave block, we stood outside the barracks, waiting to fall into formation.

Echo Company's new chain of command was in the company office building and would be out to announce who was going where at any moment. I imagined that something akin to the NFL draft was taking place inside and hoped to God that all the effort and work I had put in over the last cycle was enough to keep me in second platoon, at least. But becoming a team leader was what I really wanted.

Our one-hundred-man company milled about on the strip of grass in between our barracks and a parking lot that contained a supply warehouse while we waited for our new assignments.

About half an hour later, a group of four men emerged from the office and the Company scattered. The sea of digital camouflage uniforms smoothly dispersed into four groups as the new platoon sergeants joined each to introduce themselves and get us up to speed.

Most of us had a general idea of who would be team leaders. It was the most coveted billet in the infantry because you had just the right amount of responsibility: two or three dudes to keep in your hip pocket, train, and develop with very little administrative duty .

I was ready for this, full of piss and vinegar, and couldn't wait to hear my name called out.

Our new platoon sergeant, Staff Sergeant Hauz was a short, stocky guy with graying hair and distinct facial features. He had an uncanny ability to speak calmly, almost softly, one minute and the next, blast volume from his vocal cords that could shatter glass.

He stepped in front of us and read off a roster in squad and team order. He made his way through the first squad without mentioning me which was a huge blow because that was thought to be the top dog crew that always got the hairiest of assignments.

My dismay was short lived as he moved to the second squad and called my name as the first team leader to Sergeant Zach Walters.

As he continued down his list, I couldn't help but feel proud that I had been selected for the position. I would be the senior team leader in the squad. It was an honor and a massive boost to my already overly charged ego.

The only apprehension was being assigned to Sergeant Walters. He was coming over from third platoon, where he had spent the last deployment as a squad leader, so he had experience. Before that, he had come from the Security Forces Regiment in Virginia, which meant he hadn't seen combat.

Fresh out of SOI, security forces Marines were sent to Chesapeake for additional schooling, and then units with different missions, such as King's Bay, Georgia to guard key facilities or the Marine Barracks in Washington, D.C. to stand Presidential guard duty. After two or three years they came to infantry battalions, and we labeled them as a sort of bastard half-Grunts.

Many of them were fat, lazy, not proficient, and entitled. What's worse, they were typically moved directly into leadership billets because many of them were senior in rank. With the high operational tempo of the war, often, a unit would return from Iraq or Afghanistan and these fresh-faced security force Marines would be placed over a newly initiated veteran, who had proven his mettle in combat. But the big Marine Corps valued rank more, much to our chagrin. It was a far-from-perfect system.

One of my good friends, Deeno, was selected as second team leader. Wherever this was going to lead, I knew I could count on him. He had spent the last deployment in second Platoon with me, but in third squad under a team leader named McGruff who didn't take it easy on him.

Deeno was "good people," as we said. He was even considered for a position as the platoon radio operator, but a rough stutter kept him from the job. Everyone gave him hell for it just to watch him struggle to fire back a response- which he always did, sending us rolling with laughter. Deeno took shit from no one and always pulled his weight or more. He had earned universal respect because he was thick-skinned, proficient, and tough as nails.

By the time Staff Sergeant Hauz finished, we were standing in a nice, neat formation of three ranks arranged in billet order from squad leader on the far right to the last rifleman in third fire team on the far left.

Zach appeared in front of me with an extended hand. Clasping mine, he said, "Blackwell, it's gonna be a pleasure working with you."

That's when I knew he was different. My old squad leader had displayed such a calm professionalism only a handful of times and here this guy was, extending courtesy and dignity to me when it wasn't required or expected. What's more, he continued down the line and did the same with every man—boot or team leader alike.

He was about five-foot-ten, like me, but couldn't have weighed more than a buck forty and I wondered how the hell he was able to bare the weight we had to carry. Clearly, he had proven himself during the MEU. His squad always seemed upbeat on that deployment, and I couldn't help but notice the same mood now as I looked down the line. He was magnetic. Zach was not the typical Security Forces Marine.

He wasn't big or loud and didn't appear to be physically imposing at all. He sported a full mane of jet-black hair dashed with grey and had kind eyes. He was the opposite of the six-foot semi-truck of a man I had as a squad leader before. But from the jump, he was confident, well-spoken, and professional. I wondered what he was thinking about me as we stood there in our first formation as second platoon, second squad. The old platoon I knew was dead and a new one was born in its place in a matter of ten minutes. There was no time for sentiment. This was our future.

A few of the outgoing seniors stayed with us because they had more than a year left but wouldn't be deploying. It really was *our show* from now on. It was hard to believe, surreal even, that we had made it this far and grown this much. I still felt so young, like I had the entire world in front of me with endless possibilities. And at the top of that mountain of prospects was combat, which we were assured of at this point.

When he was finished going down the line, Zach sauntered back in front of the squad and took his place on my right. Room assignments were given out and we were dismissed to complete the barracks shuffle overnight. Adhering to typical military uniformity, platoons would live on the same floor and billet holders would room together, so Deeno and I shacked up in our new digs, feeling pretty good about all the changes.

Over the next month or so, Zach found ways to break up the usual garrison monotony. Not that he had to try. He looked at training differently than most and went about it creatively. He was inventive and it showed in everything he did. Our physical training plan was based on functional fitness, which exposed us to a whole new world of structure and implements to help develop our bodies.

We trained in circuits consisting of a series of stations spread all over Camp Lejeune, so everyone was always moving. Boots and utility trousers were the minimum uniform, with additional weight frequently incorporated and competition was frequently infused. For example, one team would be low crawling with each man carrying someone on his back while another team was sprinting and the third was pounding a spot in the ground with sledgehammers. Zach had a time interval set and he would rotate through each station with us until we were all smoked. The team that made the biggest crater in the ground was the victor.

The Marine Corps Martial Arts Program was something that Zach cherished. Up to that point, most of us dreaded even hearing the acronym, MCMAP, because it was conducted as a bland "check-in-the-box" item by our last command. This was different than the normal gladiatorial style ground fighting matches that we commonly fought one-on-one or one against two. It was a time block training system that typically consisted of several days spent hitting pads, punching air, and wrestling on mats.

The current Marine Corps order assigned a belt level requirement for each rank. To get promoted, you had to have so many hours of training followed by an evaluation from an instructor who determined if you moved to the next level. On the MEU, we only had two martial arts instructors, so it fell to them to train and evaluate the entire company.

None of us coveted the dull repetition that they had to endure. I imagined they contemplated jumping overboard and poking a hole in the rescue buoy when it was thrown out to them.

Zach cut out the monotony and bureaucracy. Smash mouth ground fighting was a regular occurrence for Second Squad, whether it was during morning training or down time when we were waiting for higher-ups to figure something out. Everyone fought everyone, including Zach, who was the best at it. The man wasn't scared to mix it up with anyone and he was slowly but surely instilling that mentality in all of us.

A few months into our new adventure as a squad, another boot drop from SOI brought with it a small-scale personnel shuffle. We received a few new guys to fill in the last open positions. I stayed in the first team slot with two of my guys, Gavin and Cotton. Gavin was a new boot we received at the start. He was young, smart, thick-skinned, and learned quickly. You couldn't sneak any bullshit by him.

Cotton on the other hand, came to us from the Marine Barracks in Washington, D.C. serving as a security guard for the various presidential grounds. He was a Security Forces Marine, so I wasn't optimistic when Zach assigned him to me several weeks before. Cotton was older than most of us and happily married. Mature, confident, and humble, he possessed an incredible work ethic. He was another lucky draw from the cesspool that was Security Forces.

Deeno headed up Team Two with Tracy, Todd, and Patrelli. Patrelli migrated from Third Platoon with Zach, who treated him as a younger brother. The whole squad could be seen rolling with laughter at some of the tricks that he would play on Patrelli, but God help anyone that messed with him.

Tracy was older than most entry level Marines. He had work experience on the outside that provided him with a sort of business savvy outlook on things. He carried the SAW and because of his distinct Pennsylvania accent paired with his somewhat stubby body type, he reminded us of a 1920s gangster. It was like we had inherited the illegitimate offspring of Al Capone.

Todd was a country boy and was good at working with his hands. If he hadn't become a Marine, he would've been just fine making a living as a masterful mechanic or a welder. He had a great sense of humor and a sort of innocence to him that only added to his youthful look. He was loyal to a fault.

Team Three finished off the lineup with Pappy leading Greddy, Norman, and Gunner. Like Zach, Pappy had spent the first few years of his contract in another Security Forces unit called Fleet Anti-Terrorism Security Team. He was smart, innovative, and good natured. Having similar experiences and training, he helped integrate some of the tactics that Zach had brought with him.

Pappy spent his off time studying foreign wars and famous tacticians, drawing lessons from them to teach to his team which spread to the rest of the squad. He only raised his voice if he had to. He wasn't a straight up sledgehammer unless one of his guys gave him a reason to be, which contrasted sharply with my style of constantly screaming at Gavin and Cotton for even the most trivial of infractions. He carried himself with a quiet pride and possessed a wealth of knowledge to teach, which he enjoyed doing.

Greddy and Gunner were inseparable. These two may have been the most "out there" characters that I ever encountered during my time in uniform. They listened to the type of music that you would hear in a weird indy film and acted almost like a married couple, casually agreeing on some things and heatedly arguing about small trivial differences of opinion. Gunner was madly in love with actress Kristen Stewart from the *Twilight* movie series. I never understood the appeal myself, but he defended her vehemently when we spoke about her in rough terms just to get a rise out of him.

He and Greddy knew each other well and kept each other going. Neither of them was thrilled with the opening chapter of their Marine Corps experience but they gave their best effort regardless. They were strong, independent, street savvy, and tough. Pappy helped keep them focused and, between him and Zach, gave them a version of the challenge that they had expected before signing up. They wanted combat but without the haircuts and uniformity that characterized military life-which was a common sentiment in the infantry at this time.

Norman was different from the other two, but he integrated well. He shared the same twisted sense of humor with the rest of us and pulled his weight because he cared about the team. His general positivity showed in his demeanor regardless of how miserable everyone was during long field ops. He was one of those rare guys that could find a way to make you laugh in the most miserable conditions. He was selfless and responded well to Pappy's leadership.

We had a very different mentality than my last squad and all the others in the company. Each team marked our collective personality in their own way. Zach valued our input and assessment of the Marines and made it a point to spend time with Pappy, Deeno, and I measuring their performance and attitude. We got to know each other well during these informal discussions in which we highlighted good and bad performances and debated the potential of each man. If one of us doubted a boot Marine because he struggled physically, Zach would agree then counter by stressing his maturity and life experience before the other two chimed in with their observations and on it went. It showed us which attributes each team leader valued and how we evaluated our guys.

We trained constantly. If we weren't out in the field, we could be found clearing out a barracks, patrolling Camp Lejeune, or running through attack simulations that Zach set up for us. Movement, learning, and teaching was the order of every day, which was exhausting. Most nights I was asleep by six or seven after preparing for the next day's work. Months later, after my wife moved up from Tennessee, I would wake up to her softly placing a dinner plate on my chest. I would eat and pass right back out.

Being an infantry leader can drain you, not just physically but mentally. The pressure was always on, from the time you stepped in front of your boys until the time you got home, whether it was a rare day spent in garrison, a month-long training operation, or a deployment .The challenges of teaching were new to me. I had three Marines that all learned differently, and Zach had to teach me how to teach them. The stress compounded as I struggled to relate the same tactics and skills to them in ways that each could understand.

But, over time, we started to gel. From all the sweat, pain, and frustration that we experienced we grew close to one another, and it carried over to our off time. One day while we were waiting the final word to go home for a weekend, I passed by one of the squad's rooms to find Deeno and Zach shooting the shit.

"Blackwell, what are you doing tonight?" Zach asked.

"Trying to find someone who wants to drink, but everyone's being a bunch of fucking pussies."

"Fuck it, I'll mix it up with a team leader!" He held his arms out in triumph.

And that's what started it all. From then on, weekends were filled with outings to a local steakhouse or our favorite bar. Countless nights of drunken debauchery and shenanigans ensued with Pappy, Deeno, and Zach. We spent hours draining drink after drink and talking about how we could mix things up with the squad. We analyzed our guys and talked about potential trades. To an outsider, it would've resembled something like a hilariously dark version of the professional football draft, fueled by ungodly amounts of alcohol, deeply offensive humor, and cynicism. We would spend a few moments arguing back and forth before moving on to animated discussions about tactics or gear.

Most people flee their jobs as soon as possible and many purposely avoid talking or thinking about them. We loved being infantrymen. We had made our little piece of the world our own and built it into a place where we could sweat, bleed, triumph, and grow together. We created the opportunity for happiness or at the very least, to offset the negative aspects of military life with small victories that made it memorable.

Soon the whole squad was included, and we frequented the local scene in Jacksonville together to tear up the town. "Work hard, play hard" took on a whole new meaning. Greddy, Gunner, and our other Boots were still our juniors but could relax a bit during our evening forays. They didn't have to call us by rank or stand at parade rest, just be respectful. As their team leaders, we understood that it was unacceptable to dress them down in public. The collective decompression was healthy and when we came back to work, it was strictly professional.

Up to this point, squads that shared this type of bond were mythical to me. During my Boot tenure, we maintained strict loyalty to teams, then to the squad, but that true connection that tied every member together was missing. Now we had something more and it grew deeper over time. We trusted and grew to respect one another, even when we didn't agree, which happened frequently. We had pride in the squad and that birthed a fierce loyalty of the rarest quality. This is what had been missing before and I would spare no effort, great or small, in the future to bring this element to every squad I was entrusted with. To us, this was not a job—it was a lifestyle. We breathed it, ate it, dreamt of it, and carried it with us everywhere. The squad became our passion.

After a few weeks, we left as a company for range SR6. Why they called it a range was beyond me. The place was just off a major highway and yet, the second we arrived I couldn't help but think that I was in the middle of nowhere. Normally, ranges had at least some sort of terrain variance to them, but this place was a swamp! There was one solid patch of earth, extending from the gravel road that we took from the highway to get there. Trees bordered the grassy clearing that butted up against the rocks and stretched thirty yards out to a berm, separating us from the marshy "range," which was little more than a long, mushy rectangle contained by a larger, also miserably swampy boundary. Muddy green sludge was everywhere around our small patch of solid earth, where we would bivouac.

Compared to the range, the rest of Camp Lejeune was at least partially dry and not as humid. Nor did it try to swallow you while you attempted to slog through it with all your gear and hope that your Boots didn't drown trying to keep up with you. The range was notorious and, not at all our favorite place to train.

Our command had reserved the site for a few days of squad level attacks- the first live fire that we had done together. Despite the stinking squishy conditions, I was intensely excited for the challenge.

We disembarked the seven-ton trucks, which were a rare treat for any infantryman, and staged our gear in company formation at the bivouac grounds. Shortly after, the squad leaders were called over to the commanding officer to be briefed on the conduct of the range while we prepared our Marines, gear, and weapons for the event.

Zach returned with the news that it was a straightforward squad attack—nothing sexy and no supporting arms. Dry runs without live ammunition would be conducted today, along with zeroing the optics on our personal weapons. Live fire would be the following day. We readied ourselves and our Marines and stood by while all three squads of First Platoon conducted their dry runs.

In between one of First's rehearsals, our CO called Zach off to the side and asked him why he had his dump pouch attached to the front of his plate carrier vest instead of the non-firing side. The small pouch was meant to hold rifle magazines that had been emptied during a firefight. It was designed to attach to the bottom row of webbing on our issued plate carrier vests and hang down below the hip on the non-firing side so a Marine could drop the expended magazine from his rifle into it efficiently as he reloaded. Battalion policy dictated where everyone's pouches would be situated based on their billet, regardless of if they were right or left-handed, much to our chagrin.

Zach had a knack for testing the waters. He wanted to innovate and find a better way of doing anything and everything relating to fighting a war. It had nothing to do with defiance or being disrespectful. In fact, he was the first squad leader I ever had who had truly mastered how to tactfully converse with officers.

We watched the conversation take shape just out of ear shot. He informed the CO that his setup had tactical value. The officer seemed skeptical, as if he expected something more, so Zach granted his wish. He faced the berm for safety and locked the bolt of his M4 rifle to the rear before presenting it as if to fire. The drill was set to simulate an emergency or "speed" reload when you run out of rounds in a firefight. He depressed the trigger and then the magazine release button, which allowed gravity to take the aluminum case down directly to the pouch in question as another source of ammunition was inserted and the bolt sent home.

With minimal movement and effort, Zach had answered a question from a commissioned officer and disproved a common military theory- that uniformity made a unit fight more effectively. To his credit, the CO didn't order him to change anything.

To that point, my experience had shown me that an officer, especially a CO, could tell somebody that the sky was fucking purple just for the sake of watching them have to believe it. Zach had just opened the portal to a different path, and it would guide me throughout the rest of my time in the infantry. That lesson, just like most that he taught me, wouldn't occur to me for many years.

As an added bonus, nobody drowned at SR6 that week.

Our squad had a planned approach to everything. Every bit of training was goal oriented and well thought through. We would spend days at a time clearing out rooms in the barracks with no one else in sight, which made the long periods in garrison, heckled by equal opportunity briefs and signing hundreds of rosters for everything under the sun, actually productive. We had created an atmosphere in which every second of the day was dedicated to improving proficiency because success in combat was the expectation.

Zach used his Security Forces experience to implement new tactics for battle in urban environments. Fighting a war in confined spaces like houses, rooms, and alleys had piqued my interest since I had been introduced to it during my Boot days. Our seniors, with their Fallujah experience, had given us a special appreciation for close quarters fighting.

Zach had graduated from the Advanced Urban Combat School, which exposed him to techniques I was never taught. He provided us with a new system to this type of fighting and expected us to become proficient and train our Boots in the matter as well. Aided by Pappy, with the same background, the four of us hit the ground running and never stopped.

Learning the skills required constant repetition, just like ground fighting, but on steroids. It didn't just build proficiency; we learned each other's mental process and it made us into a cohesive leadership core.

In the previous cycle, we spent days in the barracks waiting on higher ups to pass instructions. So many hours of wasted time spent cleaning or picking up trash in the company area and performing useless working parties made so many young Marines yearn for the day that they could return to the civilian world. Our team leaders had been kept on a very short leash and were essentially seen as glorified babysitters by the command. There wasn't much room for ingenuity and initiative.

But this time around, the climate was different, and we were expected to be productive with our down time. Zach brought us together as team leaders and trained us in new skillset so we could teach our boys. The underlying principle was that close quarters warfare was a thinking man's game and that if you just rushed into it, you were bound to become a casualty quickly. The latest data reflected that the first two men through the door of any enclosure leading up to or within a house carried an eighty-five percent mortality rate.

It was the chilling reality of urban warfare. Our enemies weren't going to fight on some clear plane free of obstacles and away from the populace. They were going to mix in with the locals to neutralize our superior firepower and draw us into environments they thought they could win in. So, we had to learn how to win, fighting on their terms by rooting them out while limiting civilian casualties. Close Quarters Battle skills appeared to be a partial means to accomplishing that.

Deeno and I spent countless hours practicing with Zach and Pappy, messing up every conceivable aspect of it before we eventually got it down. We had learned different ways to check doors, move in different types of rooms, and communicate so a lot of old habits had to be broken.

Now, one of us would hold security while another breached, and the third man would make entry before the other two followed closely, all moving to points of domination inside the room. Threats would be aggressively prosecuted and the next entry point identified before proceeding with the same process.

There are ten to fifteen different movements associated with such specific actions and a million and one varying factors that influence them. We began with the basics because brilliance in the basics is what separates the average from the good and the good from the best. Zach didn't have to tell us that he expected the best. He silently conveyed this message through his constant presence and guidance of our training practices. He demonstrated proficiency and trained us to the same standard. Before long, we started to gel and that meant running the drill from one end of the hotel style barracks to the other. Entry after entry and repetition after repetition until we thought our noses were going to bleed. It brought us closer together a team. We were all on the same page and shared a mutual respect for and confidence in each other that can only be earned.

We earned Zach's approval by working countless hours. Our fingers bled from thumbing the safeties of our rifles, our feet swelled from posting doors to walls, and our heads felt like they were about to explode. All the time, he was never malicious. There was something else in his demeanor and the way he taught us that stood out, but I just couldn't put my finger on it. It was the same thing I had noticed in Badams and Jolo but much more profound.

Zach and I were complete opposites as leaders. I was barely more than a blunt instrument. I constantly yelled and screamed at our Boots and gave absolutely no consideration to doing things differently, until he showed me a better way. It was odd to observe someone so contradictory to what I was used to in a squad leader and yet it was impossible to ignore his effectiveness. I began to question which was the right model for me to adopt; was it my former squad leader's demanding "rule with the iron fist" philosophy or Zach's example of demonstrated proficiency infused with creativity, saving the iron fist for times it was warranted?

Overall, we were a wild and motley crew. At the time I had no idea what it was that held such a variety of people together and I carried a certain curiosity about how it would work out in the future. The new responsibilities I had as a team leader played a significant factor in how I was starting see things, and I still wanted more. I wanted to be the best, to stand out from my peers, and be distinguished.

A few months after all of this, I was selected to attend the Infantry Squad Leader's Course at Advanced Infantry Training Battalion. The only downsides were, it would mean nearly three months away from the squad and it was held at Camp Geiger where I attended SOI. A few of the other team leaders from the platoon would be going with me which eased my nerves some. My selection to the course meant that I showed promise as a leader.

ISLC was a big deal for a whole slew of reasons. First, it was a mental and physical kick in the nuts. Completing this course was a confirmation of physical prowess; it was one of those rare instant credibility achievements. Second, we were still lance corporals. While the Marine Corps designates sergeants as squad leaders and corporals as fire team leaders in a perfect world, the Corps' history is littered with Marines of all ranks performing admirably in roles above their rank. It felt good to know that Zach and the chain of command was confident in my ability to punch above my weight. I had earned that confidence through my performance, but the massive ego boost kept from realizing how humbling the experience ahead would be.

On the last cycle, a few of our seniors had gone through ISLC and they conveyed to us that the instructors weren't too thrilled about lance corporals being allowed in. The thought process was that we weren't mature enough or even capable of succeeding. It was a reasonable argument but an incorrect generalization of every grunt lance corporal.

I knew we could hang because I'd seen Badams and Jolo make it through. I remember seeing them drag themselves into the barracks at odd hours of the night after a long field evaluation, only to roll right into a weekend-long study session that resulted in five or six hours of sleep spread over those meager three nights, before leaving in the Monday morning darkness to do it all over again. They were beat by the end of it, and part of me knew that we would be too.

Having us trained up to where we could assume command if a squad leader was killed or wounded was just common sense. Key leaders had been killed in every war in history and the reality of the Afghan campaign dictated that small unit leaders be independent, capable, and adaptable. We had to have a firm grasp of small unit tactics and command. Casualties were inevitable and none of us were able to choose who lived and who didn't.

The next twelve weeks were the most grueling training and evaluation process of my life. ISLC reacquainted me with temporary defeat. Academics weren't as much of an issue as the physical and interpersonal demands. Every man was forced into command positions for every evaluation. Putting a lance corporal with one non-combat deployment in charge of a combat veteran sergeant can make for a very uncomfortable experience. I struggled to make it through every event, and the realization that I wasn't ahead of my peers was quite the reality check.

Every day was a mental battle. Morning workouts were brutally long, without exception. During the week, there were no "light days" to recover from a rough session the day prior or time spent in the field. We got destroyed every day. The only time we trained to normal standards was when we performed the required service level physical fitness test at the beginning and end of the course. Every formal school was required to use this two-test method to measure the physical progress of the students.

The last week, however, started with a squad competition that had ten different stations spread over thirteen miles of Geiger's real estate, ending at Camp Devil Dog where the POGs attended Marine Combat Training before scattering to their various operational specialty schools. We carried, multiple forty-pound ammunition cans, five-gallon water jugs, weapons and full kit, plus a stretcher with a squad member on it from start to finish. Each station was an evaluation point on one of the skills we had been taught and everyone was put on the spot at least once. Because it was a team event, if one man failed then the whole group received a negative mark, so the pressure was on.

The following day, we ran the standard Marine Corps physical fitness test in armor and helmet. It was damn near impossible to perform on the same level with the additional forty-five to sixty pounds of gear unless you were a stud. The next day we ran the same course in standard issue green shorts and shirt, or green on green, as was dictated by Marine Corps policy for evaluation.

AITB ratcheted up the USMC standards. In order to get in, Marines had to score over two hundred and fifty points on the PFT. Passing that, he would have to endure the rigors of the course itself and score at least the same on the last day again just to graduate. It was inconceivable that a man could make it through the previous eleven weeks only to fail that standard at the end and not graduate, but it had happened before.

The weeks leading up to the rigidly structured course were no cake walk. We battled through the morning hazing sessions before receiving classroom instruction for the first part of each phase, then took a written test before heading to the field for three to five days for practical evaluation. Then the process started over with new skills. Anyone who fell below eighty percent on any evaluation was sent back to their unit, with a negative mark in their performance record that carried enough weight to block a promotion.

From an academic standpoint, I thought my brain would melt. Each of us was issued a stack of books a foot high on day one and we were expected to learn everything they contained. I had to spend my off time studying until two or three in the morning just to keep up. Then it was up at five to get physically demolished in full kit on the obstacle course or a eight mile stretcher run before class.

The first overnight field operation was a basic weapons evaluation and turned out to be one of the most enjoyable of my career. We started out calling for sixty-millimeter mortars on static targets. Mortar men, undergoing their version of ISLC, dropped the rounds for us as we called them on several shattered cars and tank hulks out in an open field. It was the first time I had seen the weapon in action, and it gave me a new appreciation for its destructive power. We always gave the mortar men shit about sitting in the rear and stroking giant tubes like porn stars. After this, I didn't care what they did as long the rounds came when we called for them.

After that, we trucked over to another range and shredded targets with machine guns, rifles, and M203 grenade launchers before hiking to the demolition range.

Each man detonated something. We had claymore mines, C4, and TNT to choose from. After we got done, our instructors demonstrated a donut charge and a linear charge on a wooden door and frame, just to expose us to a little extra knowledge. Other than fireworks wars as a kid and the grenade range at SOI, it was my first time blowing something up and I still remember the concussions of the blasts, the acrid smell that hung in the air, and the smoke and debris that sprang from the other side of the berm that shielded us.

With the first field evolution complete, we went back to the classroom the following week and moved on to basic infantry tactics and supporting arms employment. Learning how to mesh everything together was so satisfying. I had never been exposed to this aspect of infantry operations before and it opened a whole new world for me. I had dedicated countless hours to patrolling, digging defensive positions, and attacking fortified training bunkers, but I had no concept of the level of planning that went into it all.

Learning how to write and present an operation order came next. Contrary to popular belief, everything isn't always as simple as telling someone to go from point A to point B. The actual process for preparing an order is lengthy and tedious. We were assigned three orders to write and each one took nearly seventy-two hours with and totaled nearly seventy pages. Sleep became a distant memory. We turned each one in on a Monday and wouldn't find out if we had passed or failed for another week.

The days went by quickly enough as we adapted to the physicality. We got used to our muscles being tight and our joints stiffly creaking and grinding under the weight of our kit or the telephone poles and water jugs we ran and hiked with. Thinks that didn't groan or pop before did so regularly and the only thing to do was power through the training.

The instructors always had ways of injecting just the right amount of misery to make you wonder if you could make it to the end. None of us felt good about the fact that we were riding a bus out of Camp Geiger for our last field evaluation. Our destination was a little makeshift combat outpost that would serve as the base we would patrol from for the next several days.

Nobody was very vocal on the ride over. I sat in the back of the small bus and noticed the demeanor of the other students. Some of them stared at the floor of the open shuttle bus while others peered blankly out a window, lost in the distance. We were all simply ready to be done and we knew it was about to get rough, otherwise we would've been hiking.

The next four days were divided into eight-hour shifts. Two men from each squad were randomly selected as the patrol leader and assistant. From that moment, the clock started ticking and we had the remaining seven hours and fifty-nine minutes to plan, prepare, and execute. If any time was left in the eight-hour block, then we could sleep. After the first day and night cycle passed with only a few minutes to spare in each time block, we realized that sleep deprivation was the chosen training amplifier.

The corporals and sergeants were evaluated first. Time seemed to slow down as the instructors worked their way down the list, block after block, and we started to figure out that if you had your shit wired tight, they would stick to their evaluation checklist and let you run the show. But if you gave them an inch, they made you pay for it dearly. If they heard grumbling about the lack of rest, a longer patrol was issued. If people didn't want to move fast, they issued more weight. If we weren't mentally engaged on the move, they threw artillery simulations at us and induced casualties for us to carry.

I was miserable, just like everyone else, but I reached a point where it didn't matter anymore. Once I accepted the fact that it was going to suck until it was over, I was able to focus on the task at hand. It didn't matter that I hadn't slept or stopped moving or that I had an extra radio, machine gun, or ammunition to carry through the thick vegetation. The torrential downpour, that seemed to magically begin whenever we went to the field, didn't matter either.

Proving to myself and to my peers that I could be a squad leader was all that mattered at this point.

I had to admire the instructors' subtle genius. In addition to the evaluations, they had found a way to push many of us to and beyond our limits. The vicious workout sessions, sleep deprivation, and the shotgun blast of academics all combined to show us that we were capable of so much more than our units were requiring of us. It wasn't about passing Marines to meet an arbitrary pass or fail percentage. It was about making us better and more lethal before sending us back to our units. They accepted it as their personal responsibility because they understood what it took to lead a squad in combat.

Whether they intended it or not, the expectation of elevating the squad to this level of toughness, entered my mind. One thing that makes a great infantryman dangerous is his contempt for pain and discomfort. When you reach that point to where you really don't care what happens to you physically, it unlocks the ability to make great strides towards achieving full potential. It became clear to me that this is the standard that all infantry units *should* be training to.

At the end, there wasn't a single part of my body that didn't hurt. The entire three-month period was a brutal day in, day out grind and if you couldn't hang you got called out by your peers and the instructors as someone who didn't belong. My arrogance landed me in that group at the start, which forced me to develop before I could succeed.

The fact is, we deal in an unforgiving business. If you fail at a job in the civilian sector, the worst-case scenario is getting fired. If you fail as a small unit leader, it could result in you standing in front of a broken widow or an angry teenager, trying to explain to them they don't have a husband or a father anymore because you couldn't pull your weight or make the right decision.

This reality alone is justification for the most brutal training and direct correction. The infantry lifestyle takes a toll on the body, injects anxiety and stress, and causes us to question what we are truly capable of. But the guidance and example of the experienced men teaches us how to deal with it.

The point of the training is to make sure that we are as ready as possible when the time comes, and we find ourselves in a seemingly unwinnable situation. It is not only logical but morally sound to maintain the highest standards and defend them vehemently when a politician or civilian wants to reduce them for whatever reason. Lives are far more important than feelings or votes.

ISLC humbled me. It showed me that I was far from being the top dog I fancied myself to be. I had a monumental distance to cover before I could consider myself remotely close to being one of the best. Just as important, it showed me that I could still succeed. Several of the students washed out due to a lack of mental and physical toughness and I was still standing.

In hindsight, I discovered after my initial failures that I had resilience and perseverance, which ultimately carried me through. I graduated in the fourth slot in the class academically, which I was proud of. But my performance had rightly caused my peers to question my tactical decision-making. Many of them could run faster and move heavier loads more easily than I could. I had a huge uphill struggle ahead of me to earn back their confidence. The whole experience reminded me that it never gets easier in the infantry. There is always another challenge. For me, that challenge would come in the most unexpected ways.

One week later, after the final thirteen-mile squad competition and physical fitness tests, we graduated. The day marked the start of a ninety-six-hour liberty period for Thanksgiving and everyone was eager to get home. The ceremony was small and informal as most infantry course graduations are. Our classmates from other battalions seemed to have every senior staff NCO from their command waiting to congratulate them. We only had one.

Gunnery Sergeant Willard, the senior enlisted tactical advisor to the CO, stood in the back of the room from start to finish. Being the only staff member that stayed in place from our last deployment, he had observed the positive changes in the company with all of the new faces. During the MEU, he was so busy fixing the logistical nightmares that our old CO created that he probably developed high blood pressure. Being a Boot during that time, I had interacted with him very little, but everyone knew that he was a no-nonsense man.

After all the shifting and shuffling of leaders, he was able to breathe a little bit easier, having other competent Marines do their part. Although not physically imposing, he moved with a purpose and his personal carriage conveyed discipline and confidence. With his dark high and tight haircut and square jaw line, he was the embodiment of a 1940's recruiting poster Marine.

Immediately after the ceremony, he waded through the sea of officers and SNCOs who had come to see their Marines and greeted us with an outstretched hand. Dignified and respectful, he congratulated us as men.

"This is your peer group now." The power of the simple message eluded me as he went on to release us to enjoy our extended weekend. I was just happy to have completed the course. My thoughts were with the coming drunken debauchery that usually occupied the time of a lance corporal in the empty barracks during a 96.

As I left Camp Geiger and tore down the highway, I took a

second to reconsider his brief statement. I let the radio blare at full blast and started pealing back the layers of our brief interaction to discover what he meant. He was challenging us. It was time to live the part, even if we didn't wear the rank insignia of an NCO. More would be expected of us because we had succeeded.

In the not-so-distant future, circumstances would force me to realize that there was so much more to being a good squad leader than I had learned at school.

We returned to our home company area and found several of our seniors waiting for us. Badams gripped me in a massive bear hug that lifted me off the ground while wearing his signature ear to ear smile. He was so proud that I had made it. I was his legacy, and a true leader always defines success by the growth of his juniors.

A few weeks later, Echo Company jumped onto chartered buses and made the quick trip up to Fort Pickett, Virginia. On the last cycle, we spent three weeks here undergoing the most rudimentary training. There was a set of old muggy squad bays that housed us in between our forays out to the urban training town or woodland squad range.

Most of us weren't thrilled about returning to Pickett given our last experience but it wasn't like we were going to say no. At this point we were just eager to find out what our boots and the squad were capable of. We had a whole new chain of command, from top to bottom and were training for the real deal this time.

We had a brief stay in the same stale, wooden squad bays as before, and spent the night prepping our gear for the field and enjoying our last hot meal. The following morning, we rode trucks out to the fire team level range, and it became clear that things would be different this time around. Instead of an easy bivouac in the neat rows of a company formation with grunts snoring away beneath the stars under the watchful eyes of a horrified boot on fire watch, we immediately pushed off the road and established a defense. We would train, rehearse, and conduct the range in platoon time blocks. The rest of our time would be spent in a tactical defensive posture, educating our teams and cross-training with the machine gunners.

While we rotated through the range both day and night, the squad leaders observed and noted deficiencies for the debrief. It was a straightforward fire and movement range, as we had rehearsed constantly on the softball field back at Lejeune, but with more real estate and live rounds.

It felt good to be back with my fire team. Deeno and Pappy had kept a track of them while I was at ISLC, and we picked up right where we left off.

The day runs went well due to Cotton's smooth manipulation of the SAW and Gavin's liberal use of forty-millimeter grenades. Grunts love live fire training. When you jam magazines full of rounds and load your weapon to storm an objective amidst the recoil and blast of weapons fire, it makes all the other times where you didn't have ammunition worth it.

Returning to our positions on the perimeter, we watched our sectors for an imaginary enemy. A few hours later, another squad would assume our positions so we could rehearse for the night attack or get our boots some time with the machine guns.

The sun began to fade, and we alternated donning night vision goggles and checking the lasers mounted to our rifles. Hollywood action films make these devices seem phenomenal but they're awkward when you first start using them. Night vision depends on ambient light, which means that on nights like this one, with decent clouds overhead, they' re only going to work so well. The monocular lens takes away almost all depth perception and requires constant adjustment of the filter when transitioning between differently lit environments. It's not like playing a video game where everything is constantly crystal clear.

First platoon took their time during their rotation, and I became anxious as the time drew near for us to get another crack at it. My mind raced through the full action of the trial ahead from start to finish repeatedly until our turn finally came.

We moved up to the staging area and drew our ammunition from Gunny Willard before I briefed the team on my expectations. Cotton was always to keep the light machine gun in action. He and Gavin were to take their cue for movement from mine. I wanted loud, clear communication, and violent action. They listened and took a moment to let it soak in before we were called up.

We set up in a wedge and began to move forward, each man scanning his designated sector through the NVGs and waiting for the inevitable simulation of frontal enemy fire. The ambient light wasn't strong, so I had to strain my eyes to keep track of Gavin's and Cotton's silhouettes. I felt a cool breeze pass and breathed anxiously, knowing that Zach and the company staff were all behind me scrutinizing my every move and decision.

The human shaped targets shot up out the ground with pulsing lights to simulate enemy fire and we hit the dirt as I yelled out my initial command. "Contact front, one hundred meters, enemy fire team, rapid rate!"

I held for a quick second to ensure the targets were dropping down after being shot, then popped back up and sprinted forward, which told the other two it was time to start moving.

The team picked it up just as they were supposed to, and we were closing the distance in alternating bounds to the sound of consistent fire. In what seemed like seconds, we neared the enemy position and passed through it. We ceased fire, having destroyed our plastic adversaries and I screamed out for the team to move back.

The same movement began in reverse order and as I turned to move back under the watchful eyes of Cotton, who had kept his SAW in action without any trouble, I spied Zach's purposeful saunter moving among the formation. He whispered to take longer bounds, which he wasn't supposed to do, and I echoed it to the team. We moved as fast as we could, one buddy covering the others until we reached the starting point.

Zach was stoked. After we unloaded the few remaining rounds, he pulled me off to the side and said, "Blackwell, your boys look like fucking studs out there!"

I felt so proud, I couldn't wait to pass the compliment onto the team. Zach instructed me to return to the defense and then stood by to watch the other two teams.

Back in the defense, I took a second to mentally recap the attack. Movement and communication were good but could've been better. Marksmanship was solid. Every time I saw an Ivan target pop up it was quickly hit by accurate fire. We called them "Ivans" because we were told they were developed a long time ago when war with the Soviet Union seemed imminent. They were roughly in the shape of a human head and torso. I say roughly because they kind of resembled a cross between a fat cartoon character from a children's television program and that chick at the club on St. Patrick's Day who clearly doesn't know she's too big to be dressed the way she is.

A few minutes later, Deeno returned, and we quietly shot the breeze for a minute before Zach got back. The word came down for each platoon to establish an observation post and man it all night. We dispatched a pair of men to a small hill across the road and pitched the bug nets that the company had provided us, which were a miraculous relief from the nagging mosquitoes that lived off us all day and night.

With security posted, the rest of us bedded down in our fighting positions until it was our turn on watch. I was on cloud nine, so happy with the gleaming compliment from Zach and a few of the senior personnel and passed out exhausted, thinking about the challenges that tomorrow and the rest of Fort Pickett would bring.

In the morning, we packed up and jumped on seven-ton trucks that took us to the same mock town we had visited last year. There was a growing suspicion that were riding trucks so much because there was a brutally long hike scheduled for the end of training.

Regardless, this is what we had been looking forward to. We were confident that no other squad in the company trained on close quarters skills like we had, and we were eager to prove it.

The first day was dedicated to training briefs and receiving an operation order for an attack we would carry out the next day. It was different not being a boot and seeing the process from start to finish, outside of an academic environment. Receiving an order from an officer was long and somewhat boring at parts but also eye-opening. On my previous deployment, the staff viewed team leaders as glorified babysitters and never let them sit in on an order. The squad leaders received the orders and then had to pass it to everyone else.

This command was different. We were expected to know what was going on, and if we didn't, to ask questions and learn. Being a team leader meant more than not having to stand fire watch at night, participate in working parties, or just teach and discipline your boots. There was a higher sense of responsibility and expectation that should've been present all along.

When the brief was done, we scarfed down a meal and then turned to team level training while the squad leaders and staff stayed behind for additional planning. Deeno, Pappy, and I found a nice sized building that was unoccupied and took the boys inside to continue drilling the close quarters tactics. Having run similar drills with them over the previous months, they knew what was expected. It was time to inject some stress and see if they could perform under less-than-ideal circumstances.

We were relentless. If there was any infraction in the process, we kicked them out of the room to try again. For three hours, we exploited every mistake: hesitation, timidity, lack of communication, gaps in coverage, not covering your buddy's blindside. We didn't cut them one ounce of slack. They would do it right or not at all.

We kept it simple with two, three, and four-man entries. When darkness came, we mounted NVGs and kept right on rolling. We could tell the constant screaming and pressure was getting to them. I could just barely make out the mannerisms of tired and pissed off men inside the dark enclosures as they tried again and again to get it right, if for no other reason than to get us off their case.

To their credit, they started to make progress towards the end when Zach finally returned. Instead of stepping in and taking control of the exercise, he watched, observed, and guided us through it. Micromanagement wasn't in his vocabulary, and we knew his expectations for training. He let us run the show.

We carried on for several hours, watching the boys sweat in the damp, humid structure while we demonstrated the proper techniques to them, answered their questions, and observed the countless repetitions until Zach put us down for the night to be well-rested for the platoon assault the following afternoon.

———

The next challenge was a transition from urban training back to "green side" as we called it. Having successfully completed the attack, we left the mock town and moved to a squad level attack range. It was an impressive set up. Each squad was given a pair of M240B medium machine guns and a sixty-millimeter mortar to use at the leader's discretion.

Zach tasked me to run the support by fire position. That meant that I was responsible for ensuring that the machine guns kept steady accurate fire on the targets while he maneuvered with Deeno's and Pappy's teams to assault the objective. I felt as if electricity was coursing through my whole body. It was another challenge; another opportunity to excel. I had never overseen a support position before, so it was new territory, but it wasn't rocket science. I had Cotton and Gavin with me along with the guns and their team leader. All we had to do was secure the sight while Zach and the other two teams maneuvered around the left flank to the last concealed position. Once we opened fire, Cotton would supplement the 240s with his SAW as necessary.

Our two elements separated at a designated release point and we halted briefly to give the assault team a little lead time since they had more ground to cover. Zach cleared us to move over the radio and we started towards a small wooded incline with the machine gunners in tow. We wanted to occupy by stealth if possible. If we gave up the ghost early, the rest of the squad would have to sprint several hundred meters and immediately assault.

We cut in between a small gap in the trees, drawing closer to the elevated piece of terrain that was to be our position in a V formation. Cotton brought up the rear with Gavin and I at the points, while the gun team followed us. The sun was at our backs which would have played to our advantage if we were fighting real enemies.

Ivan targets popped up as we approached the base of the slope and Gavin and I dropped them, rushed up to the top of the berm and secured the flanks. Cotton landed right in between us and let loose with the SAW as I called his targets to him.

There was a trench line about three hundred meters away to our ten o'clock, just outside of the tree line Zach and the others were maneuvering through. Cotton delivered his first burst of about twenty-five rounds from right to left as the machine gunners landed on either side.

Their team leader must've trained the hell out of them because they had the guns up quick and took over the suppression from Cotton. They timed their bursts between the two guns so there was always lead going downrange and they still conserved ammunition. Cotton jumped in when one of them had to reload, his weapon spitting muzzle flash and ejecting a steady, controlled stream of links and brass out the right side. I hung back behind the gun line and kept track of the surrounding area to make sure we didn't get caught off guard by any simulated enemies.

Looking over my right shoulder, I spied a green fireball arching up out of the tree line three hundred meters away. It was the signal to shift fire right as the assault team emerged into the clearing. I dashed back to the guns to ensure they were focused on the right half of the enemy position and any deeper targets we could engage.

Straining to see across the open ground, I saw the team spring from the trees. One man sprinted behind another to a position and once settled, begin firing. The teams peeled out like this until they were in a sort of staggered line that angled towards the left flank of the enemy defense.

Soon they started moving forward in bounds, first by teams and then by pairs until they reached the position and flooded through the left side into the chest-high trench. We ceased fire and redistributed rounds so everyone had something. The machine guns were almost out, but they were broken down quick and ready to move.

The assault element's firing died off almost instantly and we saw a white fireball shoot straight up. That was our cue to move to them, so we hauled ass down the front side of the hill, covering the three hundred meters as fast as we could. As we arrived at the trench, Zach assigned security sectors and we fell into place between the other two teams.

I felt like I was breathing fire and sulfur as my lungs heaved beneath the weight of my kit.

Snuggling up next to a dead Ivan, I peered over my rifle and took a second to breathe. Checking my left and right, I saw that Gavin and Cotton were locked in tight, scanning their sectors with stable firing positions that minimized their exposure. The adrenaline started to wear off and I couldn't help but feel great.

There's nothing like a good range. The electricity before, the toil and adrenaline during, and at the end, knowing that you'd done it right. You feel like you're on top of the world. The scent of spent ammunition combines with the expectation of future action to construct a moment unlike any before. Action produces an appetite for more action. Later, your mind replays it all and you start to take note of what went well and what went to shit.

That was the last range I'd ever run at Fort Pickett.

This experience was much better than our first. We had gotten better and continued to grow as a squad. The boots were coming along nicely, and we were operating smoothly together. We had progressed to the point that we didn't have to explain every detail. Expectations were clear and everyone did their part. Nobody had to say things like "cover right" or "cover left" because someone already had it locked down. We watched each other's backs and developed a healthy respect for one another based on our capabilities. It was good to be back in training with the unit. I wasn't slated for any more schools before the upcoming deployment, so I could focus completely on team development and painting the town with the boys.

Back at Lejeune, we congregated at Cotton's house for a squad cook out with the wives, which was a blast. Cotton was a huge hockey fan which suited Greddy, Gunner, and Norman just fine. Pappy and I just wanted to get hammered, which we wasted no time doing after being dry for several weeks in Virginia. We grilled out, laughed, drank, and decompressed together. The prospect of the upcoming field ops and the deployment didn't worry us much. We had each other, which was more than enough, and looked forward to what the future held.

Moments like this, when a group passes a test and validates its training practices, become treasured memories. We had made mistakes and learned from them, but just as importantly, we had started to reap the benefits of our work. These moments remind us of what it means to be an infantryman. It's when we get to reflect on the countless hours of clearing out barracks rooms, running attack drills on a softball field, and the pain we put ourselves through to get better that we realize that this is not a job, but a lifestyle.

We lived it, ate it, breathed it, and drank it. The conversation naturally steered itself back to what we did wrong and how we could be better but without any dreadful connotation. There was a sense of hunger that accompanied it. And we loved it.

A few months ago, after the post-MEU shake-up, Zach took over a squad of grunts that had never worked together before. Some of the boots had trouble keeping up on runs and hikes and everyone knew different tactics. Now, we knew each other's mental process and capabilities.

The Boots had hardened up physically and learned quickly. Deeno, Pappy, and I had grown close and recognized just how different we were and how we could help each other out. He had found a way to integrate all of us into a unit that maximized our strengths, while challenging us to grow.

October rolled around and I was selected to compete in the Battalion's meritorious corporal board. Everyone involved was a team leader, so we were already doing a corporal's job, by Marine Corps standards. The winner would sport an extra chevron on his collar and the famous blood stripe running the full length of his dress blue trousers.

Only one from each company was competing which meant that each command was sending their stud, instead of just throwing a name out to satisfy the new sergeant major. I had one week to prepare, and I was separated from the daily workings of platoon life to focus solely on the competition.

I had a basic idea of what was coming but no idea how much tedious detailed work it was going to be. My time was filled with cramming every piece of knowledge that even remotely pertained to the Marine Corps into my head, from uniform regulations to close order drill, the Uniform Code of Military Justice, history, and anything else I could get my hands on. A lot of it was stuff I had learned in recruit training and discarded to make way for the flood of infantry knowledge.

Half of each day was spent with a team leader from our last deployment named Matt, studying and preparing uniforms. He was a lot like my former team leader, Badams, in that they both wanted to move on with their lives, but they wouldn't let themselves turn into lazy scumbags in their final months wearing the uniform.

We spent hours scouring books and ironing on small strips of tape with my last name perfectly stamped on them to every single piece of clothing I owned, from black dress socks to white briefs and service and dress uniforms.

Our preparations carried well into the night, leaving two or three meager hours of sleep. Matt knew I was tired, but he didn't let up one inch. His efforts and demeanor conveyed the message that he approved of me being promoted, even if it was much earlier than most of our peers, and he was willing to sacrifice his own time to help me earn it. I never asked him. He simply took it upon himself.

When he wasn't there, Staff Sergeant Troy was. Troy was an old salty platoon sergeant with multiple combat pumps to both Iraq and Afghanistan under his belt. He was one of Matt's and Badams' seniors and spent the MEU as First Platoon's senior enlisted man.

No one wanted to piss this guy off. He had a relaxed manner until someone crossed him and then he just calmly made life hell for that individual. He had a sarcastic way of answering questions that prompted you to find things out for yourself instead of risking embarrassment which was very effective. To top it all off, he was a walking encyclopedia of Marine Corps knowledge.

Troy consistently ensured I was putting in the work and kept me up to date on the evaluation events as they became known. He was the inside man who appeared out of nowhere to drop another book in my lap or tell me I had incorrectly marked a uniform item. Between him and Matt, there was no time for anything but preparation.

I was running on fumes by the time Friday finally rolled around. It had been a long week and today would be the longest of all.

We started at 0500 with a standard combat fitness test, which all of us scored nearly perfect on. The CFT was still relatively new to the Corps and was supposed to measure the individual Marine's fitness level when performing combat related tasks. It consisted of an 880-meter sprint, max ammo can overhead presses in a two-minutes and finished up with a short circuit of various movement and load bearing activities for a timed score.

I didn't know it at the time, having not been to combat yet, but this didn't do a very good job of accomplishing its intended purpose. What it did do was make POGs feel like they did something Infantry-like and it conveyed the false message that a high score could be equated to battlefield capability. Most of us had very little faith in its validity because there was no ruck mark for time.

After the CFT, we had a small window to shower up and change into Service Alpha uniforms to await one of the company first sergeants who would inspect us and the cleanliness of our living quarters. It was a painstaking examination of our wall lockers, as well, in which the first sergeant looked for everything he could find to deduct points, even going so far as to produce a small ruler to measure the folded shirts and black dress socks to ensure that they were within one eighth of an inch of the manual's allocation.

A Service Charlie uniform inspection followed in the battalion conference room, and close order drill came after that. We ended the day with an appearance before a board that made the final decision. Each of us would be called into a room to formally report in and respond to questions asked by each of the company's first sergeants and the new battalion sergeant major.

Between the six of them, there was about ninety years of professional military experience and each one of them was scrutinizing every detail of our appearance, bearing, and knowledge the second we walked in the room.

Now, behind the scenes, promotion boards often boiled down to which first sergeant could argue their cases best. If their representative won, then they had bragging rights over the others. All the other events helped but this one carried the most weight. If you bombed the board, you had no chance in hell. The key to success was your bearing. World War III could be erupting right outside the door, but if you stood tall, looked immaculate, and answered their questions directly with confidence you were golden.

Admittedly, it was a little neat to be competing in something completely new to me. This was the side of the Marine Corps that took a back seat to what really mattered to us. Most of this stuff had absolutely nothing to do with winning a war. It was just how the organization had always done things, so the tradition carried on. I had done everything I could and win or lose, after this was over, it would be back to reality where shooting, moving, and communicating defined success, failure, and worth.

After the board was over, I joined my fellow competitors in the hallway to await the final decision. Eventually, we were called in and informed that the team leader from Fox Company had won.

I was pissed; probably more than I should have been.

The rest of the company had been out in the field while I was back in the rear playing toy soldier, and I didn't even walk away with the win. It seemed that all my frustration and the dry, tedious studying had resulted in nothing of value.

My first sergeant pulled me down to his office afterwards and told me that my responses to the board questions made me seem overconfident and aggressive. Why in the fuck these were considered bad qualities for a man bound for combat was completely beyond me.

Regardless, it was over, and I could breathe a little easier. Matt couldn't believe it when I told him why I had lost. He seemed angrier than me, which was some consolation. Staff Sergeant Troy on the other hand, spent the next month addressing me as "Not-a-Corporal-Blackwell."

"Good afternoon, Staff Sergeant." I would customarily say in passing.

"Good afternoon, Not-a-Corporal-Blackwell."

"Hey Staff Sergeant, can you help me out with this?"

"Sure, Not-a-Corporal-Blackwell."

I would've bet my next paycheck that he was never going to let me live it down. It was his way of simply reminding me that failure had consequences and I got the message in the clear yet hilariously sarcastic way that he chose to convey it.

In any case, I'd be sporting the single chevron and crossed rifles of a lance corporal on my wedding day the following month.

I returned from a week-long leave to find things exactly as I had left them. The platoon leadership concluded a brief meeting down on the narrow patch of earth beneath the barracks and our platoon commander approached me afterwards. I smartly saluted and he returned it only to extend his hand and congratulate me on my recent marriage. We exchanged a few pleasantries before going our separate ways to conduct the day's business as usual.

A short while later, Staff Sergeant Hauz called me to the company office to see the first sergeant. Afternoon chow had just been concluded and we expected to secure for the weekend in a few hours. I made my way down the flights of stairs at the western end of the barracks and across the grass to the southern entrance of the building, right by the first sergeant's office.

The company office, also referred to as "CP," was quiet. It was about 1300 and it seemed the platoon leaders were wrapping up a few last-minute administrative tasks before they passed the word and cut us loose to destroy Jacksonville again. I knocked on the wooden door and the first sergeant told me to grab the red binder from a plastic mailbox attached to the cream-colored wall on the right side of the frame.

My pulse skyrocketed as I removed it from its holder and presented it to him. Only two things come in those red plastic sleeves that bear the golden Eagle, Globe, and Anchor emblem: awards and promotion warrants. I was wary, still remembering the loss of the board roughly a month earlier. Handing it to him, he opened it to reveal my promotion warrant to corporal which bore the word "meritoriously" in parenthesis next to the rank.

I was so shocked I could hardly believe it. Rank didn't matter in the sense of "power." Corporal was special because it was admittance to one of the proudest peer groups in all the services. A Marine non-commissioned officer bore a certain amount of prestige for many reasons. It was the first rank in the enlisted structure that you had to compete for. On top of that, corporals were known as the spine of the entire organization.

The ranks of private through lance corporal were given once you accrued a specified amount of time in service, but to become a NCO you had to accrue points based on your annual rifle qualification, physical fitness tests, and time in grade until your total was greater than the score that the Corps had in place to promote people. The problem was that the "cutting score" that came down from on high every month changed constantly. More often than not, lance corporals would end up chasing it for several months and even years before they actually got promoted.

I can't count high enough to illustrate the number of times I stood in formation to witness a comrade's promotion when he had no more than a month or two on his contract before leaving the service to become a civilian.

Meritorious promotions, however, had only a minimum time-in-service requirement. So, theoretically, a Marine could earn a meritorious promotion, having only spent a few months as a lance corporal, if he had been on active duty for at least two years. That was rare but not unheard of for many a solid Grunt who had a brief spate of trouble and been busted down in rank.

I had been in just shy of thirty months, so that wasn't an issue. But I could still hardly believe it. Most of my seniors had pinned on corporal chevrons right before they got out or on their last deployment and I thought I would end up the same way. Lo and behold, here I was holding my warrant in my own two hands and looking at the NCO Creed on the other side of the binder.

The first sergeant congratulated me and told me to find chevrons because the ceremony would be in one hour, right before we secured for the weekend. I shot out of the building like a bat on crystal meth, beaming with pride across the patch of earth that separated the two buildings. Badams wasn't in his room but responded to my phone call to let me know he would be there to pin me. I hit up Zach next and told him the good news so he could be my second.

In every promotion up to that point the CO or presiding officer pinned the new chevrons onto your collar but getting promoted to corporal carried the tradition of the Marine choosing anyone he wanted to do the honors. It was his way of recognizing those who had trained, mentored, and influenced him the most. Badams had been my team leader on the last deployment and laid the foundation of any success that I would have for the duration of my career. He was disciplined, tough as all hell, and loyal; truly a man of honor I respected. Zach had already made such an impact on me that it was undeniable. I valued his opinion of me and respected him as a leader and mentor for his skill, professionalism, and lethality. I wouldn't have chosen anyone else.

When the time came, I was standing behind the company as they waited in formation. This was the only thing in between them and a weekend. Nobody wanted to drag it out.

I pulled out the corporal chevrons I had earned from Badams months ago and removed the golden backings from them. It was tradition for a team leader to bestow a pair of chevrons on one their Boots when their performance warranted increased responsibility. It was a blessing of sorts. I had carried this set, pinned on the inside of my MARPAT 8-point garrison cover for nearly a year as a prized possession waiting for this day.

The first sergeant called us to attention and took his post to the back left of the CO before calling me to report. I was nervous, thinking to myself as I marched that it would be a gas if I tripped on a rock and bounced my face off the ground in front of the whole company.

Thankfully, I made it without incident. I listened as the warrant was read aloud and Lieutenant Winston, our acting CO, asked me who I wanted to promote me. I gave him the names and Badams and Zach arrived with smart salutes on either side of me. They saluted and I produced the two black insignias.

Zach handed me a small roll of red fabric tightly bound in neat plastic packaging about the size of a baseball. It was my first set of blood stripes which acted as his equivalent of Badams' chevrons. In the two years I had been in the Corps, I had never seen a mentor present this to someone during a promotion ceremony and I gripped them so tightly no force on heaven or earth could've ripped them from my hand. The two removed the lance corporal chevrons from my collar and hurled them into the air, as is customary, and took the two I held in my upturned palm.

With pride, the two worked the insignias into the fabric of my MARPAT blouse.

I braced myself for what was to come and welcomed it with a slow inhale. Badams finished first and making a fist with his right hand, which was notorious for leaving scars when he hit someone, drove the spikes through the camouflage blouse. They pierced my skin just below the collar bone. I felt every detail of the initial sting and the accompanying burn as Zach followed suit. The two shook my hand and saluted Lieutenant Winston smartly before returning to their places in the formation. The CO released the formation, and every single man made his way forward with an outstretched hand and congratulations.

Matt scooped me up afterwards and we hopped into his jeep to grab all the beer we could carry from the little exchange just down the road. By the time we got back, everyone had changed clothes and they were ready. I settled into Matt's room with several others, as he got into civilian attire for one of the best and oldest of Marine traditions. It was also considered one of the most egregious forms of hazing by higher commanders and punishable under the UCMJ. The fact that an organization centered on wholesale enemy destruction, classified what was about to happen as "hazing" was comical.

Blood striping and pinning, as the tradition was called, was a ritual that involved the newly promoted Marine receiving a hard knee strike to the outer thigh by every corporal or above in the whole company.

Once everyone had contributed, the new NCO would bear the reddish black bruises the full length of his outer leg, where the blood stripe of his dress blue trousers would rest when worn. Zach had given me my first set of NCO blood stripes for my uniform, but every single NCO in the entire Company would give me my real ones throughout the course of the night.

McGruff, Badams, Jolo, and Matt were first to do the honors. A man on each side supported me beneath the arm and the knees found their mark. The strikes made an odd sort of sound that reminded me of someone hitting a melon. Every NCO got one strike to each of my legs. A blast of heat rushed through my body, and it quickly became difficult to stand up.

The chevron pinning followed immediately, each man offering praise, congratulations, and his words of wisdom as the spiked insignias pierced my chest each time.

My legs felt as if they were on fire. They had started to swell already which took away from the seven or eight miniature punctures I had beneath each side of my collar bone. The alcohol we had been liberally consuming finally kicked in.

There was nothing demeaning about the informal ceremony. No one was cruel or condescending. This wasn't like a college fraternity rush week with some pretty boy class president making a freshman chug a bottle of dip spit because he thought he was powerful. This was pure. The pain that was racking my limbs and oozing out of the punctures at the top of my chest was meant to serve as a reminder that I had a responsibility to carry on our legacy of leadership by example.

My seniors' contributions were a physical manifestation of their blessing to go forward and live up to the title. They were proud and to receive such an honor was one of the most humbling and daunting experiences of my life. It highlighted the infinite responsibility that I had earned. Experiences of such high quality are of the rarest kind and meant to be cherished, not classified as barbarism and publicized as horrid hazing sessions. Very few things in life can compare to proving yourself to an elite tribe like the Infantry and receiving the endorsement of quality mentors.

The following week of recovery was agonizing. My legs swelled to the point that I couldn't fit into blue jeans. My roommate grabbed chow for me and brought it back to the room. I did my best to walk normally when I had to avoid any undue attention.

Staff sergeant Hauz knew exactly what had happened. I told him I had pulled a muscle in the gym, and he acknowledged my bull shit with a polite form of sarcasm that was rare for him. He didn't press the issue and no one else seemed to notice anything unusual.

By the end of the week, the bruises were still visible but the tenderness in the muscles had largely subsided. It was good timing too because we were out in the field again for another quick one-week op to brush up on close quarters marksmanship skills. The week passed quickly enough and then it was home for a few days before a two-week-long battalion field exercise followed by Enhance Mojave Viper out in California.

EMV was a major test for every battalion. If a unit did well, word traveled across the Marine Corps and the chances for a good combat deployment rose, so everyone wanted a grand slam performance. We had heard horror stories of some of the ranges we would be running, which were all most of us had to go on, but I didn't think any of us were really that nervous about it. We had a good platoon, and the squad was tight as hell.

Every day, we got better and became more cohesive. Tactical movement and communication were nearly seamless and fluid, especially in an urban training environment. We had developed a notable confidence and I looked forward to the formidable challenge in California.

All around the barracks and surrounding battalion area, posters had been put up summarizing Operation Moshtarak in Afghanistan's

Helmand Province. Word on the street was that it was turning into a tough brawl with a lot of casualties on both sides. If that's where we were going, there was no doubt that it would be just the type of deployment that every grunt signed up for. For now, we focused on EMV, with the looming deployment and the ultimate test of a breathing, thinking, and calculating enemy lurking just beneath the surface.

About a week before we left, Zach brought us the news that we were getting a corporal from Security Forces in the squad. None of us were thrilled because the spots were already filled, and it meant that either Deeno or Pappy was going to lose their billet to this cat. It had nothing to do with skill or proven leadership and everything to do with rank. They were lance corporals and he had an extra chevron on them, so he automatically got the nod. It was a reminder that regardless of how strong the infantry was, we were all still subject to big Marine Corps thinking.

What we worried about most was the potential negative effect it could have on the entire squad. We were a tribe within a tribe, and we expected outsiders to conform to our standards because the whole mattered more than the individual.

The assignment was dictated by men much higher than Zach, so there was absolutely no way around it.

We were lucky enough to have a solid crop of guys from Fleet Antiterrorism Security Team. Zach, Pappy, Cotton and even some in the other platoons had established good dependable reputations. We were fortunate enough to have them and we were hoping our luck would hold with this new addition.

Corporal Andy had arrived in the battalion a few months before and had been promoted shortly after. He was a big guy, six feet two inches tall, and built like heavy-weight boxer. I don't think I ever heard him scream at his team and it was obvious that he had a more democratic approach to leadership than I. He caught on quick and second team with Patrelli, Tracy, and Todd hardly missed a beat.

We had a few days before going to California and we took full advantage of it. Andy observed a lot and jumped into the mix with his guys without any reservations. He was calm and well-spoken, but not timid. That much was abundantly clear during the squad fights and barracks training.

The downside of Andy's arrival was that Deeno got moved to another squad. It had been great having him with us and I still wasn't sold on Andy. He had big shoes to fill.

Deeno stayed in the platoon and there wasn't any bad blood, although he was pissed about being caught up in the game of musical team leaders and not being able to see things through with his guys.

He had put in countless hours of development, training, and mentorship to make his team top notch and he had succeeded, without question. Now he had to start all over again with a new set of guys, break old habits as he saw fit, and then replace those with what needed to be there. Additionally, his new squad leader had a different philosophy. No two leaders are exactly the same. There are always variations in the way they go about things, what they expect, and the standards they have and hold everyone else to.

On top of all that, the way team leaders interact with each other as peers plays a huge role in the success of any squad. If there's any animosity, it's felt on every level. Given the amount of time and effort spent together, it's oddly similar to a marriage and the kids, or Boots in these cases, always know when mom and dad are fighting. The fix for that is a squad leader who knows how to arrange his people based on their strengths and weaknesses and leverage them appropriately.

Zach brought Andy right into the fold. He came out with us on the weekends and his personality found its place within the squad. The changes were so microscopic that I could hardly notice any at all.

Zach's reenlistment ceremony said it all. Much like a promotion to corporal, the Marine who has signed on for another term gets to choose the manner in which the ceremony is conducted. Some are very simple and straight forward, while others can be outrageously elaborate. Stories abounded of Marines having their entire company tread water in a training pool while he and the presiding officer floated in the deep end reciting the Oath of Enlistment. The reenlisting Marine can request the specific officer he wants, too, even if he is outside the direct chain of command. He can choose time, place, and uniform.

The only thing that is always the same is the reading of the certificate of reenlistment and the recitation of the Oath of Enlistment to reaffirm commitment to the Constitution.

Zach kept things modest. He didn't want anyone in clean, pressed uniforms or a massive audience. He requested our current executive officer, Lieutenant Winston to preside and only a few of his closest friends would be permitted in addition to the squad. Zach's girlfriend came and stood off to the side as we gathered around in a small semi-circle at attention for the formal portion, which was clean and quick.

The fact that no one else in the company was present spoke volumes about Zach's priorities. It wasn't that he didn't like the rest of the unit, but he most valued us and what we had built together. The scene had a certain intimacy to it that whispered to us that we were what he was most proud of and we were the reason that he signed the contract again. This squad was not *his*, but *ours*.

He requested Lieutenant Winston because, his knowledge of and respect for Afghanistan's history and culture made him someone we sought out and learned from. Zach chose well because Winston would be invaluable on the upcoming deployment. As I put it all together, I realized that Zach's ceremony summarized this portion of our lives.

Lieutenant Winston represented the importance of what lay ahead, and we all welcomed that challenge because of the spirit that we produced together as a squad. We had prepared for one of the most complex combat environments in history, one that would leave its mark on all of us. Being selected by Zach to be a part of such a significant event was humbling. It was also one of the best feelings in the world to be a part of something so genuinely great.

We touched down at March Air Force Base in sunny California and jumped on chartered buses for the journey out to Camp Wilson. Grunts from California had always bragged that they were physically superior to east coast Marines and from the bus windows, we all took in the landscape they thought made them invincible. The steep imposing hills were marked with nice houses that we guessed belonged to adult film stars.

"That's definitely a porn star's house!" someone yelled.

"Yea it's yours, isn't it? Somebody told me you're due for another gang bang later today!" the reply came.

The twisted banter played out just like it always: coarse, without any filter, and accompanied by wild laughter. Grunts take pride in having the sickest sense of humor on the planet.

About an hour and half later, we pulled through the main gate at Marine Corps Air Ground Combat Center in Twentynine Palms, home to the Seventh Marine Regiment, which was rumored to be the most proficient in the infantry. The environment around me made it believable.

There was nothing to do at this place other than train. The bus turned left after passing the main gate and proceeded down the road for a few short miles.

Panning the rugged landscape, after we disembarked confirmed that we were in the middle of nowhere. Camp Wilson, little more than a few rows of Quonset huts and a small exchange store, was set in an open patch of desert. The hardened terrain sprawled out in all directions, rising to brown and black spotted mountains a few kilometers in the distance.

Having this kind of real estate meant you could destroy anything you wanted, but you were probably going to lose your sanity when you weren't training. The place had a menacing post-apocalyptic vibe to it that contrasted with the congested vegetated layout of Camp Lejeune, which felt like it was right in the middle of Jacksonville.

It's a common belief among Marines, regardless of MOS, that Satan himself built this base specifically to watch Marines suffer. The heat had already begun sapping our energy. There wasn't a major city or main attraction remotely close by. And the place just looked so god-awfully ugly.

We set up shop in the platoon sized Quonset huts and spent the rest of the first day unpacking and preparing our gear. On the outside the structures looked like metal semi circles jutting out of the ground, as if the desert floor had swallowed half of them. The floors were concrete slabs supporting two rows of olive drab Vietnam Era style cots. No climate control or privacy.

The next twenty-four hours were a miserable drag of going to countless briefs as a company; everything from an orientation to the base to the rundown of the wildlife in the area and instructions about everything that we *weren't* allowed to do.

I shuffled around with everyone else, moving from one classroom to the next and in and out of the quaint little chapel that sat across from our huts. As the day drew on, the lecture subjects became more and more ridiculous, especially as they pertained to dumb shit that Marines had done in the past. As I heard the laundry list of various and quite inventive chicaneries I wondered, "Can someone really be that stupid? Please tell me this hasn't actually happened before. There's no way. Well, this is why we can't have nice things." The trouble that Grunts get in to when we get bored will never cease to amaze.

It culminated with company formation at around 2200, so we could receive a class on how to deal with the infamous desert tortoise should we encounter it. This particular species, being very small and particularly vulnerable, carries with it the innate burden of urinating heavily when frightened and thus dying of dehydration almost instantly. Apparently, California wildlife experts and animal rights activist groups were so up in arms about the alarming death rate of this poor animal at the hands of the barbarous and savage invading

Marines that they had bitched to high heaven about it and gotten what they wanted.

We were informed that if one was to cross our path on patrol, in the assault, while mounted in vehicles, or at any juncture at all that the exercise would be halted immediately so that trained experts could come out and remove the endangered animal before we could continue.

The astronomical stupidity of it was comical. The entire company rolled with laughter in disbelief at the sheer jackassery that we had just been exposed to. The officer who stood before us was so depressingly detached that our reaction didn't faze him a bit. He spoke in melancholy tone that confirmed he had briefed other companies on the subject and simply didn't have any more fucks to give about this precious creature he was required to introduce to us. I felt bad for the guy.

The thought that it was acceptable to some people to value the life of a small tortoise over the realistic training of a group of men bound for the most violent places in the world was so idiotic that it triggered uncontrollable laughter. Clearly it didn't have the desired effect that the wildlife protectors wanted because a bet went out that very night to see who could get the first desert tortoise kill. It was game time.

The following day consisted of white space training, meaning that Zach had the whole day to train us however he wanted.

We ran three to five miles every morning to get used to the dry heat that was very different from the humidity of the Carolinas. Strips of engineering tape were staked in the ground to create the outline of houses for close quarters drills. The activity helped us channel our tactical Chi to Zach's liking and soon enough we were getting creative with it.

Several months earlier, Zach had purchased a set of small

adjustable bipods and mounted them on the bottom of his M4. Now he added his bayonet. It was the first time I had seen anyone practice room clearing with the knife attached and I wished I had thought of it first.

White space was a driven squad leader's favorite time. He could use it to shape his boys into whatever he wanted them to be.

Today, it gave us a chance to get our new corpsman up to speed. The Army produces its own medics to care for the wounded during battle. The Marine Corps does not. As a department of the Navy, we receive that support from them usually in the form of one corpsman per platoon. We already had one assigned to us, but nobody was going to complain about having another.

Naval corpsmen have a special place in the infantry's heart. They go where we go, fight the same fight, endure the same hardships, and have saved countless American lives. Most of them divide their enlistments by serving time in a "blue side" environment, like a battalion aid station, and a "green side" environment, attached to direct ground combat units like ours.

Their green side time is considered a rite of passage. Once they have completed an assignment, we no longer view them to be a part of the Navy. Rather, we look at them as Grunts with advanced medical capabilities. Corpsmen must be every bit as capable as a rifleman and carry the added responsibility of preserving the wounded in dire circumstances. No one and I mean *no one*, takes better care of wounded Marines than corpsmen do.

Doc Wilkins was joining us for what would be his first deployment. Clearly, he joined for the right reasons because he could have requested to be attached to a BAS and floated through his enlistment performing mundane tasks like administering the six million shots given to Marines before every deployment. But here he was, fresh out of Field Medicine School and picking up on things fast.

The man wasn't intimidated, that much was obvious. He jumped right in and learned everything he could, and in turn taught us the latest and greatest about combat trauma care.

Doc, as all green side corpsman are called, stood at average height and weight with light brown hair. He had an easy-going personality and shared our dark, fatalistic sense of humor, which we appreciated. He would prove a solid addition to the team in the coming weeks and although he was considered a platoon level asset, he gravitated to our squad. To say the least, it was a mutually beneficial relationship.

After the tape house warm-up, we moved on to patrols which is what we spent most of our time on. We got a few minutes to check our gear and ensure our teams were prepped and ready before we stepped away from the huts. We changed formations constantly and communicated as we thought we would in a real combat situation. Nothing was overlooked as too small or insignificant. The goal was to continue to hone the basic skills of navigation, movement, and communication that would make us successful on the upcoming pump, which we knew at this point, would be Afghanistan. We just didn't know exactly where or when.

We spent a few hours at it and then took a break to shoot the shit and grab some chow. The rumor mill, or "bum scoop," was in full swing, as always, and word on the street was that once we left Wilson, we wouldn't be coming back until the entire three-week exercise was complete.

The PX got bled dry of all tobacco products first, which is standard practice. You could order grunts to patrol on the surface of the sun with no water and if they had nicotine, they'd be okay. Dip and cigarettes are the infantry's gold and silver.

The other amenities like soap, laundry detergent, electrolyte tablets, 550 cord, map pens, protractors, field notebooks, socks, and anything else considered even moderately useful were taken next.

The word came down that we would be departing the next day late in the afternoon to one of the forward operating bases . From there, we would truck or walk out to the ranges and live wherever we trained.

When we disembarked the vehicles a day later, I took a tour of the small outpost to scout a section of the birthing for our squad. The place wasn't so bad. There were enough small plywood hooches to house the company and a small combat operations center enclosed by a Hesco wall about twelve feet high with four guard towers arranged at the corners. In total, it was about the length of a football field and there was an open area we could use for additional training right by the front gate.

We got settled into the new digs just after nightfall and everyone bedded down for what we were told would be our last good night's sleep. Zach and the other squad leaders set up a post rotation, so the towers and radios were manned before settling into his spot between me and Gunner.

I drew the middle shift from midnight to 0200 as Corporal of the Guard. I got out the minimum amount of gear as per usual and crawled into my bag to try and pass out before watch.

The small structure was still alive with people talking and laughing about the EMV experience we'd had thus far. Someone was playing '80s rock from a small device and the tunes gave things a strange sort of vibe. To an outsider it would've seemed as if we were preparing for an alcohol fueled epic instead of a war. The only light we had was from the full moon outside.

Zach and Gunner got into a philosophical debate. Zach loved to play devil's advocate just to see how we would react, and he did so every chance he got. He would pose a question, listen to a response, then pose another or offer an alternative to see what kind of wild turn the conversation would take. Gunner made a sarcastic remark about religion and a struck a nerve. Zach shut him down hard and it killed the entire mood. The laughter died instantly, the music stopped, and everyone shut the hell up.

Zach rarely ever raised his voice with any emotion attached to it. I could count on one hand how many times it happened. Unlike many leaders, he didn't have to establish dominance through volume. His performance and his leadership merited respect, so he didn't have to be the boisterous drill instructor type so commonly associated with this profession. Because of its rarity, when he did raise his voice or show anger, the effect lingered and hung over the entire platoon like a storm cloud. The worst part about pissing him off was never his anger or wrath, it was that we had somehow disappointed him. I was glad I wasn't Gunner in that moment.

We didn't go straight to the ranges. The first phase of training was to be conducted in a small town a few hundred meters away. We patrolled on foot instead of taking trucks and settled into a small courtyard overlooked by a grayish building constructed to look like a school or some other public institution while we waited for our instructors to arrive. It was early in the morning, and we shed gear to grab a seat and light the first cigarette of the morning while the sun was still rising.

The instructors, known as coyotes, showed up and gave us the rundown of the day's events. We'd start off patrolling through the city, which was built solely for this purpose. Unbeknownst to the taxpayers, they had paid handsomely for facilities all over the country, like this one, to be filled with paid actors that would add an element of authenticity to our training.

The coyotes were a professional crew and impossible to miss due to their bright orange tactical interceptor vests that had been standard issue during the opening stages of the Iraq campaign. The vests had rows of black webbing and reflective tape that made them look like tactical traffic cones, which easily distinguished them from the rest of us with our new plate carriers.

After the briefing, we formed up in a tactical column and set out on patrol through the city. It was a straight shot through the town's busy marketplace which we could see was teaming with people moving back and forth. As we neared the beehive of activity, my hands clenched the rifle I carried and my eyes darted back and forth, scanning everyone's hands and clothing in search of anything that could be perceived as a threat.

Everyone else seemed calm and reserved. Gavin, Cotton, and the rest of the squad maintained their dispersion and scanned their sectors while the villagers darted back forth peddling their merchandise. They dressed as Afghans and spoke Dari or Pashto fluently and loudly.

Buildings rose on both sides, lined by the small wooden stalls that the vendors scurried to and from to make their daily living. The busy street narrowed as we drew further away from our starting point and the people added a sort of claustrophobic feel to it. I wasn't used to people moving through our formations, so the set-up made me anxious, as if I was compromising the squad's security by letting them carry on their business. I wondered if this is what was in store for us overseas. It was everyone else's calm that kept me calm and controlled throughout the exercise, and it ended without incident.

The whole point was to expose us to these things to limit the shock factor that we would inevitably experience once in country. It was simple psychological preparation.

While we waited for the other squads to patrol the city, the coyotes set up a "kill house" in a small structure made from shipping containers linked together to form hallways and rooms.

Kill houses, when done properly, were among the best training scenarios for grunts. Typically, a handful of guys would get the chance to go into the designated structure and practice rendering medical aid to various common battlefield wounds on a few dummies that had red paint spilled all over them. The Coyotes pulled out all the stops on this one, however and it gave us a chance to stand back and observe our guys work under pressure.

The boys stacked up behind a wall a few meters away and one of the coyotes tossed an artillery simulation into the building to kick off the exercise. The whistle of the small dummy munition ended abruptly in a tiny but loud explosion and screams filled the air as the boys sprinted to the doorway.

The actors were made up of several actual amputees who were covered in theater blood, bellowing their cries of pain and agony as our guys moved passed them to secure the area.

They cleared the rooms of any potential threats and established security as the role players thrashed on the ground and cried out, groping their ankles and begging them for help. I was impressed by how seriously the role players took the training.

They screamed as horridly as they possibly could and some fought our guys when they applied pressure to the simulated wounds. The boys had to work the whole time to keep them restrained so they could apply tourniquets and pressure dressings. Gallons of fake blood spurted out of the severed limbs onto the floor. The walls were covered in it and the actors were nearly swimming in it. Our guys slipped and fell and had to keep going from one victim to the next. The blood was meant to rattle them, to make them freeze up and make mistakes like not applying immediate direct pressure or failing to tighten a tourniquet enough to stop blood flow.

We could see slight nervousness in a few of them, but that was it. We had practiced these skills a million times, just without all the theatrics and props, so they knew what they were doing and didn't let it mess with their heads.

No more than ten minutes after the artillery simulation had been thrown, the building was secured and every casualty, about five or six in all, had been treated. A coyote moved to each casualty inspecting the medical gear applied and quizzing our Boots to ensure they understood why each injury required the specific treatments prescribed.

It was good realistic training aimed at preparing the mind and the spirit for what could happen in the future, and it was a good honest day's work. We finished up with the coyotes and they released us to patrol back up to the FOB, about a mile away.

Zach settled in up front with the point team and left me at the back as his assistant patrol leader to control the other two teams. There was about one hundred meters of space between them and us.

There were two reasons for establishing the space. First, when the lead element got hit, he would be right where the action was and could quickly pass orders back to the rest of us who would immediately maneuver into a more advantageous position.

When he introduced the strategy to us a while back, he told us that the separation aspect came from his study of the famed Selous Scouts who fought in the Rhodesian War back in the 'sixties and 'seventies. We watched some footage of their work on the Nyadzonia raid in which they slaughter over 1,200 enemy terrorists and, since then, had worked to incorporate some of their tactics. Our seniors from the last deployment cycle had moved similarly in Fallujah and taught it to us, so it wasn't entirely foreign.

Secondly, if Zach was ever killed, I needed to take his place. The distance between us increased the odds of at least one of us being alive after shit hit the fan. If I bought it, squad command would fall to Pappy and then Andy. We constantly discussed this scenario and reinforced the possibility of running through this succession of command, as we called it, so that by this point it was memorized by everyone.

Grim though it may seem to constantly be planning for your own death, it was necessary. I always took it seriously because at that point, if I was dead, I didn't matter anymore. But one fatality or casualty is better than two or three and everyone else needs to focus on killing the enemy before the situation got worse.

Before I knew it, we were back at our little EMV vacation getaway resort and in the bag with lights out. The next day we were moving out to the ranges to start the live fire portion of the exercise which I was looking forward to most.

Mechanized integration in urban environments was the order of the day. We had spent the last work-up and deployment as the Amtrac Company, so it wasn't anything new to me, Zach, or Patrelli. For the rest of the squad, who arrived after that deployment, it was all new territory. Anything with wheels or tracks on it that could move us and cut down on the distance we had to cover on our broken smashed up feet and crunching knees was a blessing.

We stood by the green mechanical monsters, savoring a quick cigarette, or sipping the water from our hydration pouches that was made scalding by the oppressive heat. Moments such as this provide a unique opportunity for us to mess with each other. It keeps the mood light and someone typically takes things too far and complete hilarity ensues.

Patrelli, standing beside one of the green tracked vehicles, had joined in a lively conversation with Pappy, myself, and a few others. Zach was unusually quiet and staring at Patrelli as if something was wrong with him; as if he didn't have his kit right or had gotten a fucked up hair cut before we came out here. He stared at him, through his ballistic sunglasses, with such intensity that it was almost eerie.

Casually, he stepped across our close little circle and unbuckled one of the shoulder straps on Patrelli's plate carrier. The action halted the usual coarse banter almost instantly. The rest of us passed around a "what the fuck" look and broke out into hysterical laughter as Zach proceeded to continue to rummage around Patrelli's kit and release buckle after buckle.

Patrelli stood there helplessly, knowing full well that he could resist but it would still end with his gear all messed up and he would be much more tired after the fact. His face portrayed a sort of melancholic pleading for an explanation from our leader, who had remained emotionless, stepped back to admire his work amidst the uncontrollable laughter and tears of joy from the rest of us.

Patrelli just stood there in the heat, with his arms hanging at his sides like a helpless child with his gear dangling from his body by one or two straps. Zach, observing the Marine as a sculptor applying the finishing touches to a masterpiece, stepped forward and tilted Patrelli's dark lensed glasses to the side. It made Patrelli look like a cartoon character that had just been hit in the face with a shovel. He had an expression of utter hopelessness that drove the rest of us to hysteria.

Zach didn't hate him. He was always messing with Patrelli because they had history. They had been together longer than anyone in the platoon and maybe even the company. They had a big brother, little brother connection that usually resulted in some sort of discomfort for Patrelli.

The randomness of these occurrences was one of the things that made them so special. For instance, Zach would have the squad gather in a room for a meeting in which we expected some crucially serious news and when he arrived moments later, he would issue a swift Hollywood karate chop to Patrelli's neck. He'd then proceed to pass us the news over Patrelli's feeble gasps for air and mercy. The hardest part for us was to not laugh and pay attention.

Zach made Patrelli fight multiple opponents back-to-back or simultaneously, which we all did. It was just more fun for us to see Patrelli's misery for some inexplicable reason.

Infantrymen delight in each other's suffering. It's not because we hate each other. It's because we all know that no matter how miserable, tired, pissed off, or deflated someone gets, everyone else has either already been that low, or will be shortly. The many miseries inherent to infantry life, like hiking in the rain, barely sleeping, or losing time with family, become more bearable when you know everyone else is equally miserable.

Conversations between grunts typically recall the most miserable times shared together in some fighting position out in the middle of nowhere standing in two feet of mud and snow or freezing rain next to someone who is just as depressed as you are; or watching a Boot on his first hike struggle because he doesn't want to get messed with for falling out. These conversations are shared amidst hysterical laughter as the fondest of memories.

The infantry lifestyle, one of hardship and privation, produces an endless supply of these experiences. And sharing them is what binds a team together. The ensuing nostalgia and humor are a result of overcoming extreme adversity and the confidence it builds.

On any given day a Grunt is more likely to recognize that he got better at something because of the struggle. He can do that thing better than any POG on the planet, and that is just one of the many things that makes the suffering worth it.

Live ranges at Twentynine Palms were awesome. Say what you want about the living arrangements, when it came to training there were far fewer constraints out here than there were back at Lejeune. Everything was bigger, from the number of objectives per range, the ground to be covered in between, and the space we had to maneuver and roam free on patrol.

Ranges 410A and 401, arguably the most infamous in the Marine Corps, did not disappoint. We used dry creek beds, rock formations, small hills, and slight rises in elevation to mask our movement or designate positions to support other teams by fire. The terrain delivered a hard right cross to the balls for most of us, running them for the first time, but they were still fun. Lejeune was flat and forested, which made it more difficult to use our weapons and the terrain as effectively.

The trenches on some of the ranges offered us a chance for close quarters live fire, which was an incredibly rare occurrence. I had been on active duty for over two years now and this was only my second time firing in an enclosed space, which was ridiculous. But any day we get to shoot live rounds and blow something up is a good day in the infantry.

In Twenty-nine Palms, we were introduced to a unit that could help us out with the latter.

Combat engineers are a breed all their own, another Marine Corps sub-culture. It's standard for a group of them to attach to a Grunt battalion during the latter stages of a work-up. They have a different set of skills in their toolbox like construction, demolition, and heavy machinery operation.

Just like any unit, regardless of occupational specialty, it's a toss-up: you could get a group of hard core POGs who hate the fact that they aren't in the infantry and make everything as difficult as humanly possible, or you could get a bunch of wildcats who can build a mockup of Fort Knox using a shovel and some rubber bands, only so they can blow it sky high just for the hell of it. Thankfully, we got the latter.

Sergeant Ross, the engineer team leader, was an infantryman trapped in an engineer's body. A seasoned combat veteran, he had the same unapologetic sense of humor, but it was punctuated with wild superstition. The man was absolutely horrified of white cigarette lighters. On multiple occasions, we would be sitting around waiting for orders or just passing time and one of us would purposely conceal one of these small devices as we lit a cigarette, knowing he would ask for it to light his own. The Marine would quickly toss it over only to see Ross recoil in animated terror and jump back, spewing a multitude of curses so colorful it would make a sailor blush.

Superstition is common on the small unit level. During my first two years as a boot, the colorful hard candy from our field meals called Charms was outlawed because it supposedly brought bad luck. This had been passed on to us from our seniors, who had received it from theirs, and so on and so forth. This belief in the ominously, but irrationally, significant can be found in many militaries and conflicts spanning history. As an example, just prior to the assassination of Afghan President Amin in 1979, the Soviet Spetsnaz unit assigned to secure his palace pissed on the wheels of their armored vehicle for good luck.

On top of his white lighter phobia, Ross sported red hair and skin as pale as a sheet of printer paper that was littered with freckles. He claimed the name "ginger" with pride and argued the price for his glorious sandy red mane was his very soul. All this, along with the fact that he absolutely loved to blow anything to kingdom come, made him fit right in. He had rubbed off on his boys, one of whom we called Joker because of the frighteningly profane and hilariously vulgar stories he told.

These men are the types of characters that make the melting pot of personalities that are infantry units so special. It's these relationships that animate it and show us how to appreciate differences, so long as they don't limit our lethality. The small petty differences that divide other cultures are set aside for the pursuit of a common goal and we learn not just to coexist, but to thrive through shared effort and humor.

Our platoon was tasked with one of the longest movements on the company level assault range. We were supporting first squad's attack along with a group of engineers. The scale of this range, with the entire company moving and clearing multiple objectives simultaneously, seemed almost infinite to me.

We hoofed it in our usual order: Zach up front with Pappy and his boys, followed by Andy's team and then mine, with the engineers tucked in the middle. One of them tripped over a rock and face planted into the scorched stones that everyone else ahead of us had trudged over. It sucked more for this guy because he was carrying an eighty-pound explosive pack.

The anti-personnel obstacle breaching system, or APOBS, is an awkwardly shaped crude backpack that contains a line charge with fragmentation grenades. It also weighs over one hundred pounds. When he hit the ground the weight lurched forward into the back of his Kevlar helmet, which shoved his face into the rocks.

Several Grunts jumped over him and sprinted towards our objective. Sergeant Ross screamed at his man to get up and not be a pussy as he passed by. The order bounced off the walls of the rocky canyon as the engineer struggled to his feet and stumbled forward, his chin bleeding heavily as he spit out teeth. Several of us stifled laughs as our chests heaved beneath the weight of our armor plates and ammunition.

The brownish canyon we were sprinting through veered left and rose slightly before leveling out into a rocky ridge overlooking the objective. Zach pushed up to the top first and called up the engineers who must have been elated to rid themselves of the APOBS that weighed them down. The only positive thing that goes through someone's mind when their body is breaking under the weight, is how awesome it will be to use it. There's also the urgency to move regardless because we must have it to win.

They emplaced it on the rising slope of the ridge, and it shot out the heavy-duty string of grenades, which made for quite a boom on the forward slope. The rest of us rushed into the falling sand and rocks that the explosions rained down and ripped into the objective with accurate directed fire from the ridge that Zach and Pappy had claimed moments before.

Patrelli launched an AT-4 rocket into a bunker a few hundred meters away which was no easy task. Rockets are a funny thing because most shooters don't account for the arch of the trajectory and over or undercompensate. Patrelli was a crack shot with both types of disposable rockets that the infantry used.

The flash and concussion of the rocket colliding with a nearby bunker marked the end of the action for us. First squad passed through ours, flowing into the trench system to destroy the hated Ivan army, ending the exercise.

It took three or four hours to run the range from start to finish and the walk back seemed like an eternity. Our bodies were readjusting as the adrenaline wore off and seemed to force time to a screeching halt. It was a good chance to decompress and laugh about all of us who had fallen on our asses or looked like we hated our lives while we were running the whole length to the support by fire position. It also gave us a chance to discuss what went wrong and make sure that everyone was pushing water and scarfing down a quick snack on the move.

After a night beneath the stars in company formation, we hopped on trucks and moved out to the defensive portion. I'm not sure which fucking genius decided on the specific site that we ended up in, but at the time I wanted him to be shot in a public venue. Whenever units come out to big training spaces like this, they're confined to certain areas by the base staff. Likely, our commanders, who had proven quite competent, didn't have much say in the site selection and there was some nerdy Marine staff weenie laughing his ass off at us back in the rear.

Again, out in the middle of post-apocalyptic nowhere, we were told to dig. We were on a rock shelf backed by jagged hills with a valley to our front.

When we started digging with the small, issued entrenching tools, we realized it was solid rock all the way down. Not a layer or two on top but all the way. We worked like dogs for the first day and most of us barely dug down a foot and a half.

Zach was the only man that completed his position. He was always ahead of everyone else, and I still don't know how. Looking across the squad's line at our barely scratched out fighting holes, and then back at his dug chest deep, was comical. He made it look so easy and the rest of us were smoked.

The Company had to send someone back to fetch pickaxes and other various tools which were shared around but to little avail since there were only two or three per platoon. Eventually someone in their Godly wisdom decided that enough was enough and heavy-duty tractors came in to break the scorching rocks.

The place was bright underneath the oppressive sun and almost completely devoid of vegetation. Our small shelf, overlooking an expanse of open ground that ended at the base of a ridgeline several clicks away, boiled in the heat.

After we settled in around the machine guns, the gun trucks with anti-armor missile launchers pulled into their various positions throughout the company, and we waited for nightfall before the show began. I was in the center of more firepower than I ever imagined, and I began to think that the previous thirty-six hours may turn out to be worth the trouble.

As the sun fell, the coyotes began moving around, and I could feel anticipation in the air. I stood in the fighting position next to Cotton, noticing that he was calm and focused as always, which reassured me. The darkness had brought with it a light, blissful breeze that contrasted with the day's heat and the stars provided excellent illumination through our NVGs. The stage was se, so I took the chance to go over one last rundown of the fire plan with Cotton and Gavin, who were both ready to let loose.

The scenario was that we were defending against a numerically superior force. To offset the notional enemy's advantage, our company had been given air and artillery support plus anti-armor gun trucks. Our little rock shelf, nestled beneath high rocky ground to the rear and left meant that we could only be attacked from the front, right where all our guns were pointed. The scene reminded me of battles from the Korean War where our predecessors slaughtered droves of Communist human wave attacks.

Several minutes later, we heard the distant scream of an F-18 and the far ridge lit up with the sparks and concussions of close air support. A pair of Cobra helicopters followed behind spewing bright tracer rounds and rockets that stitched the imaginary enemies with death and destruction. I thought about how awesome it would be to see it real life with actual bad guys on the other end.

Our ninja opponents surged forward as described by the coyotes and our indirect assets opened up along with the long-range rockets mounted on the trucks. It was like living a modern-day version of the Battle for Hoth in *Star Wars,* only a lot warmer and without any Tan Tans.

The unstoppable enemy pressed his assault. Soon we were all joining in with our personal rifles and grenade launchers. The machine guns within our lines increased their rates and grenades went out to repel the imaginary troops to our front. Clusters of Ivans, emplaced on long sticks the day prior, stood a few hundred meters out. I pointed them out to Cotton, who engaged with accurate controlled bursts from his SAW. Gavin was pumping out high explosive rounds from his grenade launcher like it was his favorite candy dispenser.

Slowly but surely the lethal laser light show died down. We were told there wasn't anything left of the enemy.

We went about our typical communication, confirming we still had all our gear and how many rounds each man had remaining. The reports travelled up the chain and orders came back down to remain at fifty percent security for the time being. At least one man per hole could sleep at a time.

I was completely awed by what I had just seen. Never had I beheld such an awesome and forceful display of firepower. For the last two years, I'd studied and read and wondered. Now I had a visual reference. It was incredible.

We took our shifts on watch throughout the remainder of the night and dawn was accompanied by the call to end the exercise. Cigarettes were lit and Marines went about tending to their gear and grabbing a quick bite.

Zach called us over to his hole for a quick team leader pow-wow. The rest of the day would be spent filling in the positions with the same rocks that had been so laboriously removed and we would bivouac as a company before returning to our EMV resort FOB and our final training block.

Everyone was in high spirits. Our stay at Twenty-nine Palms was almost over and the last phase was a three-day mock war in the same small city that our FOB overlooked.

As we filled in the positions beneath the ever-watchful eye of the sun, someone started snapping pictures. There was always someone with a camera on big ops like this and we had been bullshitting for months about making a squad calendar. Each man struck a pose that he thought was common to male models dressed as fake firefighters or policemen. We intended to compile them into an actual calendar for our wives or girlfriends before we deployed. It helped pass the time and keep the mood light while we worked.

The next day, reveille sounded shortly after the sun had begun its ascent. I lit a cigarette and enjoyed the first deep inhale while I was still partially wrapped in my poncho liner and water-resistant bivy sack. There wasn't any rush, so we took a few minutes to massage our still swollen feet, shave, shit, and get our gear packed up as a small open-backed vehicle pulled up and the staff offloaded vats of hot breakfast for us to enjoy.

The hair on my neck shot skyward when I heard Zach's voice rise over the tables to our left. A heated confrontation had broken out between him and first platoon's staff sergeant.

I had no idea what had started it, but I was ready to wield my rifle like a baseball bat on a collision course with this guy's face. Several times since his arrival a few months ago, the platoon sergeant had drawn Zach into bullshit arguments that always ended with him pulling rank and threatening administrative punishment because he would say something stupid or even downright provocative and Zach would make him look like the idiot that he was. This time was no different and I could clearly hear the staff sergeant tell Zach that he if said another word he would have him busted down.

The Uniform Code of Military Justice is one of the most fairly and clearly organized systems on paper. There are articles that forbid adultery, larceny, unlawful violence, unauthorized absence, sodomy, rape, murder, and nearly everything else under the sun that a normal and sane individual would consider socially or morally unacceptable. There are even more comical and irrelevant sections like article 114: Dueling. I'm a little unsure of the last recorded instance when two cats loaded up flintlocks and marched ten paces before turning to defend their honor with muzzle loaded death, but it couldn't have been a recent occurrence.

Like any justice system, however, most of the flaws are not the black and white parameters themselves but how they are applied once subjected to human interpretation. If the administering officer and SNCO advisor are sensible men, there isn't a whole lot to worry about. But there is a chance that one or both of those guys could be a total scumbag and use it to punish Marines for every infraction no matter how great or small. Nothing except a living, breathing, hate-filled enemy can kill a unit quicker than a commander who relies totally on the UCMJ to maintain good order and discipline.

For most commanders, non-judicial punishment was typically a last resort, reserved for high visibility situations. If a Marine initiates a high-speed pursuit with the local law enforcement, pops on a drug test, gets a DUI or does something equally as stupid then its unavoidable and warranted. Judgement, for the offender and adjudicator, is really what it comes down to.

In every organization, even the infantry, there are always a few who use the black and white systems to mask their insecurities . Zach's superiority as a Grunt and a leader, threatened this particular staff sergeant. And he was intent on letting every know that he thought he was the big man on the block because he held a higher rank. Instances like this made him universally hated by the entire company. I felt sorry that First platoon had to put up with him. The situation died down and we finished chow as the trucks arrived to take us back to the FOB, which we left shortly after arriving to conduct the three-day mock war.

The exercise was filled with situations designed to evaluate how the entire battalion operated. We patrolled among the actors, saw scenarios that tempted Marines to fire their weapons when they shouldn't, and acted or reacted to a developing tactical scenario that kept the hands on the clock moving until finally it was done, and we found ourselves back at Camp Wilson cleaning our gear and standing by to migrate back to the other coast. The work up was essentially over, and the word came down from the top that we had scored a touchdown, which felt good to hear.

We had a long leave block ahead and about a month of final administrative work to wrap up before deployment.

A few days after we got back, Zach volunteered to go on the

advance party. He'd be leaving for Afghanistan a few weeks before the rest of us to get his feet wet and feed us intel about the situation. The advance party consisted of several squad leaders, the CO, and a small contingent of support personnel.

Since the War on Terror was just shy of its ninth anniversary, this was nothing new. It was standard procedure for units to push a small group ahead, so the key leaders got acquainted with the environment and the transition between outgoing and incoming units was smooth, theoretically.

I would have interim responsibility for the squad until we got to Afghanistan. I went home to Tennessee to enjoy the three weeks of leave with my new wife and family. The time was brief, but it was a good rejuvenation period. I took advantage of every second of it, bearing in the back of my mind that it could be the last time I ever saw home.

My mother, sweet and calm as she always was, seemed nervous. Her mannerisms betrayed anxiety below the surface. My older brother had been fighting in Afghanistan with Third Battalion, First Marines for several months now and they had taken quite a few casualties. She did her best to mask it and stay busy, but it was wearing on her. The lack of information concerning the well-being of her boy understandably unsettled her. She'd had, and would have many more, sleepless nights praying for our safe return.

I admired her stoicism and wondered if I would be able endure that pressure with the grace that she did. It was astonishing. For all the hardships that we endure as fighting men, those of our women and families back home are still some of the most astounding and daunting, without question.

I noticed a similar demeanor in my young wife. I admired her strength and enjoyed every second of warmth and happiness that she shared with me. She never asked me to stay. I imagined the thought must have crossed her mind, but she never voiced it. She expected me to be an honorable man and perform the duty that I freely signed up for. How I ever got so lucky, I'll never know.

Much too quickly, the leave block ended, and we all returned to Lejeune. The final ten days or so was reserved for last-minute gear inspections and the myriad of pencil-pushing tasks we had to complete before "crossing the pond." We shuffled through the base gymnasium a short walk away from the barracks, to fill out our Service Member's Group Life Insurance policies and make out our wills.

It felt strange to be filling out the paperwork for a last will and testament at age twenty-two. I had thought about it so little before and it dawned on me that I was doing this about forty to fifty years sooner than most people do.

The thought melted away as quickly as it had entered my mind. I had bigger fish to fry right now, primarily making sure the squad got back to Zach ready to fight. The guys were in good spirits but appeared a little anxious. Internally, we were asking the questions that every man asks himself before he goes to war for the first time. "How am I gonna measure up? How is this going to end? Will I ever see home again? If I die, will my wife remarry? How is it going to feel to get shot at?"

Fear is normal for every man, even the ones who have fought before. It became clear very quickly as we counted the remaining days that being afraid doesn't make someone a coward. Acting out of fear and running away from responsibility does. I felt it just like everyone else and we discussed it openly as a squad.

Pappy, Andy, and I had our own conversations about it. No one had any intention of running away or feigning injury or mental illness. We held each other together through honesty and the bond we had built during the preceding months. I knew if we stuck together, even if some of us were killed or wounded, we would be alright. Zach had glued us together in a way that only he could. The men to my left and right knew what to do and we were as ready as we were ever going to be.

Chapter 4

June 8, 2010

I passed through the main gate of Camp Lejeune like always and made my way through the usual traffic towards the company area. I was focused on the last-minute paperwork left to complete, and hoping for an early release so I could rush back home to my wife. We were five days out from the great beyond and it was a scorcher of a summer so far. The daytime highs were stretching into the high nineties and the humidity soaked us with sweat.

Staff Sergeant Hauz assigned us a few rosters to be filled out and some working parties to complete before we could go home. Several Marines from the platoon needed to be taken to various locations around the base to complete some administrative work with the POGs. It looked like we would be out before noon, thankfully.

Andy, however, was roped into an additional duty. He was a "chaser," which entailed escorting Marines from the brig about the base to complete their out processing. Why they had the man out on that kind of goat rope less than a week before he went to didn't make any sense, but it was unavoidable. We just put the lotion in the basket.

I scooped up Gavin and another cat to take them over to POG

country so we could cross another task off the list. We walked down past the barracks and crossed the two lanes of paved street known as PT Road to the parking lot where my Ford Ranger was parked.

Every single commuter in the battalion hated walking from that patch of asphalt to get to the company area whenever we had a formation or any sort of task that involved the back-and-forth trek. If you were running late to work you had to screech into a parking spot, if one was still there, and haul ass across the street, hoping that you didn't get splattered across the pavement on your way to get your ass chewed for being late. The only positive about the whole setup was the small body of water that lay on the other side and fed into the Atlantic. It was a bit of peace in a hard place.

I broke my gaze from the dark blue water and noticed that most of the company was streaming down to a small grassy area on our left where the parking lot ended. I hadn't gotten a call about a formation and if there was one it would've been in our company area we'd just left. Something was up.

Our company first sergeant had just jumped out of his car, and he was *moving*.

First sergeant Payton came to us from the Air Wing several months ago. He was a model version of his peer group in many ways: professional, motivated to high heaven, and well-versed in administrative matters. Unlike most of his peers, he understood there was a time and place for everything. He wasn't the type to scream like a drill instructor at a Marine for having chipped chevrons or ripped cammies after being in the field for a month. He knew there were times when getting dirty, shooting, moving, and communicating took precedence over appearance. Zach described him as, "being as much of a first sergeant as I can handle."

Direct and straight to the point, he noticed our group. His eyes lit up as he asked us where we were going. I said we were headed to over to the base administrative area and before I could finish, he cut me off.

"No, you're not! Get over there in formation!" he barked.

There was something other than anger in his voice that I couldn't put my finger on. It just didn't feel right. He was rushed and almost nervous which was unusual for him. We stepped it out over to the rest of the company and everyone, absolutely everyone, was either there or en route. Pappy had gotten the squad assembled and Staff Sergeant Hauz told me to get Andy down here ASAP. He didn't care if he had to bring the incarcerated Marine with him.

It took what seemed like an eternity to get all of Echo company assembled on this small patch of earth right near the shimmering water. It was hot and people started asking questions as we baked in the humidity. Could they have moved up our deployment date? What the fuck could bring everything to a screeching a halt? For all we knew aliens had invaded Jacksonville and we were being tasked with retaking the city. They could've told us the sky was falling and it probably wouldn't have phased most of us. We just wanted answers.

Days from now, we were leaving for one of the most violent places in the world, many of us for the first time. We had trained hard, suffered, bonded, and committed to the road ahead regardless of how it turned out in the end. The urgency that came with the natural anxiety of combat made us impatient.

We were ready for anything except for what we were about to hear.

A small entourage of unknown officers joined us after what seemed like an eternity. Payton drew the assembly in close as the strangers hovered a few yards behind him with these odd looks on their faces. They were calm. They almost seemed compassionate, and that was the oddest thing yet. We were unusually close to our first sergeant, as if waiting to hear a secret. No formations or formalities, no reports to be given or salutes rendered; something serious had come down the pipes.

I was on the left side of the semi-circle to Payton's two o'clock with a few Marines in front of me and Staff Sergeant Hauz just behind my left shoulder. Payton opened his mouth and uttered the words that none of us will ever forget for the rest of our lives. His broken uncertain voice drove to the depth of my soul, portraying a singular piercing emotion: sorrow.

"There ain't no easy way to say this, so I'm just gonna say it. We got word this morning that Sergeant Walters and Sergeant Shanfield were killed..."

The sound of his voice dropped off as if someone was turning the volume down. Staff Sergeant Hauz had his hand on my right shoulder and lowered his forehead onto my left as Payton's words reached me.

I wasn't sure if I could believe what I was being told. My eyes darted back and forth to the faces around me. The spectrum of every negative human emotion was on full display: emptiness, paralysis, shock, fear, uncertainty, anger, and rage.

Zach was dead.

One of the officers who had accompanied Payton was a high-level chaplain, who moved forward, offering his condolences and a few words of comfort. He was speaking but I couldn't hear him, or anyone else who spoke. I was lost in the words that had just confounded me. I knew what Payton had said and I didn't doubt him or question his honesty. But *Zach?*

They told us we were free to move around but no one was allowed to leave the small patch of grass and under no circumstances were we to use our cell phones.

The squad naturally gravitated to a spot on the far back left of the area. I stood there watching them, some more emotional than others. Patrelli sat down silently, staring at the ground in front of him with his forearms wrapped around one knee. Andy was across from him in much the same position, wiping tears away from his reddened face. Pappy silently kept to the fringes, holding firm with Greddy and Gunner. Cotton was solemn. His face portrayed a certain solidarity that I tried and failed to mimic. Gavin looked uncertain, unmoored, and that was how I felt.

I wiped away my own tears as Lieutenant Thomas approached. I asked them what had happened, and all the young platoon commander could offer was that an IED had killed them both. They were on patrol with First Battalion, Sixth Marines, the unit we would be replacing. He had no tactical details, and that lack of information released a flood of questions and a flash of anger. Two of our best were just killed before the rest of us even got in the fight and that's all they could give us. *What the fuck?*

The guys had started to speak intermittently now, and members of the company trickled over with outstretched hands and open arms. Some offered condolences and others promises of vengeance.

Andy was in tears again, pushing through his sobs to speak to the assembly. His face was beet red, and he had to squeeze words out when his heaving chest allowed. He reminded us that Zach would not want this deployment to turn into a crusade to kill Afghans.

I thought it was such a stupid thing to say at the time. Those people had just murdered a man that altered my life trajectory and earned my respect. I realized that I was thinking very differently than the squad was, guided by Andy's words. I couldn't know for sure how they all felt, but in that moment, I wanted to butcher the entire country of Afghanistan. My vision was one of a world on fire, serenaded by painful screams and malice.

I didn't give a shit if our country, or the even world, thought it was wrong for us to crave vengeance. Their mentor hadn't been killed and they would experience none of the hardships of this war.

But Andy was right. As much as I hated to admit it, Zach wanted us to *win*. That didn't mean torching every village we came across, as appealing as it seemed to me in that moment. Ending up with our mugshots plastered all over the news as war criminals would be the supreme disgrace to his legacy.

He would want us to think; to operate with the coldhearted efficiency and control necessary to single out the terrorists, then slaughter them without mercy or compassion. That was the job. Wanton destruction and emotional violence wasn't the answer. His emotional control served as the example to reinforce that. I knew that it would be monumentally difficult to emulate or even remember that, as I grappled with the emotions inside.

Time froze while we were down by the water, like we were caught in some sort of haze that rendered the very concept irrelevant to reality. Was this still some sort of twisted nightmare playing in my subconscious to prepare me for potential loss?

We were back in the barracks now and several hours had passed. Time had not stopped, and Zach's death was not a nightmare or some twisted joke. It was real and no amount of reflection or any question answered would change it. It was cold and absolute.

One of the machine gunners stopped by to offer his comfort to the squad, which was huddled in Pappy's room. He slapped a large wad of cash into my hands. His platoon had been saving for months to fund a massive party before our departure. It was several hundred dollars and he asked if we could do something for the families.

Hesitantly, I agreed. I had no idea how to comfort a grieving mother, especially one who had seen her boy grow strong and fearless only to be extinguished so violently.

We met up with Derek's team leaders to pull something together. They had lost their leader too and deserved to have a say in how the money was spent.

As we waited, the next battery of questions racked my brain. Did he suffer? Was it quick and painless? Did 1/6 lose anyone or was it just our two? On and on it went for a few brief seconds and then shut off abruptly, as if someone had pulled the cord on a television that was too loud for comfort.

First Sergeant Payton informally gathered us in the quad to release us for the day. We huddled around just as we had, hours before the learn of Zach's and Derek's deaths. He cut straight to the point, announcing the time for morning formation and then asked me if we were going to see Zach's girlfriend. I said we were. Zach's mother had been notified already so there was no reason to keep her in the dark.

At the bottom of the stairs, our third squad leader, Sergeant. Bart stopped me. He was a FAST Marine like Zach and had arrived earlier during the work-up, going straight into his billet. He fell into the group of solid dudes we got from that small demographic and was, in my opinion, nearly as good as Zach.

Bart had a headful of thick jet-black hair. He carried his tall frame with confidence and spoke with a distinguished New Jersey accent. He ran a tight ship and like us and didn't have to raise his voice much. I respected him as a man that led from the front. Putting his arm around me, he pulled me around the corner to offer some advice before we departed.

"I respected Zach; I looked up to him and wanted to be like him. He brought me under his wing a taught me how to be a squad leader and that's what I'm gonna do with you. Don't ever let your squad see you cry."

I listened with my head held low and nodded that I understood. It was good to know that I had his help going forward but I felt detached as if stuck in an out of body experience; like being on autopilot.

I climbed into my truck with Pappy and a few of the boys and headed over to Zach's storage unit, to meet up with Misty. She was short with shoulder-length black hair and tattoos. Zach had met her at our favorite bar and the two spent a significant amount of time together. She was always lively and quick-witted, sharing the squad's sense of humor. It was obvious to me early on that she kept him on his toes and that it was a serious relationship, even though he didn't propose before he left.

She was in tears, having heard the news before we could tell her, as we lifted the bay door of the small unit. Zach's 1987 Salene Mustang was parked in inside. He had painted the car black in a way that he said reminded him of his favorite post-apocalyptic film, *Mad Max*. He was a mustang fanatic, but this one was the perfect expression of his identity.

Loading Misty's belongings into her small sedan, we said a brief goodbye and promised to keep her posted on any new developments. Like us, she wanted answers that no one had.

I had sent a text to my wife earlier and told her to stay off social media and stay in for the afternoon. Then I had gotten so caught up with everything that I had forgotten all about it. She must've been worried sick to the point of anger wondering why I was acting so strange. Our messages went back and forth until I said, "Fuck it" and just called her to break the news.

It was nearly dark before I got home, and she was waiting for me in the bedroom when I arrived. She wasn't in shambles or falling apart. She didn't grip me fearfully or beg me to stay home to avoid a similar fate. She listened and observed and comforted me, suppressing her own fears and offering me the understanding that only a loving wife can.

As we sat there on the bed in silence, neither one of us knowing where to go next, something started to slowly creep its way into me. It was something foreign yet familiar at the same time. Something coldhearted lurked beneath the veil of secrecy that shrouded the spine-tingling sensation.

I was in the comfort of my own home with the woman I loved. There was no one to judge or scrutinize me and evaluate my reaction to this giant ominous mess.

And yet, the subtlety of this phantom feeling made me suspicious. Then the dam broke with a furious wave of new and dangerous questions that slammed into my consciousness with such concussive force that it was impossible to stand firm. What was going to happen to me? How could any of us expect to survive if they had killed Zach? Who had killed him? What had happened? Why?

The initial questions ceased abruptly, and a sudden realization set in. I was a squad leader now. I was Zach's successor. This is why he was so keen on drilling the succession of command in training.

Was I capable of living up to him as a Squad Leader? Was it even remotely possible? Could I even hope to do half as well as him? How many eyes had noticed me today after we found out and thought that

I wasn't up to the task? Had I shown the squad the strength that they needed to instill confidence in them?

This was doubt. Not superficial nervousness that would pass quickly but true genuine doubt. The onslaught was so unnerving that it drew me into myself, blocking out everything around me, to include my wife. I felt subdued and overwhelmed.

The phone in my pocket buzzed against my hip and broke me free from my fugue. A wave of relief washed over me. It was Don, one of my team leaders from our last deployment. He, Badams, Jolo, and Matt had been the strongest and most positive influences I'd had before Zach, and they had each set a solid example for me to follow.

Badams and Don both called almost as soon as they heard the news. They were both civilians now and lived in Virginia. Neither one of them portrayed an ounce of fear when we talked. They were attentive, understanding, and confident in me. I admitted my doubts to them and wondered if it was a cause for shame. It wasn't about being killed or being good enough to get even with Zach's killers. It was about measuring up to him. How the hell was I supposed to do that? It's like wearing a size nine boot and realizing that you have to fill a size fifteen in an instant; a comparison that I would constantly be reminded of every day for the next seven months.

Neither one of them chewed my ass or told me to "be a man" but instead said everything I was feeling was perfectly normal. In fact, something would be wrong if I wasn't asking these questions. They exuded strength and courage from several hundred miles away and it sustained me.

Badams offered me one small but monumental piece of advice that I would both struggle with and live by sooner than I expected. He said, "Remember, you're there to be their squad leader, not their friend."

His true meaning was something that I couldn't understand at that moment. I had kept my distance from all the boots, especially Gavin and Cotton, but I was close with Pappy and Andy was my friend. How was this going to work? It seemed that Zach never had to draw the line between professional and personal relationships. We all knew when it was time to work and when it was time to play, and we had grown so tight that the two seemed to merge effortlessly. Should I take the same approach or just be me and figure it out?

I called my father next to tell him what had happened, having no idea how Mom would take the news. She already had one son in Afghanistan who had lost several buddies, and she was about to hear this. I wondered how she would survive the stress that we caused her, not to mention the emotional roller coaster she would endure with the lack of information afforded to families.

He was deeply sorry that I had lost such a close friend and mentor. I knew he would have to have a much harder conversation with Mom after this one was over. He didn't lay out any elaborate expectations for me or fire my spirit for vengeance or anything like that. He simply wanted me to do my best and come home. He didn't care if I was the best squad leader in Marine Corps history or if I won medals or installed our family name in America's shrines of martial bravery. His expectation was the same that day as it had been all my life: do your very best at everything you do.

The following day, I crawled out of bed still groggy from the day before. It had been emotionally exhausting, and I still felt completely drained.

We had a memorial service for Zach and Derek at the chapel across the street from the Sixth Marine Regimental area. I stood in the front row at rigid attention and listened to First Sergeant Payton ceremoniously call role for the company. My eyes moistened as I listened to the dutiful replies of several Marines until he called out the two names we all knew were coming.

"Sergeant Walters... Sergeant Walters... Sergeant Zachary J. Walters! Sergeant Derek L. Shanfield!"

Nothing. The room echoed with the sound of his voice and a lonely hollow chill crept up my spine. The silence seemed to scream out to each of us, reminding us of the gravity of the situation. This was real.

The sound system crackled to life as Taps played and I spied the two rifleman's crosses at center stage just below the altar. I wondered how many more we would see before it was all over.

That afternoon the first sergeant took volunteers from ours and Derek's squad to go with him and receive the bodies with the families at Dover Air Force Base. I went with several others including Pappy, Lieutenant Thomas, a few team leaders from Derek's squad, and their platoon commander, Lieutenant James Zimmerman. I hardly knew James at the time, but his demeanor and reputation made him the platoon commander everyone wanted. He didn't micromanage his guys, had an easy-going carriage, and was proficient and humble.

We piled into a government-issued van and drove the six-hour trip to Delaware almost without stopping. We arrived at the hotel, just outside Dover Air Force Base, and changed into cammies before heading down to a conference room to meet the families.

I had no idea what to expect or how to act. I just tried to be sympathetic. What could I possibly say to a grieving mother who had just lost her son so unexpectedly? What words could ease her pain or compensate her for her loss and bring at least some form of happiness to her shattered world? It seemed an impossible task.

My anxiety abated the moment we met Ms. Walters, who had travelled from Texas with a dear friend of hers. Staff Sergeant Hauz and First Sergeant Payton made the introductions then retired to the back of the room as we sat with the two ladies. Sitting at the large round table in the empty room, we listened to Ms. Walters' fondest memories of her dearly departed boy.

It was comforting to see strength in her. She was devastated and yet seemed more concerned with our well-being. She wasn't bitter or angry. She didn't blame us for Zach's decision to extend his service or for his death. In a way, she looked relieved to see us. It felt like a family funeral that reunited distant relatives.

We used the money that Weapons Platoon gave us to have a professional photo album made of Zach's best pictures. She wiped away her tears, looking at them carefully and asked questions about his gear and what he was saying and doing. To my surprise, she met a lot of our responses with laughter, instantly recognizing her boy from our descriptions. Despite her sadness, she seemed comforted which made the experience much easier for me. I would've had absolutely no clue what to say or do if she had been angry or bitter.

A few hours later, we left with us for the Air Force base, beneath overcast skies and threatening rain.

When we arrived, a Marine escort brought us into a small building. We stood behind Zach's mother who sat next to the mortuary Marine who would prepare Zach's remains. We learned that even she would not be able to view the body because there was so little left of him. Later, through a good friend of mine, I would learn that the 1/6 patrol on site used one body bag for both Zach and Derek. It sparked images of my friend with half of his head seared off and what little remained of his body charred black. No gear or weapon or limbs still attached existed in my mind. Just half of a cold blank face with a neutral expression staring back at me.

The Marine placed a small box that contained Zach's personal effects on the table. His demeanor was that of a doctor with good bedside manner. He seemed to put Ms. Walters at ease with his kindness and good nature. In the infantry, we kept to ourselves so completely that it was difficult to identify with other Marines. This man was clearly very good at what he did, and I recognized how different someone had to be to exist in the realm of loss and pain without crumbling completely.

Ms. Walters shared a few words with him and thanked him before we adjourned to the edge of the airstrip.

The C-130 bearing flag-draped coffins had landed, and we lined up in two ranks to render appropriate honors and sing the "Marine Hymn" as the caskets were offloaded, per Ms. Walters' request. I stood at attention with the first sergeant on my left and Pappy on my right as the procession began. We brought up a slow salute and took Payton's cue to begin the verse as the caskets rolled out of the large back door of hulking bird.

I remember the somber mood, the grey sky and the slightly darker plane that sat on the asphalt with its tail door resting on the deck. The long cold metal boxes emerged from the opening, escorted by a small detail of service men. My eyes followed the vessels, dressed in the Nation's colors, as they inched further away from the aircraft.

It's one thing to see a picture in a newspaper of a flag-draped coffin or to watch a movie that plays this scene out. It is an entirely different ordeal to see it in person, especially when it is someone that you've actually known.

As the long, decorated rectangles rolled slowly past us, twenty-five yards away, I wondered how this could be all that was left of them. They had been so real, so animated and full of life and now this was it.

Nothing, and I mean absolutely nothing, can compare to the complete and utter shocking finality of combat loss.

The song faded as we closed the first verse, and we slowly lowered our salute back to the position of attention. Payton put us at ease after our Fallen had passed. We said our goodbyes to Ms. Walters before changing back into civilian attire and heading to Lejeune.

We only had about three days left to finish our preparations before we deployed, and it was time to put this behind us. Nothing could change it. It was as simple as that. But how could I move one? Was I supposed to grieve before or after the deployment? Could I really turn all this off and get on with the business at hand?

I didn't know what to think so I just resolved to lock it all away until we got home. I could grieve then. I didn't seem normal, but neither was having one of your friends get blown into a thousand pieces so small that they couldn't all be collected.

We got back to LeJeune quickly and I went home to spend what precious little time I had left with my wife. She would've been well within her rights to demand that I stay behind instead of going to Dover in the first place, but she offered not one word of protest. If ever there was a dutiful wife, it was her.

She must have been so afraid, but no one would've been able to tell. The fact that she displayed such strength and solidarity, despite having a husband too caught up in events to be attentive to her needs, is beyond me. It allowed me to focus on what lay ahead, knowing that she would be okay.

I wondered how different my experience was compared to others who had lost friends killed in combat. The fact was, I still hadn't been in combat yet. Losing someone at a distance had to be tamer than being next to someone in their final moments.

In a way, I wished that I had been with Zach at the end. At least I would've been able to kill the people responsible for his death instead of having to wait and wonder. I wanted revenge. I didn't care about their culture, their way of life, their sons or fathers or husbands, or their religion. Fuck them. They murdered my friend, and I would repay them in time.

The big picture in Afghanistan didn't much matter to me at all. It was beyond my control and left to generals and politicians to sort it out. I had made up my mind. I wasn't going on a killing spree of civilians, but I was not going to go out of my way for their wellbeing and especially not for their fucking comfort. Risking our lives so they could have running water, schools, and other modern amenities is unacceptable and why our country viewed those objectives as morally forthright is senseless.

The fight was what mattered to me. I wanted to burn the enemy's whole world to the ground. I'd have to fight internally to restrain my emotions. Patrelli, Pappy, Gavin and the rest of the squad didn't deserve to spend the rest of their lives behind bars because I lost control. Nevertheless, I was going over there to kill the enemy. Any goal beyond that was non-existent.

Chapter 5

Afghanistan

The morning of 13 July 2010 found us cruising through the clouds en route to Afghanistan. I sat in a window seat with Pappy to my right and a pile of weapons and gear in between us, looking out the window. I was replaying the images of saying goodbye to my wife and taking pictures as a squad on the same grass where we'd learned about Zach and Derek. One look at the photographs would've betrayed the fact that something was missing.

Families had milled about the area with their Marines, absorbing everything about the final moments they had before we boarded the buses in the late afternoon. It was one of the hottest days North Carolina had seen in years, breaking triple digits on the thermometer with high humidity.

Several of our seniors, including Matt, traveled from their homes to see us off, which meant the world to me. My brother had told me stories of some people hurting themselves before deployment or simply not showing up and I had since wondered who from our unit would choose self-preservation over honor. But here we were with every single soul accounted for, ready to go to war. There wasn't an overwhelming sense of fear either, but something else in the air. It was hunger. The entire company was ready to go to war. That, coupled with the small host of unit alumni that turned out, displayed the character of the American fighting man, and spoke volumes about the type of men we had in 2/6 Echo.

As we touched down and taxied into the gates at both European layovers, my thoughts drifted back to my final moments with my wife. I wondered if they would in fact be final. I remember her saying how much she already missed me and the feeling of her body against mine, her warmth, her smile, and her tears.

Night turned to day as we made our final stop and donned our kits for the last leg into Afghanistan aboard a C-130. I had shelled out a pretty penny for a custom-made chest rig that had space for everything I needed as a squad leader. Ironically enough I didn't even know that I would be one when I ordered it. It had pouches for thirteen magazines that rested on top of a drop-down map pouch attached by parachute cord and flanked by two large sacks for medical supplies and additional machine gun ammunition. It also had spaces designated for grenades, pyrotechnics, writing utensils, chow, radios, and batteries. The only problem was that it was fucking huge. I took crap from other team leaders because the outline of my body resembled a tactical sumo wrestler. But it was durable, and I was determined to get every penny's worth out of the damn thing.

There were still some nerves but for the most part I was calm enough to grab some shut eye on the bird. My last deployment was similar and every future one would follow the same pattern. Saying goodbye was the hardest part about leaving and once that was over with, getting to the destination was cake. Whatever was going to happen would happen, and that was that. We were already on our way.

We touched down in Kandahar for a quick layover that provided the chance for us to see the city that our country had erected on foreign soil. And it was just that—a small thriving city, built in what I could only imagine was the deepest circle of hell temperature-wise. The heat hit like a blast furnace as we disembarked the bird en route to our temporary quarters. The sudden change in temperature, accompanied by a gust of wind made it seem like I was walking into a blast furnace.

I stayed in the tent to get some more rest before we moved on. I heard comments about all the American restaurants and the various exchanges that our Allies had built for their troops as I struggled to get sleep. I figured I would look back on this moment in the future and be happy that I had taken advantage of the opportunity and time would prove me right.

Two or three hours later, the tent had thinned out. The Company left in waves for Camp Dwyer where we would remain until moving into our area of operations. Then it was our turn and before I knew it, we were airborne again. Kandahar to Dwyer was a short enough trip and out we stepped, right back into that forceful heat wave, and made our way off to the side to count heads and equipment, just as we had done every single time.

As we stood in our nice, neat ranks looking across the airstrip, a small element of First Battalion, Sixth Marines was boarding our plane. Their uniforms looked ragged, as if they had been worked into the ground for so long that their appearance didn't matter to them anymore. I read anxiety and stress in some of them. Others were animated and excited, picturing the triumphant return that awaited them, while others seemed not the least bit affected as they shuffled forward to begin the long trek back to The World. I couldn't help but wonder if that's what we would look like seven months from now. Would this experience really change us that much?

We moved off the tarmac and passed through a small opening in the HESCO wall that separated the landing field from a maze of giant insulated tents. Single file, we moved as if playing follow the leader, taking in our new environment.

Dwyer seemed massive to me. It was another of the many

Coalition settlements that had been built over the last nine years of warfare and had nearly every modern amenity we could think of. There was a barber shop of course, a decent PX, and contract chow hall that made real food, and an infinite number of large tents for troop housing, briefings, and so on. The small city even boasted a penitentiary-style weight room beneath staked canvas for the POGs, who stayed here in relative safety and comfort for their deployment.

They had air-conditioned trailers that housed their offices, close to the main chow hall. Dwyer had at least two locations to feed the myriad of troops on site, one being a twenty-four-hour facility. It seemed out of place to have something so American in such a foreign place but that was the way it went, and every grunt harbors at least a small amount of jealousy over it.

Among the thousands of troops here, only a small percentage of us would actually fight. But people back home didn't know, or much care, about who was doing what. They didn't differentiate between the POGs who spent their deployment in the A/C with three hot meals a day and the grunts who would live and fight like animals, far away from all things modern. To the outside world, we were all the same. To us, their deployments were just poorly chosen tax-free paid vacations and we took every chance we could to make sure that they knew it.

The chow hall was decent enough with cold drinks and food prepared by local contractors and I had stocked up on all the tobacco products I could carry earlier. Satisfied, I lay down and passed out thinking about my wife and wondering what Afghanistan would have for us in the future. We were here and in about two weeks, we would be moving out to walk in Zach and Derek's footsteps.

The following day we woke up and ran a few miles as a squad before we showered up and went to chow. After we returned to the hooch, Lieutenant Thomas came in and told me to grab my shit and come to the CO's briefing with the squad leaders which struck me as odd because we were told before we left that a Sergeant Marshall would be taking squad command and that I would remain his first team leader.

I was torn by the decision at the time. On the one hand, I was livid because I had trained, worked, and developed with this group as Zach's second and by succession of command, this responsibility should have fallen to me just as it would have if we had been together on patrol when he was killed. On the other hand, Sergeant Marshall was an experienced squad leader with multiple combat pumps under his belt and had agreed to extend his contract when he heard what had happened. Our battalion sergeant major had to jump through some hoops to get his paperwork processed and he had to stay behind to get everything squared away, so until he got here, nothing had changed for the squad.

As long as I got a crack at the guys who killed our friend, the billet I held was of secondary importance.

We crossed a few rows of tents and slid through the large dusty flap of one that served as a sort of conference room. Several neat rows of chairs sat off to our right and with a small plywood stage the far end. We settled in the open space by the entrance, which contained a large chalkboard covered in maps and erected on wheels. All twelve squad leaders, plus the platoon sergeants and commanders were waiting for us to receive the operation's order from Captain Brock, our CO.

He was a much better officer than our last company commander who, after seven months on ship with us, still hadn't learned everyone's name. During this cycle, Captain Brock made a conscious effort to get to know us. He spoke to us like men without, absent any false bravado, and wasn't a horrendous micromanager. He wasn't an overbearing man, but he didn't exactly exude confidence either. He seemed cautious.

Brock began his brief of the current situation with his usual calm. The AO was huge, or at least it seemed so to me. There were several maps that covered the boards and provided us with as much geographical clarity as possible. Marjah was a farming community roughly the size of Washington, D.C. that had been designed by the U.S. in the 1950's and was not at all the heavily urbanized Fallujah where my seniors fought. Settled about twenty miles to the southwest of Helmand Province's capital, Lashkar Gah, it resembled a checkerboard in the ariel photography. Lines of canals ran along the major dirt roads and divided fields of corn, wheat, and marijuana. The predominant crop, however, was poppy, which many of the roughly 100,000 inhabitants were dependent on.

Marjah was important because the Taliban used that poppy as its chief exports to fund its terror campaign against the Infidel at the expense of the local populace. Years from now, General Stanley McChrystal would write his memoir, *My Share of the* Task, detailing the strategy that we were now a part of. He would explain that securing Marjah was a small piece of controlling the Helmand River Valley and linking several Coalition controlled areas to the provincial capital and eventually to Kandahar.[1] Marjah was different from the provincial capital and Kandahar because it had to be *taken* from the Taliban, whereas the other two were not firmly in enemy hands.

Operation Moshtarak was the most recent step taken towards that end and is still recognized as one of the toughest operations of the Afghan campaign for many reasons. For starters, it had been under Taliban control since September of 2008 and was home to over sixty tribes, each with their own agendas and loyalties. Tribal rivalries complicated and even prevented some partnerships, specifically a unified front of armed resistance to terrorist aggression. On top of all that, for many years prior to Moshtarak, Marjah's local government administration was full of corrupt individuals who extorted and raped the citizenry. By the time Coalition forces arrived, the only thing that united the tribes was their hatred for both the Taliban and the former governor of Helmand, Sher Mohammed Akhundzada, and his pedophilic police chief, Abdul Rahman Jan.[1]

The main force, comprised of U.S., British, Afghan, Canadian, and French troops, was preceded by smaller operations that shaped the situation through direct-action raids by specialized units, intelligence gathering, and information operations in the form of dropping anti-Taliban leaflets to disrupt their social support network. In wars past, major operations like this usually included massive amounts of preparation fire from artillery and aircraft to soften the enemy before troops hit the ground. However, such fire was cut off all together to reduce collateral damage and in hopes of persuading Marjah's population that we weren't there to destroy everything. A secondary aim was to demonstrate that we could win man to man, without our superior advantage in weaponry.

The plan of execution called for forces to secure key terrain that controlled access to and from Marjah, before inserting the previously mentioned forces into critical positions. Once on the ground, they would neutralize, at least temporarily, some of the Taliban's prepared defensive positions. With the enemy encircled, two companies of Marines partnered with Afghan National Army soldiers would touch down in Marjah proper, and the clearing phase would commence.

Progress was slowed by the enemy, as it normally is, who proved themselves proficient insurgents who utilized complex ambush techniques, according to McChrystal.[2] The term "defense in depth" describes a tactical posture in which a force utilizes multiple layers of passive and active security measures to destroy or repel an attacking force. A prime example was the company defense exercise we conducted in California with air assets striking the notional enemy as far out as possible and then artillery taking over followed by mortars and finally direct fire weapons as it drew closer to our physical position.

However, counterinsurgency campaigns and even partially urbanized areas such as this require a twist to the doctrinal methods. In Marjah, the Taliban employed IEDs in concert with direct fire weapons and the terrain itself to maximize casualties and leverage a psychological advantage. Terrorists had used similar tactics everywhere up to this point in the war.

The thought of going into a situation like this without employing a healthy amount of preparatory and supporting fires seems like a good idea from the outside. In fact, many of us hated this approach. It's not that we wanted to destroy farms and houses and kill civilians, it's that we simply valued American lives more than the homes of people who lacked the will to stick up for themselves. It's a cold-hearted approach, but when the infantry deploys, the gloves need to come off. 1/6 had supporting arms and they used them to great effect when necessary. We would have a few more constraints to operate within.

None of the strategy and very little of Marjah's history was known to me at the time. Standing in front of the maps, all I knew was what Captain Brock was telling us.

A few months after Moshtarak began and the initial units were set to return home, we arrived to relieve 1/6's haggard Alpha Company, who controlled a piece of turf in mid-western Marjah. Also unbeknownst to us, the site was just a few miles down the road from where some of the footage for the HBO miniseries *The Battle for Marjah* was captured.

The territory extended west to a desert-like sector known on our maps as L1C. The estimated enemy strength still in Marjah numbered over one hundred fighters armed with the standard terror kit of AKs, PKM machine guns, RPG 7s, and improvised explosive devices.

IEDs, like the one used to kill Zach and Derek, were the enemy's preferred weapon because of their psychological effect. The crude contraptions could be made from almost anything- from a used rocket casing to an empty tobacco can. They understood that leveraging that against us and Americans back home would degrade popular support for the war, just as the North Vietnamese and Viet Cong had done. It was one of the keys to achieving their long-term goals.

Our sister Companies, Fox and Golf, would be operating to our north and south respectively with Weapons Company to the south and east of them. Company HQ would be located at Combat

Outpost Kelly in roughly the center of our sector, with the platoons positioned spread throughout. First platoon would be stationed at their own patrol base to the southwest and Third would man COP Kelly until a new patrol base, called Shanfield in remembrance of Derek, was constructed.

Our platoon was going to detach from Echo Company. Further south, Weapons Company had a larger area of responsibility and needed more men if they were to saturate the area sufficiently. Second platoon would independently man and patrol out of Combat Outpost Narea.

Supporting fire would be more limited than in the opening phases of Operation Moshtarak, which we were now a part of. The probability of getting clearance for artillery was slim and mortars were not permitted. Air assets would be the primary and our battalion's vehicular units were next in the pecking order. Driving mine resistant ambush protected vehicles, or MRAPs, with mounted medium and heavy machine guns, they would respond to units in distress. Each platoon would give up a few men to form a Company "Mobile" platoon, outfitted similarly and headed up by Gunny Willard. Our Company's mortar men, machine gunners, and assault men would be divided up and attached to the platoons for the duration of the deployment.

After the brief was over, Lieutenant Thomas told me that because the AO was too big for three squads, he was making a fourth that I would lead. He eased my initial skepticism by telling me that I would stay right where I was with Second Squad. But there was a catch: each squad would have to give up two Marines to form the new one under Sergeant Marshall, when he arrived. He recommended Gavin and Cotton because, as of that moment, I wasn't their team leader anymore and the two had worked with each other for over a year.

That sent a flash of anger through every fiber of my being. He wouldn't accept creating a squad made only of Weapons Platoon guys, he said, because he wanted mixed experiences. That made sense, but I still didn't like it. The guys I had helped train and build up were going to go to someone else who didn't even know them, and I wouldn't get to see how they turned out up close and personally. It felt like watching your boys practice and perform all season long, only to miss the championship game.

On top of all that, we were no longer Second Squad. I was now the junior squad leader in the platoon so that meant Marshall and his boys would move into our old spot and we would become Fourth Squad, call sign 2 Delta.

The term "mixed emotions" doesn't even begin to cover how I was feeling. At least we were going to retain the same guys from Weapons Platoon who had been attached to us during training. Bittle, from mortars would carry the M32 grenade launcher and Karl would bring his 240B to add some extra firepower.

I got the boys together and gave them the rundown. The fact that most of us were staying together helped keep it smooth. Nobody seemed particularly anxious about it and Sergeant Marshall, who would arrive shortly after squaring away his extension papers, would have a fresh squad waiting for him.

I pulled Cotton and Gavin outside the tent for a few parting words. It wouldn't be right to just cut them loose after all we'd been through together. I made it clear that this made the most sense, despite my reservations. They didn't have a team leader anymore and had worked together extensively.

What I didn't want them thinking was that we were getting rid of the trash and didn't want them around. The fact is they were solid dudes and Marshall, who hadn't trained with any of us, would need a few heavy hitters to round out his line-up. They were disappointed and a little apprehensive, but they accepted the decision and didn't make things difficult, which I still admired. Some dudes would bitch and moan and complain about being moved around until someone made them shut up. But these two stayed professional.

I lit up a cigarette after they ducked back into the tent and thought about what had just happened. The picture of everyone's faces looking back at me stayed in my head as if I was holding it in my hands. I had this strange empty feeling like I had just lost something. I took a deep drag, focusing on the mental snapshot of our crew, and exhaled. Norman had gone to the battalion commander's personal security detail. Gavin and Cotton were moving over to Sergeant Marshall. Bittle and Karl were now permanent, and Zach was gone. Just like that the second squad we had built together didn't exist anymore.

Fourth squad, 2 Delta as we were now known, wasn't a completely blank canvas. We didn't erase everything up to this point, just shuffled the deck of cards a bit. All the training and experiences we had, and the way Zach had formed us around his leadership would be the base on which we would construct everything moving forward.

As we continued to train for the next few weeks, my confidence grew, and I started to believe that I could actually do this. I could follow Zach's example and be a great leader; the one that the squad needed and deserved. Pappy, Andy, and I had a good working relationship and we communicated well.

Everyone was honest about feeling fear. There isn't a single man past or present who can honestly say he never felt it at some point in war. Anyone who does is full of shit. Despite that, there was no doubt that we were ready to leave this glamor camp to the POGs and do what we came here to do.

A few short days later, I was in total darkness, crammed in the back of a CH 53 helicopter, sailing through the pitch-black Afghan sky. I could barely see the man across from me. Faint outlines of half the platoon over the mound of our rucks piled in the middle were barely discernable.

The heat, even at night, was still astonishing. The wind that passed over the helo as we sped towards the unknown was overpowered by the warmth generated by the machine. The drone of the rotors drowned out everything except for a few random sharp pinging sounds that reminded me of throwing rocks at a tin can. I constantly attempted to move my legs, which were crushed beneath the weight of our gear, so they wouldn't fall asleep. I had no idea what to expect on the other side of this trip.

I always hated flying. It didn't matter if I was on a civilian airplane, a C130, a helicopter, or a giant Martian spaceship, I absolutely hated flying. Countless times I boarded planes to fly home on leave to see my wife and family and with the slightest jerk, shudder, or unexpected movement of the aircraft I'd have a vision of the flight being yanked out of the sky, pinning attendants to the ceiling as I was I ripped in half by my seat belt only to see a wall of fire rushing straight towards me followed by a cut to black. I've always thought flying to be a gamble in which we value speed and convenience over rationality and safety.

But on this trip, I felt nothing of the sort. It was strange; almost as if it was fated for nothing to happen. How much sense would it make for us to fall from the sky and roast in the wreckage before we got a chance to fight in the war? That would be ridiculous.

This flight felt different. There was something deeper about it and still shrouded in mystery and adventure. This wasn't a wrestling match or a football game and it damn sure wasn't a first-person shooter video game. There weren't any "get backs" or "do overs" or "resets" and life wasn't measured by an energy bar in the lower right-hand corner of the screen. This was real now. We had trained ourselves to the brink and back for this. Countless hours had fallen off our lives as we labored under the heavy weight of the infantry, peeling layer after painful layer of skin from our feet, and seeping sweat out of every pore in our bodies for this moment...and it was here. It was finally here. This is what I had been searching for my whole life.

The world continued without us. People would continue living out their days working, playing with their children, and struggling to make ends meet or basking in wealth and prosperity. But we were about to do what less than one percent of Americans in our time would ever do: land in a combat zone. Not making it back didn't seem to matter anymore. I was at the top of this pyramid I'd been climbing since my youth and about to find out what sort of prize awaited me.

I crawled back out of my head and noticed the outline of Kevlar helmets with raised NVGs darting to the left and right before settling towards the back of the aircraft. We were slowing down, and the rotor wash was blasting dust and natural debris all over the place as the landing gear set down onto the earth.

Our rucks were averaging about 120 pounds, and everyone grabbed whichever one was right in front them as stumbled over each other out the back ramp. Standing up had sent a feeling of pure glory through my legs as the circulation resumed.

I could just make out Staff Sergeant Hauz standing at the end of the ramp counting everyone as they passed him and made their way through the darkness off to the right.

I careened down the ramp and the last Marines bounded off right after me. The platoon sergeant was leaning over a pack trying to see if it was his. Above the sound of the helo, I could make out his curses as he screamed at the last of us, trying to find out who had his gear. Apparently having *his* specific pack was of monumental importance and couldn't wait the five minutes it would take to just grab the damn thing and get it into the COP. So, he just left it.

I couldn't fucking believe it. Seriously? Tracy had messed up his ankle coming out of the helo and was being helped by Doc. Someone had grabbed the other side of the abandoned ruck and helped me stumble forward in the darkness.

The terrain was crusty and irregular. We were moving through a dried field and every step was on a small rise or depression of the rows that had been tilled to grow some form of sustenance for however many years before 1/6 had arrived and staked their claim. The CH 53 was long gone now, and it was deathly quiet.

I looked to my right and saw the shadowy figure of a Marine

standing on top of a berm that surrounded the area known as "inside the wire." He wasn't wearing gear or NVGs like the rest of us. In the faint light of a nearby burn pit, I could hardly see that he didn't even have a weapon or a uniform on. The flames illuminated the pale complexion of his body, covered only by dark, silky shorts. This dude wasn't even wearing boots.

What kind of place did we just drop into? The whole scene gave off this sort of *Lord of the Flies* vibe and I half expected him to light a torch and blow into an oversized conch to warn his buddies that we had arrived.

What the fuck? I thought. Well, we were here... and in the most anticlimactic fashion possible.

Things moved quickly over the next few days. The top priority was getting 1/6's Marines consolidated so they could leave, which meant that several of their squads dispersed throughout the AO had to be relieved. Gunny Willard transported us out to a small observation post situated at a T intersection a few miles west while the remainder of the platoon headed back east to link up with Weapons Company.

Marjah was a place forgotten by time. The fields were farmed by the toil of the native inhabitants with the most rudimentary of tools and simple techniques. As I stood at the OP, looking north across the dirt road we had just driven down, I could see a farmer working his land. It struck me that he didn't care about our presence in the slightest. He simply went about his business.

The road intersection was to our right. Main supply route Jessica ran the length of our AO from the east to west. Route Wolverines formed the bottom part of the T and traveled south. The road had a steep grassy ditch cut into the center of it and mud brick huts on both sides as far as I could see. Several hundred meters south, First platoon's patrol base rested on Wolverines. That was the closest friendly unit to our position.

1/6 had chosen this spot because it provided good visibility in all directions of the T intersection. The post was nestled in between the left corner of the crossroads and a small mud brick hut that could house about five of us. In front, lining Jessica were two rows of waist-high sandbags with a small gate next to Wolverines.

It felt like more a dog kennel than a tactical emplacement. If we were engaged, everyone would have to get small very quickly. Our only cover was the small fifteen-foot area we were standing in and the abutting hut to our left.

I didn't like feeling so confined. I wanted freedom to move.

As the other squad packed up their gear and got ready to step off, I spoke to the squad leader by the northern wall. He told me that we were standing in the very spot where one of their lieutenants had been killed by small arms fire. We stood there pouring sweat and baking in the heat, as he identified the tree line about two hundred meters away on the far side of the field where the farmer was working. He emphasized that the Taliban had used it frequently as a machine gun firing position. With a handshake, he wished us well and just like that, we were all alone in the wild, left to our own devices.

We stood around the intersection for an hour or two before we realized that there was very little vehicle traffic. Occasionally a small dirt bike would jet by, loaded down with two or even three passengers, or a small 1980s sedan would bounce along the unimproved dirt roads. I noticed that regardless of the mode of transportation, it seemed that the locals had figured out how to extend its maximum capacity for personnel and cargo by untold amounts. They had these large flatbed trucks that would be jammed full of crops, people, and random crap stacked over six feet higher than the metal railings. It didn't matter how rough the poor dirt roads were, they never lost anything or anyone over the side. It was amazing.

Darkness came quickly and we downgraded our security posture, manning the machine guns and radios that we had. The nighttime quiet allowed us to adjust to our new surroundings. It was early July now, well into the summer fighting season, and the fields seemed so dry that I couldn't imagine how anyone could find enough water to cultivate anything.

The the dusty roads and small houses with brown mud brick walls made it seem like a place that had stood still while the rest of the world advanced. The only vegetation I noticed ran along the canals lining the roads and the irrigation ditches separating the fields. There was barely any shelter, save for our tiny room and the temperature was well over one hundred degrees.

We developed a reaction plan for enemy contact and those who weren't on post were able to drop their gear inside the small enclosure and rest or eat. Weapons and kits would always remain within one arm's reach, just as they had during training.

The squad's mood was surprisingly light. The usual banter played back and forth between Pappy, Andy and the rest of the boys. I half expected everyone to be on edge because we were alone together in a combat zone for the first time.

We bedded down for the night rotating through on the post positions until a squad from first platoon showed up to relieve us in the morning. I shared the fire plan with the squad leader, and we loaded the MRAPs, heading east on route Jessica, past the company position at COP Kelly to link up with the rest of the platoon at another patrol base.

After we arrived, the boys turned to checking their gear before our first combat patrol in country. I dropped my kit and ducked underneath cammie netting supported by several ten-foot poles to join the platoon leadership. They were waiting for me, along with Captain Gibson.

I knew him already. He had been our company commander on the last deployment, after his predecessor was relieved for incompetence. What I still couldn't figure out was how this guy didn't remember me. We had been on the same ship, gone to the same countries, and trained together in the same Company for over a year before he rotated to Weapons.

He introduced himself with a handshake and I reminded him of our history before we dove right in. We were going to patrol south as a platoon to our new position, several kilometers away situated on another main intersection. There wasn't a whole lot to discuss, and it was far less formal than the orders process I had learned in school. It was simple: everyone would walk in one giant tactical column until we got to where we were going. Thomas and Gibson would coordinate any support we needed and Hauz would be there to take care of the casualties. All I had to do was control the squad and follow everyone else.

As we stepped off around noon, I couldn't help but feel strange. We had plenty of guns. But something about being the last squad in formation felt like chasing the older kids as a boy and trying to catch them.

I looked around the formation constantly. Everyone was alert. Every second that I wasn't watching the boys and the few locals we passed, I had my eyes glued to the front to make sure we didn't get left behind.

The hours melted off the clock and the heat drained pounds of sweat from my body. My anxiety about being last in the order of movement faded a little more each time I looked to the front and saw that Bart's squad was still there. We still had a few hours of daylight left and were due to arrive before nightfall, which I was grateful for.

Night operations have a certain discomfort to them. Despite our modern advances in technology, visibility is severely limited. Tack on the fact that most Americans grow up sleeping at night and that alone brings a whole new set of psychological issues into play: we're tired, we can't see well, we're thinking about a nice comfy bed, and the darkness is always accompanied by a unique sense of detachment from normalcy. It takes a while for most of us to become accustomed to doing daytime things outside of daytime hours.

This patrol was about as simple as it gets though. We only had three combat vets in the platoon, and I assumed they were more worried about the fact that the rest of us were experiencing all of this for the first time.

The terrain didn't change much as we marched. It was a bit more vegetated, mainly along the canals and drainage ditches that lined the fields. A few small saplings sprang up here and there but aside from that and the clusters of mud brick compounds we came across, there was very little cover or concealment.

The fields, however, took on their own bipolar personality. We passed through one that was dry and barren only to jump a wadi and walk right into another that was lush with head high corn stalks.

Slowly but surely, we made our way through this place that seemed as if it had no idea that the rest of the world had advanced beyond the Stone Age, save for a few vehicles and the occasional generator.

About four hours later, we arrived at COP Narea. The place wasn't too shabby. Enclosed by a triple stacked HESCO wall with two entrances, one north and one southeast, it sat on Route Elephants which ran south to north, ending at MSR Jessica. More fields surrounded the post as far as the eye could see with a few compounds scattered here and there. Another main east to west road lay two fields to the south. Beyond that to the southeast was a more urbanized area that fell under another company's responsibility.

From here we would saturate the area with patrols and find the enemy. We had our own operations center and two tents with air conditioning. Climate control was the last thing I expected to find here so it wasn't disappointing to find that they were no match for the heat and humidity. Man-made remedies weren't tough enough to survive here. It seemed to laugh at our feeble attempts to outmatch it as the machines simply churned out hot air that felt like a blast furnace every time someone came or went.

We shacked up with Third Squad for the first day or two before realizing that it was better to spread out. There was plenty of room in the compound for it. We had a second set of double HESCOs that separated us from the twenty or so Afghan National Army soldiers who lived on the other side.

We chose a nice little spot nestled in between the eastern wall and Third's tent, which we covered with a sheet of camouflaged netting. As we strung it up and lined the wall with our cots, it reminded me of building forts as a kid, but with a lot more guns.

Over the next two days, the other squads went out to test the waters and all had contact with the enemy. We worked the post rotation and passed time cleaning weapons and keeping our gear tight. All the while I kept asking myself why Thomas was keeping us for last.

First squad had gotten into a nice little fire fight at the end of their first time out, followed by Second, and Third. I started wondering if the man just wasn't confident in us, or in me specifically. When I asked him about it, he assured me that we would patrol just as much as everyone else. He had gone out with two of the other squads, so he clearly wasn't an armchair quarterback.

Sure enough, he made good on his promise. I got called into the COC the next day to receive my first brief from him as a squad leader. I listened intently and asked a million and one questions, most of which were irrelevant and the product of only having done this in a school setting.

Fuck it—we were here and the excess movements from one position to another and post reliefs were over. It was time to do what we came here to do. No more waiting. It didn't matter anymore that the others had gone before us. We had a massive chip on our shoulders and a score to settle. They killed Zach and now it was our turn.

Word from the lieutenant was that there was a terrorist detachment led by a one Lal Muhammed that had set up a training camp in our area. We didn't exactly have their daily schedule, but it sounded like they weren't your typical run of the mill terrorists. They were training, coordinating, and clearly not afraid to fight.

Thomas was sending us northeast to a small village, designated

Tango 3 on the map, to speak with the locals and ascertain Muhammed's whereabouts. As I understood it, the villagers in our wanted this guy gone. We had all been told, for as long as I been a Marine that the Afghan people hated the Taliban and were willing to help us get rid of them.

I came out of the COC and passed the timeline to Pappy and Andy. We were leaving first thing in the morning, so everyone went down knowing that we were on deck. I had thought about this moment countless times over the past three years and imagined the restlessness that would come with it. I'd expected the presumed anticipation to keep me awake, unable to tear my thoughts away from what lay ahead.

Instead, I slept like a giant sweaty baby.

So many things thus far were less forceful than I thought they would be. Our insert flight didn't end in a catastrophic crash or a massive firefight. Marjah didn't seem like it was in perpetual turmoil or a constant state of overwhelming violence. It was almost peaceful and boring.

What I couldn't know was that tomorrow's events would shatter that façade. I had no idea how this would turn out. But I did know that it was time to test my mettle and I would never be the same after.

It was the hottest day of my entire life. Our little area inside Narea was a beehive of activity. The Marines were moving back and forth, checking optics, gathering ammunition, and lubricating weapons. The team leaders spent the final moments having last minute conversations with their boys while I filed a patrol report in the COC.

A few moments later I stepped out from beneath the green canvas tent to find the squad assembled and ready to step out into the great unknown. I drew the charging handle of my weapon back as one of our SAW gunners applied lubricant to the inside as Andy and Pappy gave me thumbs up.

"COC, this is 2 Delta. Request permission to depart friendly lines with one-one packs." I said into the radio.

"Roger, permission granted," came the scratchy reply.

I waved the patrol forward and we moved towards the northern entry point, falling into formation on the move. I looked up at the nearly medieval design of the HESCO walls with manned guard towers perched atop. A first squad Marine curiously peered down on us as if he was contemplating how we would measure up. The exit, about fifty meters to our front, seemed like it was miles away.

We broached the concertina wire gate, pulled off to the side by a Marine from another squad. All eyes seemed locked on us. It was only natural for them to wonder how we would do. Zach was admired by everyone, but he wasn't here anymore. The other squads had already proven themselves and they knew that we were hungry for our chance.

Following the bend of the walls to the right, we crossed route Elephants. And just like that, we were outside the wire, steadily moving away from the perceived safety of Narea.

We moved cautiously and deliberately, observing the entirely new realm around us, alone for the first time. It was so surreal. I looked forward to the point team, then back to the team behind me, as we moved across the first barren field, crunching the dried earth beneath our weight.

We are finally here. We are actually doing this, I thought to myself. Nothing else mattered anymore, not the oppressive heat or the politics of the war, not even family and friends back home hoping that I didn't meet a violent demise the next time my foot hit the ground. The only thing that mattered was doing what we came here to do: fight and win.

Pappy's team was spread out in front of me in a skirmisher's line moving towards the next field and I could see the heat, visibly rising from the top of the infernal corn stalks. It was like seeing the heat waves waft off a charcoal grill. We stepped through the first rows and into the oven that was to be our battlefield for as long as we lived.

Our feet sank into the mud to the ankles with every step in the well-irrigated farmland. Moving quickly would be difficult. Despite the struggle for us to maintain decent footing, everyone was alert and scanning their sectors as we moved. We felt relatively safe in the fields, reasoning that the Taliban wouldn't mine them, attempting maintain good faith with the locals.

Andy's team patrolled behind me in a tactical column. Together, the two groups formed a T-shape that afforded us flexibility if we were engaged from the front or sides. We had turned northeast, towards our objective which was the Tango 3 district only a few kilometers away from the COP.

The squad radio attached to my left shoulder beeped and Pappy alerted me that we were closing in on the village. I checked the small GPS on my wrist to confirm. Being in unfamiliar territory didn't faze him one bit. He knew where we were going. Nearly one hour had elapsed since we departed Narea.

We passed through a small cluster of compounds lining an east-west running wadi and a long lane of open alternating green and barren patches lay in front of us. The expanse was bordered by our target village on the left, which was lined by a shallow irrigation ditch and a few small trees. Across the field to the east lay a column of thicker vegetation with minor undergrowth and a smaller cluster of compounds, punctuated by a single two-story mud brick structure.

We maintained fifty meters between the teams, planning to enter the hamlet from the northern end. As we neared the entrance, the ditch that traveled the length of the wall branched off to the east towards the adjacent tree line. Pappy's team veered off the imaginary line of advance and settled into the small off shoot, while the rest of us stayed moving forward.

I settled in with Pappy and his group as Andy's Team One passed through the break in the walls. The ditch, forming a natural L shape, offered us thigh high cover and the ability to move laterally. I was impressed with how smooth the movement had been.

Team One, accompanied by several ANA soldiers, was now obscured by the ten-foot-high walls. Staring across the dried field, I crouched down behind my rifle with Pappy's Team Two, waiting for the enemy, daring them walk into the trap. We lay there, offering ourselves as bait for what seemed like hours, hoping they would be stupid enough to take it.

The silence was snapped by a high pitched series of rapid pops right overhead that sounded like massive sheets of bubble wrap being twisted. *Game the fuck on!*

"Contact front!" I screamed.

The team around me let loose on the eastern tree line with everything they had. Machine guns and rifles went cyclic instantly. I burned through my first magazine so fast it would've given a competition shooter an erection.

"Kill everything!"

We kept firing, pouring a solid wall of fuck-you lead into the location. Andy's Team One sprang from the village behind us and set up to our right in the north-to-south running section, our little trench. I was in between the two teams at the bend of the L shaped wadi. The enemy fire intensified as we exchanged magazines and slid new belts onto the feed trays of the guns.

We started controlling our fire and moving slightly right and left after bursts, overwhelming the enemy's output. I glanced left and right and heard the boys calling targets as the enemy moved among the trees.

Doc was the only one not adding to the hail of bullets. I crawled to him, using the ditch to shield my body, thinking he was hit. Tracy was kneeling in the wadi next to him, still blazing away with his SAW.

Draped over Tracy's calves in the ditch, I realized Doc's rifle had been shot while running from the village to the wadi. The enemy projectile was lodged in the upper receiver, millimeters above the chamber. It was worthless with the round still sticking out of it.

Holy shit.

If his rifle hadn't been there, the bullet would've gone into his chest. The initial excitement began to wear off and we started to settle down a bit. Our fire became more controlled, and communication passed up and down the line as the enemy element darted back and forth three hundred meters away.

The two-story structure to my two o'clock across the field was occupied and our rifles weren't going to do anything to it at all. We increased suppression as Bittle prepared the shoulder-fired, collapsible Light Anti-Armor Weapon he had carried with him. The rocket misfired and we slowed our rate to conserve ammunition. The enemy fire was still coming in close but in far less volume. The rocket misfired a second time and then a third, making it useless.

Bittle shouldered the extended tube and resumed firing with his M4 while we shredded the Taliban a short distance away. They had set up right in the intersection of our fires and we made them pay for it. As they crawled and struggled under the weight of our suppression, the 240B machine gun, on Team One's left, spit out rounds that shredded their limbs and drove the enemy from cover for the rest of us to finish off with grenade rounds and rifle shots.

Through the din of modern weaponry's wondrous performance, I sighted in on a muzzle flash next to a large haystack, nestled between two trees. I saw the dust kick up and the flames leave the muzzle as the gun burst in futile desperation. I caught my breath.

Inhale, exhale... slow, steady squeeze.

The firing stopped after my third well-aimed shot. I tore my eye from the optic and jumped over Tracy, screaming over the fire for Team One to hold in place. The rest of us maneuvered left over the ANA soldiers and Karl, still firing his machine gun, to assault the terrorists on the opposing wadi.

We crouched and moved low and steady, to the end of the trench. By this time, we had been trading rounds for hours and had no idea.

A section of the battalion's Combined Anti-Armor Team had pulled up behind us on Route Elephants, bordering the western edge of T3. Lieutenant Thomas must've called them from Narea, where he was monitoring the situation.

The section leader from CAAT called over the radio. He was coordinating an airstrike and needed me to mark our position.

The teams stayed put as I rushed back through the wadi in two long bounds to where our ANA comrades lay looking about and occasionally firing their rifles. With my chest heaving and my heart throbbing through my chest, I realized I had just taken a huge unnecessary risk. Thankfully, the enemy was reeling from the casualties we'd induced, otherwise they could've easily sent me to an early grave.

I lay on my back in the ditch, sweat-soaked and covered in mud head to toe, as I yanked a smoke grenade from my chest rig and hurled it to my left for the pilots to identify our position.

I got on the radio and told Team One to increase their rate of fire again. After the initial volley impacted across the flat, battered field, Team Two moved past me into its old position and attempted to mark the enemy with a smoke grenade from an M203 launcher. After several attempts, we realized the enemy had moved further south. It looked like they'd consolidated in the larger structure.

Despite my foolhardy sprint, the pilot overhead didn't pick up the smoke from several minutes earlier. We didn't have any more, save for the red canisters reserved for friendly casualties. One of the local soldiers with us volunteered to take off the bright baby blue T-shirt he wore underneath his web gear and wave it around to attract the attention of the bird overhead.

What the hell. I figured.

My radio crackled to life with a voice from CAAT 1 telling me the birds were inbound as the Afghan shed his gear. We sent another wave of bullets at the trapped enemy while he waved the cloth around over his head before dropping back down into cover.

We peeled individually back towards T3 so the birds could drop their bombs. I ended up right back where I had started, in between Tracy and Doc when an automatic burst sawed right over our heads from behind and heart rates skyrocketed. The continuous burst forced us completely into the ditch and we started crawling towards Pappy's team. We were so close together that the three of us looked like one muddy mass. The ditch we had occupied for the entire fight seemed to shrink as the rounds ripped mere feet overhead.

An overexcited turret gunner from the CAAT section had opened fire on the enemy position, not knowing we were in between. His fire passed through a break in the village wall then over us, en route to his target. We crawled through the small half-tunnel in the humid, soggy mud as I screamed into the radio to find out what was happening.

The firing ceased a few seconds later but it felt like it lasted an eternity, as if the clock was moving in slow motion and the machine gun was on steroids. I breathed a little easier and team two rebounded with controlled, consistent fire. Expletives came out as fast as automatic fire when I told them not to return fire to the rear. I wasn't sure if they were pissed about it or just as relieved as I was.

I scrambled back over to Team Two and we alternated firing and changing magazines for the upcoming move. The air assets had both positions, but we were still too close for comfort. Team One was ready shortly thereafter and sprinted back towards T3 as soon as we took over the firing. Once the whole squad was consolidated, the birds would be able to drop without any chance of hitting us.

The enemy continued their intermittent firing to tell us they weren't done yet. I looked over my shoulder and saw the barrels lining the ditch that ran the length of Tango 3's wall. The rounds kicked up dust and debris as they ripped over the field off to our four o'clock and Team Two clawed their way out of the ditch towards the new position.

Pappy and I hauled ass just behind them with the ANA soldiers. Stumbling over the rough field and rebounding, I looked to my left to see the Afghan soldier hold his rifle over his back and burn through an entire magazine as he ran alongside me, having no clue where he was shooting. It was as if the destination just kept moving further and further away from me as I ran in between the ANA soldier and Pappy. The field was now dried and clumpy, almost rocky, from the mid-day sun. Rounds snapped past our heads and sprayed dust and fragments of dirt clods by our feet as we made our way towards the relative safety of the new canal and fell in.

I looked up to the northern end of T3, a few meters away, to see the CAAT platoon sergeant calling in the air support. He stood in the road next to his vehicle, casually talking into his radio. I moved back down the wadi and settled in between the two teams. Being in the middle gave me a feeling of control.

Both teams were redistributing ammo in anticipation for the next phase and maintained a consistent pace of rifle fire until the bomb finally dropped. The earth shook and rumbled, reminding me of just how small I was in the realm of modern warfare. The bomb zoomed in and impacted with a terrible bang of dust, debris, and invisible force that engulfed the entire target area instantly. The sheer power of it was astonishing, even without the massive fireballs portrayed in movies.

After the initial awe of the airstrike passed, I glanced down at my watch and saw that it was after two o'clock. We had been at it for about six hours and the effects were showing on all of us. The sun and the terrain seemed to add more weight to our backs. I was so dehydrated that my muscles were cramping with each contraction and every movement was performed in slow motion.

We were spent, and still had to be ready for another fight on the way back if it found us.

After a moment of indecision, I called back to Narea, requesting the quick reaction squad to come out and support us. We looked like beaten zombies lining up on the road in front of the CAAT section's vehicles and started to shuffle back towards the COP. A few hundred meters later, we spotted first squad set up in a blocking position, covering our return to friendly lines. I requested permission to enter before we passed under the overwatch of the guns up in the HESCO towers.

It felt like walking through a Roman Coliseum gate with falling rose petals and a roaring crowd in the background. The triumph felt overwhelmingly awesome, as if electricity was coursing through my veins. We had passed our test and left no doubt.

The squad collapsed on the cots, and I headed for the COC. Pulling back the covering of the green canvas tent felt like handling a baking sheet without an oven mitten. Sergeant Marshall and Lieutenant Thomas were standing over the map table.

The second I walked in, Marshall shot up and clasped my hand, offering his praise. The lieutenant told me that the air assets counted at least seven enemy dead. The pilots could identify their litter teams moving casualties off the front line as we put them down throughout. And we had no friendly casualties.

Shortly thereafter, the leadership from the CAAT team showed up and we exchanged handshakes and congratulations. I moved outside to our squad area and dropped my gear next to the cot that I called home.

The squad was elated, passing back exchanges of what we had all just done. Our generation of Marine been told from the beginning that the final phase of recruit training, The Crucible, was the last rite of passage for all Marines. After the fight we had just been through, and seeing the elation of the squad now, I couldn't believe that.

Every part of my body ached, every muscle was entirely spent, and it was as if my lungs had swallowed fire and my throat had been parched for a decade. But I felt the strongest pride of my entire life in that moment, one that dwarfed all others and could never be taken away.

The day was ours. Everything else felt inconsequential. We had lived up to the infantryman's legacy and passed our initial test, our initiation into the most natural world of man.

Sergeant Marshall stopped by in his gear, ready to push out on patrol with his boys, and congratulated the squad.

"Now you can go back home and tell Sergeant Walters' family that you got 'em," he said.

He left after another handshake, and I sat down. Time seemed to stop dead in its tracks. The adrenaline was flooding out of our bodies and exhaustion took its place, along with a torrent of suppressed emotions that flooded the senses. Soon the whole group was fast asleep. I'd never been so tired in all my life, and I fell in line with the rest as my body shut down under the hundred-degree sun and a feeling of accomplishment that dwarfed all those before.

That first meeting with the enemy would set the tone for the rest of our time in Narea. Countless hours were spent patrolling and occupying the observation post we established to the north on route Elephants. Long fire fights, close air support from F-18s and Cobra gunships, and the COP getting harassed by small arms and machine gun fire were all regular occurrences. Quiet, uneventful days were few and far between.

Day in and day out, it was a tactical chess match of maneuver. We were feeling the enemy out and they were learning about us. The environment taught us to appreciate the gravity of small things on patrol. The random cold turn of the stomach, the hair standing up on the back of the neck or noticing a once busy village street suddenly become empty and deadly quiet, all warranted close scrutinization.

Everything had a meaning. We halted frequently to scan piles of trash and cracks in mud brick walls for wires and IED components. We searched houses and found urea nitrate and other materials typical of the bombs but weren't allowed to seize it unless it was a massive quantity. One of the prime ingredients in the enemy's most deadly weapon was protected by our own bureaucracy because "it was essential to the economic livelihood of the Afghan farmer." So, we carried on and just looked at the materials in passing, wondering when it would be crafted into some crude and clever apparatus that would disintegrate some of us on the next patrol.

Our ANA counterparts were largely useless. Laziness, timidity, and negligence were rampant among their ranks, save for a handful of individuals. Their commander, however, First Sergeant Rambo, was invaluable. The corrupt Afghan National Police had a small outpost just across the southern road from COP Narea, which they manned whenever they felt like it.

One hot, sweltering day, when COP Narea came under fire, the Afghan police fired a .50 caliber machine gun within a few feet of one of our posts that was engaging the enemy, which prompted Rambo to threaten them at gunpoint the next day.

On similar occasions when Narea took fire, he had a four-man team follow behind him, weapons loaded, as he mounted the perimeter walls to return fire. These four guys formed a chain to pass up weapon after weapon to him as he sprayed rounds in the general direction of the suspected enemy position. Despite Rambo's lack of precision, we respected his spirit. The man didn't back down from a fight, unlike most of the ANA troops assigned to us.

One of his troops eagerly followed his example and found a way to set the world record for most RPG rockets fired in a minute. When Rambo mounted the walls, this guy followed suit, launcher on his shoulder and a backpack full of rockets. He would fire, then reload, then fire again until he was out of ammunition. I never once saw him look to his rear to clear the back-blast area of friendly troops, or even check his left or right, like we are taught when we fire rockets. We loved having this guy out on patrol, but in an uneasy way. If you could direct that eager aggression towards a terrorist or two, the effects would be devastating. Just don't be behind him when he lets loose.

Interpreters were another hit or miss asset that we worked with closely. Lucky was the main guy and the best one we had. He spoke decent enough English and his translations were honest. Plus, he didn't crap his pants and curl up in the nearest wadi during a fight like some of the soldiers. He was a tough customer, and everyone respected his endurance because he worked like our medical corpsmen did. Interpreters and Corpsmen patrolled multiple times nearly every day because it was an operational requirement to have one of each on every movement.

Lucky's peers, however, were a different matter. They spoke barely perceptible broken English and regarded their duties with nonchalance. The only consistency we had with most of them was that they didn't give a shit. One of them even angrily promised to conceal IED positions from us because he didn't like us entering local homes.

The fact is many of these guys didn't care what happened in Marjah. Most of them were shipped in from other provinces. It was evidence of the tribal mentality that permeates all of Afghanistan.

For the locals in Marjah, if an issue didn't affect their specific tribe or their little patch of land, then it didn't matter. The concept of a national identity, like that shared by Americans, was nonexistent or completely, depending on who we spoke to. The collective benefit of the country wasn't a priority to most of them.

Consequently, I viewed the ANA as extra baggage and didn't trust the villagers. Whenever they pointed out compounds supposedly housing terrorists, we had to wonder if it was true or if he was aiming us at an old family rival. As for the soldiers, we kept them at distance, trusting only the ones who had proven their prowess, like Lucky, Rambo, and the Rocket Man.

It had been nearly three months since we set foot on Marjah's soil and the stress was taking its toll. Lieutenant Thomas divided our days into eight-hour blocks. One squad would be patrolling, another would serve as their quick reaction force in case they got into a jam, and the squad would man Narea's entry points and machine gun towers. We kept the small observation post, further down route elephants, manned by a squad around the clock, rotating through. Everyone had something to do always.

There was never an easy day. We had pushed our bodies beyond extreme limits for years to prepare for this and were still smoked after every patrol. The humidity in Marjah's fields added a sweltering effect that made Camp Lejeune seem mild. It was constantly stifling which made it impossible to hydrate. Meaningful sleep was difficult to come by because the enemy harassed our posts with fire, and we patrolled at all hours. My piss matched the color of orange Kool-Aid. Showers, climate control, running water, and nearly every other modern amenity didn't exist out here.

As the effects began to mount, we started to learn about ourselves and each other. We had trained together for months and gotten close, but what we were doing now added more depth. It was a natural continuation, because there are some questions that simply couldn't be answered in training. What stood out to me the most was finding out why the men in our squad thought we were here and what they valued or hated about the situation.

The mood within the squad had changed. I had noticed the intangible shift but didn't know how to confront it. It slowly became clear that I viewed this whole endeavor differently than everyone else. The excitement of getting into fire fights had faded, replaced by a more rational caution that favored survival.

From my perspective, they were tired of the constant, grueling patrols day after day, whether they resulted in action or not. It seemed that they didn't understand why I still wanted to close in on the enemy when we came under fire, instead of taking cover and calling in an airstrike. I imagined that they felt as if I was being careless with their safety.

One day at OP Elephants, Andy and I sat down on a pair of ration boxes and had a conversation about it. We had spent over one third of our time in country and learned a lot about each other. Actions during a fight followed up with simple remarks afterwards, either in jest or riddled with strong emotions, gave us a rare and raw window into the inner workings of one another.

The sun was setting, accompanied by the typically slight drop in temperature and the boys were bedding down, minus the two we had on watch. The small post consisted of a Hesco tower with a tube of concrete traffic walls extending behind it. In front of it all was an MRAP with an M2 machine gun mounted in its turret.

We sat in the back, opposite the MRAP, discussing the predicament we were in. Andy was built differently than I. Not just physically but mentally. He seemed to take pride in helping the locals and serving as a buffer between them and the terrorists. He was a protector. Many of the other typical Grunt traits remained: he was tough, he could sniff out bullshit from a mile off, and he spoke his mind.

My mentality towards the locals was opposite his. I abandoned any care I had left for them within the first month of us being here. I believed they were either willingly harboring terrorists or they were terrorists themselves. I saw everyone as a potential threat, even the children. More than once, we had gathered around the radio during another squad's fire fight, and all heard the reports of children serving as active observers for enemy fire.

Routinely, we received word from our officers about schools being built or local markets thriving in other parts of Marjah. Andy was so close to being a part of what he wanted, but it was always another company or platoon that got those missions. Results like those always seemed to be valued more than enemy deaths-especially back home in the media.

To me, it was someone else's job to provide them with modern amenities and democratic institutions. I constantly wondered why media outlets were so fascinated with the idea of us performing humanitarian tasks. Not that we had access to any of it, but that had been the message before we came here, and I had no reason to assume it had changed.

All we had done since we arrived was patrol, stand post, and fight. Someone with a microphone and an audience back home had to know that. So why were they so intent on presenting us as these champions of the Afghan people? Why would anybody value that image at all? More importantly, I wondered why Andy wanted to be a part of that so badly.

As the conversation progressed, it sounded like the idea of digging a well or building a school for a village appealed to him far more standing over enemy corpses. Maybe he was frustrated that all we had done was fight. I couldn't understand that. Infantrymen are meant to destroy, not protect. I had come here to inflict as much pain on the enemy as I possibly could. Andy, I thought, came here because he really did want to help people. This was the first moment that stripped us both to our most basic form: the warrior and the protector.

As we talked, both Andy and I recognized how irreconcilable our positions were.

Through a haze of harsh 88 Mild cigarettes, Andy and I went back and forth over what was more important. Recognizing that we were running in circles, he ended the conversation pointedly. As the smoke cleared and he tossed the burning butt onto the ground he said, "You want the romanticized version of war."

It wouldn't dawn on me until nearly half a decade later just how right he was, and the rest of the deployment would serve as a reminder of a lesson that my parents taught me growing up: you don't always get what you want.

A few days after my dialogue with Andy, our platoon was reattached to Echo Company. We were leaving Narea to take over the company headquarters position at COP Kelly. Captain Brock and First Sergeant Payton had trucked in so they could patrol back with us.

The temperature was unusually high, and the terrain turned from flat open earth to high corn fields as we slogged through the mud and sweltered in the humidity. We were in the back of the platoon, which made the pace seem agonizingly slow and frustrating as hell.

About three hours and several kilometers later, we stopped for a long security halt. The boys settled into the best firing positions possible and kept their eyes peeled for enemy indicators. A few minutes later, we got word that Third Platoon was in a nasty fight to our north and had taken casualties.

Through the company radio net, we learned that Cody Roberts, Pappy's best friend, had been wounded. The two had been together at their first duty station in Fleet Anti-terrorism Security Team and continued a very close friendship. If it had been Deeno, I would've wanted to know, so I pushed through the giant green stalks and found him to break the news. To say that he was unaffected would be a lie, but anyone else would've had to look hard to see it. He stayed focused on what was in front of us and on keeping his team engaged.

We continued for what seemed like hours, with limited information on Cody status. All I knew was that he had been shot and evacuated. Anytime you get word that a Marine in your unit is wounded it stings, even if you don't know them that well. I barely knew Cody at all, but it still didn't stop the hair on my body from standing up or my heart skipping a few beats. I was more worried about Pappy if he didn't pull through.

We caught harassing fire from our rear just outside the COP Kelly a few hours later. The outpost was no more than fifty meters to our north when the automatic bursts shattered the otherwise peaceful movement. They engaged us after the terrain had slightly opened back up and evaporated once we had consolidated and returned fire. The engagement ended quickly, and it was obvious that they were just trying to wear us down even more, after our long patrol. Despite the lack of modern communications in Marjah, everyone knew when one of our patrols went out. No doubt, the word had traveled from village to village from the time we stepped off from Narea that morning, meaning they had waited all day to pull the trigger. It was about wearing us down long term.

As we moved through the Hesco serpentine, I noticed the place was a little bigger than Narea. It had four posts equally spaced along the double height Hesco wall, and the centrally located operations center was much larger. We gathered our helmets, which always came off immediately once inside the wire, and moved towards a row of tents on the right-hand side.

Everyone was here and relatively safe, so my top priority was to get an update about Cody. I dropped my kit by an unclaimed cot and headed straight for the COC. I was nervous and I knew that Pappy was too. This was important to him. I wanted to show him that keeping him informed was a priority.

Staff Sergeant Case was the man in charge or running the operations center. He had served an enlistment as a combat instructor at the School of Infantry, so we had history. His full mane of black hair was peppered with white strands, and he looked exhausted. Clearly, he wasn't sleeping much.

I couldn't even get my out before he told me that Cody had been stable when he was evacuated. Relief washed over me as I shook hand and promised to stop by so we could catch up. Returning the squad tent, I found Pappy, having just returned from getting his boys some chow, and passed the news to him.

Relief washed over me as I prepped my gear for the next patrol. Water refilled, weapon lubricated, and old batteries changed out, I left our birthing to scrouge up a meal. My stomach roared as I turned right and crossed the small prison gym towards a plywood building to satisfy my hunger.

Lieutenant James Zimmerman, third platoon's commander, had just finished eating when I walked through the door. I thought that if anyone knew anything more about Cody, it would be him. When I asked, the commander told me that he was back in surgery now but wasn't sure why.

Lieutenant Zimmerman was calm, as he always seemed to me, but he moved smartly out of the unfinished wooden structure, which seemed odd. I debated passing the word but decided against it. I didn't want to frustrate Pappy and the guys with a bunch of back-and-forth information.

Not more than half an hour later everyone in the COP, save for the Marines on post, were assembled outside the COC and Captain Brock informed us that Cody had died. I was shocked. How the hell could he have been stable one minute and dead the next? It took me a minute to recognize the sheer idiocy of that thought. Battlefield wounds carry with them a measure of unpredictability and sometimes, the results simply don't make sense.

Fear and near panic seized me when I realized what I had done to Pappy. I had given the man false hope.

I wondered how the hell we could possibly move forward after that and whether he could ever trust a single word I said. With Zach's death and now Cody's, Pappy had lost his two best friends in the Corps.

He was more distant for a time after that and understandably so. I didn't know how to approach him. I tried to make it clear that I was there for him but that was as far as I knew how to go.

I was grasping in the dark for a way to figure out how to keep good faith with him, and it seemed like nothing would be enough. At the end of the day, this was about him. I had no idea how to console someone in a situation that I had handled so poorly. It felt different than when Zach was killed because we all knew him. We were still sharing that loss together. But I hadn't known Cody and that made it impossible for me to understand the weight of loss that Pappy felt. I couldn't fully empathize with him and that created another gap on top of the one that existed between Andy and me.

I was losing the squad on a personal level.

Pappy made it easier for me. He didn't lash out or get angry or seem to blame me for how it all happened. From my perspective, he did what I did when Zach was killed and put grieving on hold until after we could get back home. To his everlasting credit, he warmed back up to the squad quickly. To an outside observer he would've seemed perfectly normal. But no one is the same after such an experience- that much I did know.

Roughly a month before, we had been assigned a new platoon sergeant. Staff Sergeant. Beasley was an old school Marine and a behemoth of a man. On the MEU, he had been a squad leader with First platoon, and it was clear that he favored an iron discipline approach to leadership. Uniform regulations, customs and courtesies, grooming standards, and COP cleanliness were high on his priorities list. When he took over for Staff Sergeant Hauz, he made it very clear that we were to maintain Marine Corps standards in every aspect of life, from addressing each other by rank and last name to uniformly arranging our living quarters. I took this as law and instituted the changes immediately as much of that tradition had gone to the wayside since our arrival. I backed it up with my typical stubbornness and the same iron fist presentation that I displayed back at Camp Lejeune.

The change in leadership, both Beasley's and mine, combined with the physical wear and tear and constant state of heightened stress began to degrade morale. We were nearing the halfway point of the deployment and everyone's thoughts started to shift towards home. The initial thrill of war had lost its luster. I did my best to walk the line with the rules inside the COP, then discard them the moment we departed on patrol, which widened the gaps between us. I learned, after it was too late to repair, that half measures erode trust quickly. A leader must be all in or all out.

I didn't know how to stymie the flow of negative energy, so I just carried on. Not confronting it directly, allowed the uneasy feeling to fester. Andy and I abhorred each other's view of the war overall and Pappy had trouble getting over how poorly I handled the news of Cody's death. To make matters worse, it was all filtered down to everyone else in the squad. The children within a home always know when parents fight, and this situation was no different.

I didn't have any doubts about our ability to fight and win outside the COP. But I was learning that being a squad leader is about much more than fighting. Zach understood us and how to keep us together and how to push us without fracturing relationships. The human aspect of leadership is so vitally important to success. And it is one of many areas that Zach's abilities dwarfed mine.

These were the harsh lessons Marjah was teaching me. No school can bestow empathy or emotional intelligence. I was being forced to accept that the cookie-cutter robotic Marine approach to leadership eventually falls short in stressful environments. It became painfully clear that good leaders infantry leaders had to know war, but they also had to understand people.

Cody's death on the 31st of August would mark the beginning of the company's darkest time in Marjah. Lance Corporal Ross Carver was shot in the head by an enemy sniper three days later, and Corporal Phillip Charte was killed by small arms fire on September 7th. Third Platoon had suffered three killed in the span of eight days.

The number of wounded began to mount. This was a day in, day out struggle to break the enemy's will. We inflicted far more pain and loss than we received. This wasn't a battle akin to the poor portrayals of Vietnam that show high American casualties with little or no progress. We weren't frantic or horrified of our own shadows. In nearly every engagement, it was clear that we were superior warriors. But only so many bullets can miss before at least one finds its mark.

Every man's luck in combat is variable and finite.

The company had begun to suffer the weight of loss. In a group this tight, everyone knows everyone in some way. Patrelli had been in Third Platoon with Charte and Zach on the previous deployment. Pappy had lost both of his best friends, and Karl had come from Weapons Platoon with Carver. Aside from Zach, I wasn't close with any of them. I hadn't even grieved for him yet and had no idea how to help them. I should have. I was their leader, wasn't I?

Fight hard, follow orders, and don't stop. That's what I knew. It worked well when the bullets were flying but after the last round was fired, they needed more from me. My inability to help all of them deal with loss amid the fighting made it seem as if I didn't care.

I wondered how the hell Zach was so good at holding us all together. But no matter how much I thought about it, I never came up with the answer. It seemed so easy for him which only added to my frustration. Trying to fill his boots consumed my thoughts as we pushed forward through countless fights and amidst endless patrolling in this inhospitable tribal flash back. The only thing I knew for certain was to keep fighting and never quit.

The next month brought several fruitless platoon-sized operations sprinkled in with the daily squad level efforts. The heat and humidity remained, and the mud only added to the already countless knee and ankle sprains. Extended fights were fewer and occurred more distant from COP Kelly but were just as potent. I saw it as evidence of the casualties we had inflicted on them.

We had pushed the enemy back, creating a small buffer zone that extended north from the company position to Mia Kel village and west to OP Gettysburg. We had passed the halfway mark in the deployment and were now painfully aware of the fact that we still had another three months to go.

This is a crucial time in any deployment because guys start thinking about home more than usual, which makes life-altering mistakes more likely to occur. The only ways out were to win, be wounded, or die. The last choice was to fake some sort of mental disorder which, regardless of how much we hated Afghanistan, wasn't an option. None of us were going to spend the rest of our lives with that kind of disgrace. We stuck together and put the things we had to deal with on hold until we could get back home with our honor intact.

At this crucial middle phase, another significant event altered the landscape of the squad. One morning before noon Third Squad had been out mixing it up with the Taliban, several hundred meters to the northeast. We were the designated react squad, so when they called for support, we geared up to lend a hand.

Shin splints and joint pain were so common that we developed contempt for them. The heat made it impossible to hydrate adequately and our meals didn't provide the necessary sustenance to sustain us. Every muscle ached from the previous patrol and the boys were operating on roughly four hours of sleep a night, which is less than half they would need to recover from soft tissue injuries. But bitching was kept to a minimum because that was the price of admission, and everyone felt it.

We struck out east, crossing over three or four crunchy fields, then cut north and settled into a large empty compound where we could see Third's trail element off to our left through holes in the compound wall. We called them murder holes because someone had to work hard to carve them out. In a place like this the only purpose for a softball sized hole was to be able to fit a muzzle through it and maintain the wall's protection for the rest of the body. Many of them were low to the ground, meant for a shooter to lay prone and engage. Typically, as we often found after being engaged, the enemy had doused the other side of the wall with water to limit the muzzle blast from kicking up dirt and debris that we could see to identify their position.

Third Squad had the situation well in hand and I guessed that they just wanted us there to seal the eastern escape route. We couldn't see the other part of their patrol, but we heard the consistent exchange of gun fire.

They were slugging it out, it sounded like, and as the volume grew more distant and they maneuvered, we moved with them off to their right, looking for any of the bastards to try and make a break for it. With no such luck, the gun fire died out and we started moving.

A few hours passed and we wound up entering the small village of Mia Kel. Sergeant Bart's Third squad covered the eastern portion of the main road and our boys passed through them to take up the western approach.

Questioning the locals had turned up nothing, as usual. At this point most of us had just accepted the fact that most of them weren't going to give us anything useful, regardless of how many terrorists we killed, which made sense because we raised the standard of living for some. If they could survive, the current state of things was very profitable for them. Our government was pumping trillions into theirs and some of that found its way down to this small local level. They had something to line their pockets with, provided they were on the right side of the local political scene.

I had a quick face-to-face with Bart and we settled that he would move out first with his group and we would pick up the rear. We were all gassed, but they had been out here longer and there were only a few hours of daylight left.

We held in place for about an hour before Bart and his squad picked up and moved a hundred meters south, settling into the nearest wadi to cover our movement. Soaking wet and heaving beneath the weight of the humidity and our gear, we started out. Andy held his team in a wadi just outside the village to give us a small lead while I accompanied Pappy's team into the semi-dry field.

As soon as we hit the halfway point, the enemy AKs came alive and forced us to the ground before each of us bounded half right towards the fire, shooting back. Greddy and I were glued to our radios which were drowned out with a torrent of traffic. This was the worst possible spot to be in: trying to shrink our two hundred- fifty-pound bodies to fit behind small clumps of dirt with our asses hanging out in the middle of an open field.

The report of an explosion close to Andy's position added a new dimension to the fight. The enemy exchanged rounds with us and Bart's boys to our left and now another element was swapping grenades with Andy and his off to our right.

Whether we went left or right, we had to move fast.

My heart jumped into my throat when Pappy screamed out that

Bittle was hit. I looked over and saw him working with several blood-soaked bandages while Gunner ripped off a few aggressive bursts with his SAW on the other side. Greddy was next to me getting the medevac request sent up while Bart got some Cobra gunships to come lend a hand.

Minutes later, as the low hum of the rotors grew louder, the enemy fire abated. Andy reported no casualties before everything was drowned out by the Cobra gliding overhead and smoothly settling in to dump hundreds of rounds into one of the enemy positions roughly two hundred meters to our front. Watching and hearing the twenty-millimeter cannon shred the compound was one of the most awesome things I've ever seen. I was torn between hoping it killed every one of the fuckers and getting any feedback that came from Pappy concerning Bittle. A 7.62 round had ripped through his hand, shattering the bones when he got up to bound forward. The wound was wrapped, and the bleeding was controlled before another helicopter landed to pick him up.

And just like that it was over.

Bittle was alive but gone, and the scene was so quiet it felt empty. The massive information traffic jam that was my brain moments before slowly returned to normal as we slipped into the wadi with Bart's squad. Andy and his team emerged from the vegetation on the south side of Mia Kel unscathed from their close encounter to join us and we redistributed ammunition. Third's 240 machine gun was fresh out and ours was running low. We spread Bittle's rifle, the M32 grenade launcher, and his NVGs amongst the squad while Third pushed south towards the COP.

After giving them a good hundred meters head start, we followed in trace. Pappy and I wondered how bad the wound was. At least it was only his hand and not something vital. Regardless, a wound like that with all the bones nearby would have lifelong consequences. It must have been incredibly painful. Through it all I never heard him scream or fall apart because of it. Bittle was one tough hombre.

Staff Sergeant Beasley was waiting for us when we got inside the wire to assure us that Bittle was okay. The day was finally over but taking a deep breath after dropping kit didn't have the same reassurance anymore. We were down a gun now and Bittle couldn't be replaced. Someone else could be assigned to carry the M32, but he worked wonders on the morale of the whole squad. To say that he was missed for the rest of the deployment is an understatement.

Not more than a week later, we received a combat replacement from another unit. Brayden was a good-natured cat. He was sharp and respected the situation he was in, arriving two-thirds of the way through a rough deployment. Regardless, he warmed to the squad quickly and fit right in as a breath of fresh air. Plus, he brought cold weather gear in the form of a giant fluffy coat we called a happy suit. Nightfall caused the temperature to plummet during this time of year and the coat was reserved as a small luxury for whoever was standing post out at the OPs. It made life a little more bearable for the last two months.

By the time November rolled around, we were all more than ready to go home. Almost everyone had been battling random bouts of dysentery, on and off. Marines frequently rushed to the plywood latrines with space-aged looking wag bags in hand to spill their guts out of both ends, which drastically accelerated weight loss.

During patrols, we stopped as needed so Marines could relieve themselves in a wadi and if we felt the lightning-fast onset during a fire fight, we just had to let it out. Most of us didn't care because we'd seen the locals squat down and use the wadis as a toilet since we got here. The same ditches we'd been using for cover and maneuver were communal toilets for them. We'd been swimming in their shit for five months so why not add to it?

The start of November meant that I had to decide whether to reenlist or not. I had been able to speak to my wife via a satellite phone about once every three weeks since we got here, and she had told me that she would support my decision either way. My mother, who I had spoken to only a few times, had faith that I would make the right decision. It must have been brutal for them. This life that I had chosen afforded them little more than sleepless nights, stress, and separation.

Staff Sergeant Beasley encouraged me to go somewhere new to see a different side of the Corps, and that got me thinking. I loved the infantry. We had a merit-based culture, built on toughness, proficiency, lethality, and example. We valued hard training and displayed how much we cared for one another by suffering. I knew that those aspects of this lifestyle wouldn't be found anywhere else.

On the other hand, I considered the effect that this could have on my marriage and my family. The war had no end in sight and multiple future deployments were a certainty.

I briefly considered what I learned about myself as a leader since June 8th, when Zach was killed. I thought about the effect that I had on the squad and how we seemed to be less effective without our true leader at the helm.

Ultimately, it was my shortcomings that made me decide to sign the contract again. If I went back home and left the Corps behind, I would have a nice happy life with my wonderful little wife and the family we would make, and my parents could rest easier.

But I would remember my time with the infantry for the rest of my life. Did I really want to spend those years that were meant for familial bliss, looking back at this deployment as my last?

I wanted to discover exactly what type of leader I *could* be. I couldn't leave this life behind wondering who I would've become if I had stuck around and discovered something more. On top of that, I wanted to know where Zach got his "X" factor from. Where did that extra bit of iron in his soul come from? Did I have the same thing in me, buried deep inside, waiting for me to reach in and dig it out?

I decided to go back to where he started. I chose Fleet Anti-terrorism Security Team. One way or another I was going to have answers to these questions, and I committed to working myself to the bone for them. Sink or swim, I wouldn't have to wonder. "What if...?"

Within a week, my decision had traveled up the chain of command and I got trucked east to the battalion position, FOB Marjah, to start my reenlistment papers. The dysentery that had spread through the platoon hit me like a lightning bolt as soon as I jumped off the truck. I was so dehydrated that the Battalion medical staff held me there for an extra day to get pumped full of IV fluids. It was a wonder that I had eluded it for this long.

The next day, November 3rd, one of our sniper team leaders arrived while I was waiting on transport back to Kelly. We struck up a conversation in one of the large troop tents, as he staged his gear and weapons by an empty cot. He told me that he had to get blood work done. I wondered how the hell anyone would be able to do that in a place like this. The closest thing I had seen to a sterile environment was a trauma tent back at COP Kelly.

He told me that he had been searching a compound used by the enemy and gotten a few cuts from some needles that they had hidden on top of a high wall. It was just one more example of how dirty they were and a reminder that there should never be a single sliver of quarter given to them. Worse though, he informed me that Lieutenant James Zimmerman from Third Platoon had been killed the previous day.

I couldn't believe it. Every Platoon wanted Lieutenant Zimmerman as their commander. He was a good balanced leader. I never heard him raise his voice or saw him micro-manage his squad leaders. He patrolled more than any other commander in the company and seemed happy to do so. Leaving the tent, I flagged down the battalion sergeant major in passing and he confirmed the news.

We had lost another of our best.

As is so often the case, I didn't learn the details until years later. Zimmerman had taken a round to the chest just above the left edge of his plate carrier and died on the way to higher care. When the squad sent up his medevac request, a Chinook from Camp Bastion outfitted with a surgical team was dispatched instead of one of the Blackhawks from Camp Dwyer, which was much closer. He was alive roughly an hour later when the Chinook arrived, but at that point, he was beyond help.

Zimmerman's guys were solid warfighters and the corpsman who worked on him was damn good. It was a cold reminder that when a man's time is up, nothing can stop the inevitable. Bullets and bombs don't discriminate based on rank, value, past achievements, or even proficiency and prowess. There's no voodoo magic or special privilege that staves off the inevitable, and there is always an amount of chance in combat that the enemy gets to affect, regardless of how good we are. When your number is up, that's it. It is what it is.

Third Platoon's area was the most kinetic and they had sustained most of the Company's casualties. Their senior enlisted man, Staff Sergeant Grant was as solid as they come. He was on his third deployment to Afghanistan and fifth overall, having fought in Iraq as well. The man just kept moving from unit to unit, accruing a plethora of combat experience to pass on. He moved into the role previously filled by Lieutenant Zimmerman and brought one of his experienced squad leaders to fill in as platoon sergeant for the last leg of the deployment. No matter how hard a unit gets hit or who dies, the fight doesn't stop until one side surrenders or is wiped out. So onward we went.

The days grew shorter, but time seemed to pass slower as if the clock was trying to prolong our residency. Our joints ground and creaked with every movement, in or out of gear. Thoughts of simple pleasures that we had missed for the past five months grew dominated conversation. We hadn't showered or laundered our clothes properly since our arrival. We had adapted to living without small things like having dry feet, a mattress, and climate control. But the big things like safety, sex, privacy, a good meal, and not pissing out something that resembled orange soda were what most of us couldn't wait to experience again.

Still, the conditions showed me the human body's remarkable capacity for barbaric living, fighting, and manual labor. None of us looked like we had come from a modern civilization. We had all lost at least twenty pounds and added a decade to our joints. Our eyes sank back into our skulls and our rib cages stretched the chaffed skin against our armor as we labored in the fields for the last two months. It expanded on the lesson that I had learned and relearned since SOI, that we are capable of so much more than we realize.

The operational tempo persisted. We'd formed a fifth squad to help with the rotation of the three OPs we now had to man, in addition to the COP posts and patrolling effort. Nobody stayed awake longer than they had to save to check up on a buddy who was on watch. If we got the chance to sleep, we were out.

Our last true test from the enemy came early in the month. Lieutenant Thomas tasked us with pushing north, past Mia Kel to gain contact with the enemy. The area had quieted down a bit since Bittle was wounded and we had to move farther and farther away from Kelly to find a fight. We moved a few hundred meters west and cut hard north, passing the now abandoned compounds where we'd found machine guns and IED materials in the previous months.

The fields were bare now that the cold weather had begun to set in. It was as if autumn didn't exist here. In the span of a week or two, the heat had given way to milder days and shivering nights, when we crunched solid earth beneath our weight with every step. Most of the wadis were still lined with green vegetation, however, and a few small sporadic trees.

Mia Kel disappeared off to our right and a few fields later, we were further north than we'd ever been as a squad. The unfamiliar terrain made me uneasy. It was deathly quiet, and I didn't see any locals anywhere.

Pappy's team with Thomas had just crossed a wide ditch lining a road and passed in between a narrow opening in a row of small mud brick structures to our front. I saw them fan back out and wade into one of the few fields that still had waist high crops about fifty meters in ahead.

Aggressive bursts from multiple firing positions destroyed the quiet. The enemy had used the crops as a trigger line. I rushed forward and slipped on the wadi's near slope as a round ripped right past my face and collided with a tree just over my right shoulder. I took the longest, deepest breath of my life as I realized that if I hadn't fallen on my ass, Andy would be a squad leader and my wife would be getting a visit from a chaplain. We weren't fighting amateurs.

I peeked over the far slope in between the compounds to see Pappy's team firing and pealing back to the left into a compound as Patrelli and Karl moved past me and broke into the hut on the right.

Pappy was hit just as his boys left the kill zone. I rushed forward to the edge of the field, fearing the worst. The way he fell looked like an invisible giant had driven a massive sledgehammer down onto his left shoulder.

The boys had established firing positions in the compounds behind us and the enemy's volume was now limited but still too close for comfort. Pappy wasn't bleeding but the shoulder strap of his plate carrier was hanging on by a thread. He was up on his feet just after I knelt beside him, and we hauled ass to our seven o'clock while the squad riddled the enemy positions.

Once inside the small mud brick room, I saw Pappy's arm was limp and the shoulder strap was nearly gone.

Andy's team was in a mud brick courtyard with waist high walls on the other side of the gap. They identified the enemy in a small building to our two o'clock across the field and Thomas was passing everything to the COC. Just then, Patrelli sent an AT-4 rocket right into the enclosure, silencing everything.

We collected ourselves briefly while Doc checked on Pappy before we moved forward to do a damage assessment on the mosque. If we fired anything bigger than a forty-millimeter grenade, the standing order was to physically assess the damage. Our investigation yielded nothing except a few shell casings, which was usual.

My heart rate returned to normal as I checked our security posture, set up in the enemy's old firing positions.

On the patrol back, I broke away from surveying my surroundings to scrutinize every detail from the intense firefight. That enemy crew knew what they were doing.

They had pre-established trigger lines and multiple concealed positions in the vegetation of the wadi plus the one in the building, which turned out to be a mosque. From there, they knew they could cover the entire field and they used the gap in the compounds to canalize us so we couldn't maneuver. And lastly, they used the religious site because they knew we couldn't destroy it or even enter it unless they used it to fire on us. Not your typical street thugs.

When we finally got back, just as the sun was setting, Pappy went into the surgical tent to see the doctor we had living with us. He had a contusion on his left shoulder, which was oddly relieving to hear. The bruise was wicked, and he was sore as hell for weeks. I still couldn't figure out what caused it. Wouldn't a 7.62 round have penetrated his body at least? Beasley's vote was on a ricochet, but I wasn't so sure. Whether it was a ricochet, a round that didn't have enough powder behind it, or a game to some omniscient being playing puppet master for his own entertainment, I didn't care. Pappy was okay and we were a month out from leaving this place behind.

The last few weeks of our time in Marjah passed so slowly it was infuriating. We struggled to maintain our sanity at the same observation post we'd started at six months before, now called OP Gettysburg. Positioned to the west of Kelly at the intersection of Routes Jessica and Wolverines, we called it the HESCO Submarine. The structure was just wide enough for a normal man to lie down in and was roughly twenty feet long. The rectangular outpost's walls were double-stacked HESCO and the top row wasn't even filled in completely. So, whenever the post took incoming fire, enemy rounds passed right through the top row and the Marines inside were forced to simply sit down in their gear and wait it out while one or two men fired from the single post at the eastern end.

The only way in or out was a ten-foot ladder next to the single machine gun tower. That post was the safest spot because it was double lined with sandbags and had an actual roof. The rest of Gettysburg had a cammie netting sheet draped over top of the hollow Hesco walls. Add to that the small 7.62 ammo can we had to shit, never mor than a few feet away from someone trying to choke down a meal or sleep, and the fumes from the burn pit immediately outside, and you got the recipe for a very unpleasant place to exist.

The place was a fucking death trap. All it would take is one grenade being tossed in and a whole squad could be critically injured with many killed. The other squad leaders and I had voiced our concerns to various people in the chain of command for the past five months. We were told that engineer support, with their heavy construction vehicles, couldn't be pulled from whatever they were doing to fix the place up. So, we carried on. All the squads had rotated through the three OPs we had, plus patrolling out of Kelly, since we had moved up from Narea.

Several weeks prior, we spent fourteen days in OP Gettysburg. I was just as worried that we would lose our minds and slip into a twisted mix of *Apocalypse Now* and *Alice in Wonderland* as I was concerned about the tactical situation. After that, Lieutenant Thomas did his best to limit the time spent at the OPs to about three to five days.

It was November 11th, and Third Squad had just taken over Gettysburg from us. We had eagerly returned to COP Kelly for what we expected to be our last patrolling cycle before the end of the deployment.

For some reason, the enemy hadn't taken advantage of the

situation yet and we were hoping that our luck would hold for a few more weeks.

Somebody shattered that hope late into the afternoon on November 12th by using a blind spot on the southern side of the post. Whoever they were, a fanatic terrorist or a simple local farmer, they used the wadi that housed our burn pit to approach from the west and, keeping tight to the HESCO, lobbed a grenade into the machine gun tower. They would've been spotted if they came from any other direction.

Sergeant Bart was critically wounded by large pieces of shrapnel to the chest and one of his guys, Lance Corporal Twigg, received minor wounds to his feet. Luckily the grenade didn't tumble down into the berthing area before it exploded.

Back at COP Kelly, we watched the company's mobile section tear out of the gate to pick up the casualties. Twigg was lucky and was able to move assisted to the surgeon's tent once they arrived.

Bart, however, was far less fortunate. The twisted clumps of shrapnel had lodged close to his heart which required immediate emergency surgery. He was conscious and responsive as they loaded him onto the helicopter that took him to a higher level of care.

Lt. Thomas pinged us to man Gettysburg again. We were only one day into our patrolling rotation and had just come from there. Given recent events, we weren't thrilled to return. But leaving Third Squad there, after watching Bart and Twigg get blown up wasn't an option.

We hitched a ride with Mobile and pulled up to see Third squad already out of the OP and posting security for the engineers. Whatever had kept them for the last several months was put on hold so they could fix up the place, finally. The shitty thing was that it took two Marines, one of whom was a squad leader, getting wounded before that could happen. The whole situation was infuriating. We had told our superiors time and time again that this was a possibility, and we were always told that engineer support was bogged down.

But here we were, right back in the HESCO sub. At least the

place was getting an upgrade. The engineers, also called sappers, added a new section to the western side and a wooden roof with sandbags. There was nothing we could do about the blind spot, but we used a sheet of HESCO and triple-strand concertina wire to which we attached empty energy drink cans filled with gravel. Anyone attempting to get to the post would have to vault over or cut the wire and the sound of the rattling cans would alert the Marines in the tower. It was a simple approach to anti-intrusion measures.

The renovations complete, we entered the new upgraded Gettysburg, using a door at the western end. It was a simple section of Hesco wire with a sheet attached to it, but a door none the less. There was an additional watch posted and we resumed normal operations as the sappers loaded up and pulled away.

We were nearly halfway through the last full month but had lost Zimmerman and Bart wouldn't be back this close to the end. It reminded me that we couldn't stop or rest until we were physically out of Marjah. No matter how much we missed home or family, killing the enemy mattered more. The concept of modern comforts had grown so alien to us, I wondered if we would have to readjust to having running water or air conditioning and the like.

More pressing, however, was that little voice in the back of my mind that wondered how many more we would lose before it was all over with. Reviewing everyone we had lost and the countless who had been wounded, I knew I couldn't dwell on it. If it was going to happen, then it was going to happen, plain and simple. All any of us could do was fight as hard as we possibly could, never pull a punch, and keep moving forward one patrol at a time until we were dead, or we hopped on a bird back to civilization, which was so close we could almost taste it.

Christmas Day of 2010 finally arrived. The other platoons had consolidated at our position in COP Kelly for the flight back to Camp

Dwyer, which couldn't come soon enough. With nothing to do but wait, I started measuring what we had accomplished.

December had been characterized by a significant drop in temperatures and enemy contact, which was typical. Every winter, the terrorists tone down their operations and hop the border with Pakistan, their primary sanctuary, or simply hide in plain sight as farmers. They nurse their wounds, rearm themselves, or train for the next fighting season, like the one they had just shared with us.

So, the cycle went.

For us, we had the pride of knowing that Marjah was a better place. We had killed many of the terrorists and significantly reduced the Taliban's revenue from the local drug trade, having managed to convince a few farmers to grow wheat instead of poppy. Schools and markets had been built to aid the political presentation of the war. Keeping them open and secure was now the burden of Third Battalion, Ninth Marines who was relieving us.

At this point, I didn't much care what happened to Marjah after we left.

The way I saw it, this was how America measured success. If there was less fighting, more democratic institutions, and generals that could walk around a few meters outside the COP and declare the place was safe, everything was great. Add on a "capable" force of Afghan soldiers and police, and the only way the situation could be better was if we started riding unicorns on patrol and left our rifles back at the COP.

With all the bull shit being peddled back home about this war, it wouldn't surprise me if someone believed it. It wasn't that people weren't telling the truth, because many were. It was just that certain parts were either downplayed or omitted.

Marjah *was* better off than before we arrived... for now. A general could, indeed, walk outside the COP without his flak and Kevlar on... if there were roughly fifty of us, armed to the teeth as always, pushed out to security positions for his stroll. Based on the past six months of intensive combat with the enemy, we knew that no terrorist was going to fuck with that many guns.

We participated in this dog and pony show more than once and hated it with the purest passion, but the illusion of security was constructed, nonetheless. Marjah was undeniably *more* secure, but not to that degree.

The schools and markets that had been built or reopened during our tenure would eventually close down again in violent fashion many years later and the Taliban, or whichever terrorist flavor of the week, would again have the opportunity to sow its poppy and help fund its Jihad with minimal interference. It would take a few years to happen, but it was inevitable. Marjah's security was solely dependent on our presence and operations.

We had bought time. Without a wholehearted commitment from the American people and lacking a government with a solid understanding of Afghanistan and a clear goal with manageable expectations, that was the best that could be achieved.

The Afghan government forces that had been so publicly praised and painted as an organization coming into their own were the complete opposite. In late November and early December, we had conducted only ANA-led patrols. Many of these cats didn't care enough to put forth much effort, so after we had gone through the preparations check lists with their leadership at the COP, these patrols devolved into short walks towards the target zone with them in the lead. Then they would revert back to being completely dependent on us for everything. The greatest lie of the Afghan campaign was that the ANA could sustain any progress we had made.

The strategic accomplishments and failures aside, on our level we had won. The real reason why we, as infantrymen, were here was to fight and kill the enemy and we had done that. All the other "reasons" like creating a brighter future for Afghans, advancing democracy, bringing education to women and children, advancing women's rights, and whatever other bull shit was being paraded around in the States, didn't matter. Those ideals came from a people with no real understanding of this country's nature or ours.

We had fulfilled our purpose of locating, closing with, and destroying the enemy. We gained critical knowledge of who we are that most people never do. Each man left Marjah knowing exactly what he was truly capable of. We had experienced hardship and adversity unknown to our civilian counterparts, and we became better, hardened men for it.

After many months in close proximity, some of us didn't exactly like each other. But there wasn't a single man who wouldn't have done *absolutely anything* to preserve the life of everyone around him, carrying the same weight and fighting the same enemy. Discipline, toughness, selflessness, lethality, proficiency, and example all had clear and unquestionable definitions now. These are the timeless infantry values that separate our culture from all others.

Regardless of the Afghan campaign's outcome, we would always have Marjah and nothing on heaven or earth could take that away from us because we had held true to those values, just as our predecessors had from Belleau Wood to present. I had never felt true pride with such potency in my entire life after realizing that undeniable and unmistakable fact.

For the time being, as I sat on my pack in the center of the COP on December 25th, my thoughts turned towards home and the wife who waited for me. I felt easy. I was ready to leave.

So much had happened since Zach was killed and the time to face it and process everything was fast approaching. I wasn't going down that road until I was alone on home soil. In the immediate, provided a true believer didn't send an RPG round into the side of our helo on the way back, we would be at Dwyer soon.

I imagined how that would be: the sharp bank of the flying machine as it erupted into fire and an uncontrollable spin cut short by instant darkness. But it didn't happen.

As we loaded the CH-53 helicopter, I looked around and saw a few smiling faces peppered among the solemn and exhausted men I had fought next to for what seemed like a lifetime. The helicopter's rumble was accompanied by a blast of air that lifted us off the earth and towards our first stop at FOB Marjah. The force of the machine was wonderful. It was the best Christmas present of my life.

---

1. (McChrystal 2013,2014). See notes.
2. (McChrystal 2013,2014). See notes.

Chapter 6

Living Among The Snakes

The reenlistment package I signed in Marjah, had sent me to Chesapeake, Virginia to attend the Basic Security Guard School in the summer of 2011. Chesapeake had several military installations scattered in among the civilian population, which differed from the larger degree of separation we enjoyed at Lejeune. The school, however, was located at a Navy Annex out in the Virginia country with nothing but farms around. It had the basic amenities that we were used to: a gym, chow hall, and even a small restaurant right outside the gate. As students, we stayed in the open squad bays on the second floor of the barracks.

After we graduated, we would either be sent to FAST, which is what I wanted, or assigned to guard other military installations in Georgia or Washington. The course work was different. It was geared towards deterrence and reaction instead of aggressive offensive action. The instructor-led morning workouts were a mix of basic body weight exercises and running with the occasional trip to the obstacle course—hardly the intense weight bearing sessions I was accustomed to.

We only hiked once and very seldom did we wear full armor.

Academics were emphasized over physical toughness, leadership, and critical skills development.

I couldn't wait to be done with it all and on to my next assignment, which I hoped would be to FAST Company. I came here to find out if I had what it took to be a leader like Zach was and I needed to be in a similar environment to find that answer.

Additionally, the social climate was the opposite of what I enjoyed with my old unit. I and three other NCOs came within an inch of being busted down in rank, within the first month of the course because another student cried hazing.

Lance Corporal Smithers was a small, gangly looking kid in his late teens who had already failed the school once and been recycled to our class. His accusation began as a product of our harsh corrections in response to his various and consistent minor offenses. The man couldn't wear his uniform properly, arrive on time to his appointed place of duty, keep up during the very few physical activities required of us, and maintained a general "woe is me" attitude. His perceived victimhood kicked into high gear when he was corrected, rather harshly he thought, in front of the platoon by Corporal Byrd.

Byrd was a Light Armored Reconnaissance Marine and an Iraq veteran who I thought I had much in common with. We valued hard, realistic training over the schoolhouse approach to dumbed down academics and had similar leadership styles.

Sergeant Kent came from the supply community which was interesting to me because he was the first POG I had ever coexisted with for an extended period of time. He was humble and soft-spoken unless a situation required more, which made him approachable. Having very little knowledge of the infantry tactics, weapons, or culture, he consulted Byrd and myself frequently. All of us had completed a prior enlistment before being saddled together here.

Rounding out the leadership group in our thirty-man class was a lance corporal we affectionately called Slave. He was short, good-natured, and accepted his unique situation with an optimistic sarcasm. Unlike the other students, he was already half-way through his first enlistment.

Slave had been injured during his first attempt at passing the school. The command had assigned him to perform all the mundane, tedious work no one else wanted to do while he recovered. He had been stuck here for so long that he wondered if he would ever get to leave.

When he was medically cleared and came to our class, the man was ready to do anything to move on to the next chapter of his Marine Corps career. Slave brought an element of sarcastic humor to our little group that helped us keep our cool as we tried to float in the mirky waters we found ourselves in.

Unbeknown to us at the time, Marine Corps Security Forces Regiment was a completely different animal than the infantry not just structurally but culturally. Marines from any occupational specialty could put in for security forces duty. It was listed as a "special duty assignment" like drill instructors, combat instructors, and recruiters, hence the presence of Sergeant Kent.

The upside for grunts like Byrd and I was that we could get our required special duty assignment out of the way while staying close to the infantry and dodging the dreaded stint as a drill instructor or recruiter. Not many Grunts volunteered to convince teenagers to join or help turn them into Marines at one of the depots. Drill Instructors were under a political microscope and recruiters hated the grind associated with their temporary assignment.

On top of that, recruiters and drill instructors usually work about twenty hours a day. To fill these spots, the Corps publishes a list every year for eligible NCO's, telling them where they are going. The only way around it was to select one as a part of a reenlistment package.

So here I was not more than a month into school, standing tall before *the man* a breath away from losing my rank, pay, and any future in the Marine Corps, courtesy of Smithers. "The man" in this case was Major Honeycutt, the commanding officer of Training Company. He had a reputation among the NCOs and instructor cadre of being strictly by the book and almost relishing the opportunity to dole out administrative punishment. He had prohibited the use of nicotine and caffeine, the infantry's most precious commodities, at his previous duty station in Tropic Bay by saying smoking and coffee inhibited the cognitive ability of Marines. His right-hand man was a gunnery sergeant by the name of Sid, whose favorite pastime was watching Honeycutt bust NCOs.

Smithers' original accusation had mutated into a story that involved Kent, Byrd, and me standing him up against a wall and throwing knives at him. How it grew from the simple ass-chewing it was into that was beyond me. What had happened was he had shown up to the firing range with the wrong water source and Byrd had corrected him for it rather harshly. Given Smither's unwillingness to follow simple directions, none of us were going to take it easy on him.

It was obvious kid was full of shit and fishing for a way out of the Corps at our expense. He knew that he had a good chance of getting what he wanted in the environment that Honeycutt and Sid fostered. And that was the real detrimental effect of the Corps' obsession with eliminating hazing. It created these situations for people like Smithers to exploit.

The second he reported the situation, Julie, Byrd, and I were separated. Even the instructors we enjoyed a certain amount of mutual, experience-based respect with, avoided us like the plague. I didn't blame them—not in a place like this.

Word got around that whenever something like this occurred, the parties in question weren't the only ones with their dicks on the chopping block. Anyone remotely involved in or with knowledge of the incident was targeted as well. Kent and I were here because we didn't stop Byrd from correcting Smithers.

Honeycutt, Sid, and the entire chain of command had built a little paradise where the weak could prevail over the strong and we were observing the effects firsthand.

I was summoned into the office and dutifully reported in for the festivities to begin. The meeting resembled a medieval trial in which the angry townsfolk hurled rotten vegetables and human shit at the man being tried before a lord who chastised him righteously.

The major, seated in his leather throne behind a polished wooden desk, asked questions about my perception of the events and repeatedly cut off any responses with the term "irrelevant." I eventually just stood there at attention and just waited for him to get to the point. That being in any given situation regarding discipline, "Your perception as an NCO doesn't matter. The only thing that matters is how the junior Marine *feels*." He told me.

My knuckles turned white, and my jaw clenched momentarily as Honeycutt continued with what I could tell was a well-rehearsed speech. He listed the "types of authority" as physical, moral, and administrative. Being a non-commissioned officer, apparently meant nothing to this man. He gave examples of each, stating along the way that the commissioned officer was the only man who possessed any authority of any kind and highlighting the administrative as the most important of all. It was crystal clear that although this unit was advertised as still being within the infantry realm, in reality it was something else entirely.

The infantry that Byrd and I knew placed the highest expectations and freedom to lead on the small unit leader. Team leaders, squad leaders, and NCOs were *expected* to be bulldogs, hell bent on exemplifying our cultural values and holding Marines accountable. The punishment had to fit the crime and disciplinary matters allowed us a way to exercise judgement outside of a tactical environment that honed the trait.

Nearly everything that Honeycutt was preaching was contradictory to the NCO Creed, that charged us to uphold Marine tradition, train our juniors, and influence our seniors. He liked his NCOs as Robots and something in his tone and the setting portrayed an air of arrogance and self-righteousness.

The situation came to an end with Kent and Byrd joining me

before the commander's desk. What happened next, I couldn't possibly make up if I tried.

Sid stood off to our left in the corner, smirking like a jackass and Honeycutt started playing his favorite role. The two recited a short dialogue debating whether we could be "salvaged." I thought to myself, "wait a second... That's from fucking *Starship Troopers*. Are you fucking serious?!"

These guys had done this so many times that, at some point, they thought it was a good idea to act out movie scenes to send their message. And they had clearly rehearsed it. Their performances should've earned them an Oscar.

We were ordered to read the book, which was already on required reading, so we could discuss it with Honeycutt personally. Adding this to our existing academic workload left very little time for anything else. From that moment on, the three of us kept our heads low and never gave Honeycutt and Sid a chance to satisfy themselves at our expense.

What we didn't know was that at some point afterwards, one of them would call ahead to our future command to inform them of the situation. That meant we would go to our next assignment already viewed as "troublemakers" and "shit bags." As conniving and political as it was, it sat just fine with me. I loved being underestimated.

And all because a kid wasn't happy with his Marine Corps experience. I wanted to hurt Smithers every time I laid eyes on him but resolved not to give him the satisfaction. We weren't going to give this guy anything he could use against us. We were going to keep our honor intact, while he had compromised his. He hated the Marine Corps and thought that he could get out somehow by crying wolf and utilizing a system built on a civilian mentality.

We were used to solving issues without getting the command involved. That could consist of a simple discussion among those involved, physically fighting, or anything in between. There was no human resources representative to complain to in the infantry.

Honeycutt had created an environment in which the first option was the only one and anything more would be settled by maximum use of the Uniformed Code of Military Justice. This allowed Marines like Smithers to stick around and destroy the morale and trust within a unit. The UCMJ doesn't sustain the small unit in combat and if trust isn't established prior to going to war, then any unit runs the risk of incurring unnecessary casualties.

The other NCOs and I stopped inspecting the class every morning and offering any knowledge or experience to anyone. Without us to make sure he studied or showed up to formations, or conduct himself properly, Smithers wasn't going to last long. Sure enough, he eventually buried himself and everyone, even Sid, saw him for what he truly was.

He would spend another six months at Training Company, after we graduated, feigning injury before he finally moved on. Smithers taught us that no one in this bastard unit could be trusted and that we had to watch our own backs.

Difficult as it was, with the way the Corps was changing, the lesson needed to be learned as a matter of professional survival. In the new Corps, now led by General Jim Amos from the aviation community, the junior Marine would be able to get away with murder at the expense of the small unit leader.

It was a far cry from the infantry I came from, where the staff valued a leader who had to be restrained instead of kicked in the ass, and who used brains and example instead of relying on a manual or the rank on his collar. I didn't fully understand my new environment yet, but I knew one thing: this sure as hell wasn't the infantry.

The unusually hot summer of 2011 found me in Norfolk, Virginia at a small place called Camp Allen. Like most duty stations, it had fewer positives than negatives. I thought it was a prison the first time I pulled through the gate and, ironically, there was a brig just down the road. The rectangular perimeter of our camp was fenced in with chained link and strands of barbed wire running across the top. A small gate, the only way in or out, was manned by a combination of sailors, civilians, and Marines. Inside the fence was a small company office with an armory and a few platoon rooms, a gym, and a small indoor firing range.

The barracks, which were filled with black mold and lacked amenities such as hot or running water, and the chow hall were located on the far end. The whole camp looked as if it were designed to keep us in as opposed to keeping everyone else out. Civilians frequented the range and seemed to be free to come and go as they pleased. There was an elementary school across the street from the gate that generated quite a bit of traffic in the mornings and afternoons. Parents and children alike peered at us and through the fence to see what was going on.

It seemed strange to have a base that was so open to the public. I imagined that this is what animals locked in a zoo cage felt like, regarding the foreign creatures on the other side as they stared and gawked at us.

My new platoon commander was waiting for me and, when Byrd arrived the next day, we hit the ground running. The three of us strapped on old worn-out boxing gloves behind the company office to get to know each other. We rotated in, each of us fighting the other two, as our company first sergeant, a career supply Marine, stood off to the side and watched the spectacle through the smoke of his lit cigarette.

Moments like this are critical. It afforded the chance to look inside the other man across gauge his prowess, or lack thereof, and his capacity for pain. With every move forward or back and every punch thrown we got an answer about the other man. Was he weak or strong? Was he cautious, calculated, aggressive or reckless? After an hour or so, we peeled off the half rotten gloves and discussed what we'd seen in each other. Busted lips and bruised bodies were the foundation for the next chapter of my career.

Over the next few days, Sergeant Kent and Corporal Slave would be reporting in with many of the Boots from our Security School class. So, we had a bit of time to get to know one another.

Captain Willis, our new platoon commander and sparring partner, came from the famed First Marine Division in sunny southern California. His alarming level of self-confidence seemed to mask insecurity. He had a stout build and a shining shaved head, dipped tobacco constantly, and was crystal clear about his expectations.

Willis wanted hard-nosed old-school NCOs he had to restrain and emphasized that his relationship with us as squad leaders was second only to that with the platoon sergeant. His existing platoon was set to rotate to the Fleet in a few days, so he incorporated them into our discussions and training, which largely consisted of tactical decision games around a sand table.

We'd both had similar experiences with FAST Marines in our old units and wanted to produce men who closely resembled Zach and Derek as opposed to guys who lacked basic infantry skills and our values. The challenge was significant, given the treacherous climate in Third FAST Company's command.

Being away from Training Company didn't mean we were out of the woods. Our company still fell under the same regiment and the staff had the same "pen is mightier than the sword" mentality. Over the next several months, I began to understand why.

The operational blueprint for FAST Companies was vastly different than that of a normal infantry battalion. For starters, we deployed as platoons instead of entire companies or battalions, which meant that when we left Camp Allen, the staff stayed behind and simply passed us on to a different staff at our destination. Over time, this model prevented the development of consistent working relationships between commanders, administrators, and the small unit level. Consequently, matters of discipline nearly always resulted in maximum administrative punishment and the micromanagement of training practices. The command climate at FAST was such that none of us trusted anyone above the platoon level until they proved worthy of it. We did not give anyone the benefit of the doubt.

In 2/6, it was clear that you would be held accountable for your actions. However, whenever someone messed up, the UCMJ was always the last option unless the offense was especially grievous, such as a public arrest or something that drew undue attention to the unit.

It was a transitional period for the Corps, and a single black mark could be a career killer. It didn't matter if the man in question was a rock star war fighter who had earned the respect of his unit, or if he was a young man who had simply demonstrated poor judgement in the moment. Anything higher than a simple negative counseling form significantly increased the chances of being denied reenlistment. Meritorious promotions and glowing recommendations from well-connected senior staff could bring a Marine back from the brink, but it was a long shot.

Understanding this, many officers would allow the team or squad leader to handle disciplinary matters, which facilitated good order and discipline without destroying a young Marine's future. Usually, it was much more physically and mentally unpleasant but much more effective at teaching the appropriate lesson and molding men into better Marines.

I remember being yanked out my rack aboard the USS Carter Hall on my first deployment and getting beaten black and blue for being a drunken idiot in Turkey. My career as a Marine could've ended the next day but after the CO saw my face, he dismissed the prospect. If he had resorted to NJP, the next years of my life, and consequently the rest of it, would've been very different. I learned the value of disciplinary creativity because of that situation, painful as it was, and carried the lesson with me for the rest of my time in uniform.

Here, at FAST Company, there was no such mentality. Commanders passed out maximum level NJPs as often as possible without a care in the world or any thought to how it would alter the development of so many young Marines. They exhibited no desire to teach and mold, because they would have minimal interaction with or responsibility for them. It was much easier to do the paperwork and pass it off to the next staff.

We were numbers on the spreadsheet of rosters they maintained and reported on instead of men they knew with potential.

It was obvious that if Willis, Byrd, and I wanted to produce solid Grunts for the Fleet, we would have no assistance from above in instilling the proper values and skills in them. We would have to create the environment for success ourselves under constant scrutiny.

The other reason why most FAST Marines were garbage when they hit the Fleet, was a simple question of personnel. Any reenlisting NCO could request FAST Company as his duty station. Which led to Sergeants or Corporals from other communities like the airwing, supply, or administration becoming FAST squad leaders.

So, a Boot who graduates SOI, then Basic Security Guard school shows up to FAST and has a POG squad leader who has little or no knowledge of infantry values, tasks, or skills. That Boot will go to an infantry unit for the last two years of his enlistment. He is expected to be proficient and ready to lead before he arrives, even if his squad leader was incapable of preparing him.

It's no wonder a lot of these guys weren't ready. They were set up for failure by an operational structure and a climate that was culturally opposed the infantry proper. The only hope they had was to get a few solid Grunt NCOs who had the proper foundation to prepare them for what was ahead-which could be combat in Afghanistan.

This is the environment that Zach had come from. I realized that part of what made him special was the fact that he refused to be bogged down by these factors. Instead of looking at them as limitations, he viewed them as obstacles to be overcome. We saw the same will when he was with us, I had simply failed to recognize it when it was right in front of me. I'm not sure what kind of leaders he'd had but that determination separated him.

The way forward was a bit clearer.

I could either adapt and conquer or focus on the fact that the staff expected us to fail and let that crutch destroy me. All the lessons learned from my many mistakes and all my faults as a leader would mean nothing if I couldn't or didn't teach these younger guys a better way to lead. Regardless, any one of them could end up in similar circumstances with mortal consequences. Byrd, Kent, Slave, and I had a responsibility to prepare them regardless of how they or the various commands felt about it.

Fuck their expectation. It was time to go to work and find out what kind of leader I *could* be and if I could live up to Zach's legacy.

Our first deployment came a few short months later, just before the 2011 holiday season. The crisp fall weather and urban structures of Virginia were replaced by Tropic Bay's rocky cliffs, palm trees, and ocean breeze. Excluding France and Greece, it was the most beautiful place I had ever been.

We alternated with a Fast Platoon from Bravo Company, occupying guard towers that surrounded Naval Station Tropic Bay. Every now and then we were able to take some time as a platoon to train at the few ranges we had access to, and complete exercises required by the commanding officer. There wasn't much time to enjoy the ocean and liberty was so restricted that it wasn't worth leaving the barracks for.

Just before we came here, a new Corporal was assigned to our platoon. Brown Bear, we called him, stood about five and a half feet tall and had a stocky build with a crop of short, fuzzy, dark hair. He brought balance to our leadership team. Byrd was all bite, still very much in the hammer phase of leadership and I was still stern most of the time because, regardless of the promise our Marines showed, they were still so green. Kent maintained the quiet demeanor common to POGs, and the newly promoted Corporal Slave was still setting boundaries with the Marines, most of whom he'd been at school with for some time.

Brown Bear was confident and direct when teaching but otherwise relatively laid back until he had to correct someone. There was no mistaking his light mood for weakness, and he injected a bit of sarcasm to our already coarse humor. He never appeared to be stressed about anything. He was tough, proficient, and easy going which integrated seamlessly with us as he stepped into the role of third squad leader.

Major Tyranny, the commanding officer at Tropic Bay, was an entirely different character. Hailing from the Force Reconnaissance community, he stood over six feet tall and possessed a seemingly unlimited amount of confidence and poise. He carried himself as a heavy-handed NCO, which was unusual given their reputation for prioritizing fighting skill and toughness over uniforms and haircuts.

His command of the Marines was absolute, and his demeanor and actions reflected an arrogance that was apparent to everyone but him. He had his fingers in every single activity and made it known that *his* way was the *only* way. To a civilian, he would've been the picture of a military robot, appearing to have found his life's purpose in the Corps and strictly enforcing every single standard. To us, he was the perfect example of entitlement and what *not* to be as a leader.

He wanted everyone to know that he was the big man on the block every time he appeared, which was exclusively to make corrections. Nine times out of ten, he would be in violation of the very infraction he was addressing.

He dressed down Marines for every minute mistake he could find, from uniform violations to their tactical posture while standing post in the guard towers. Many times, he would bring his wife and children up the steps of a tower to behold the spectacle. After, they would descend the structure to fish and drink, just below as if it was a nice summer day back in the States. All the while, the Marine above was left to rot in the sun, having just been chewed out in front of two small children and the Major's wife. Situations like that make Marines want to leave the Corps more than anything else.

Harsh corrections are common in the infantry and are typically well-received, or at least accepted, when they come from a man who sets the proper example. However, it is universally understood that if there happens to be a family member or a civilian nearby, matters are to be handled differently and much more subtly out of respect for the dignity of the man in question.

Simply put he was a personification of the "do as I say, not as I do" mentality.

But there was something more brazenly arrogant about him. Like Major Honeycutt, he took pride in his behavior and felt he was justified. The only thing he loved more than chewing us out was busting guys down, which he did eight times in the three months we were at Tropic Bay. Only two of them, including my own, were justifiable. The rest were a product of him stretching the Uniform Code of Military Justice to exercise his power. The fact that he enjoyed it was evident in the mason jar he kept on his desk, for all to see, full of chevrons that he took from the Marines he demoted.

Most disturbing of all, however, was his negative influence over Captain Willis, who began to emulate his overbearing and demanding manner. Granted, any platoon commander who had to deal with a commander like Tyranny would have a hell of a time attempting to keep him at bay. Their relationship dynamic showed me that officers, just like the rest of us, can be impressionable and moldable, regardless of their status.

Willis would be relieved of platoon command several months later in Bahrain, confirming that Tyranny had polluted him. But that was many months away from now.

For all his faults, Tyranny did demonstrate tactical sense. He knew defensive operations and tactical site security—FAST's primary mission—well. Sleep deprivation was incorporated into every exercise he designed, along with several scenarios built to test our decision-making and task organization. Despite his direct attempts to undermine our experience as squad leaders, the Marines learned a lot. They had perfect examples of what *not* to do in Tyranny and Willis and an NCO crew that, imperfect as we were, demonstrated the opposite.

We had established trust with many of them. Most of our time was spent trying to shield them from Tyranny and his lackies, who we viewed as spies. They had noticed, but as long as we stayed busy with good training and didn't taunt them, we were left alone until the boss man felt the itch to interfere. We wanted our actions to highlight that instead of our words. The training provided them a chance to hone essential skills and kept the wolves at bay, for a time at least.

A leader's success is a product of the people around him and the effort that he puts into developing them. For me that included the entire squad with a special emphasis on the team leaders.

Marjah had taught me how crucial the relationship between squad and team leaders were. I couldn't be everywhere at once and I needed reliable, hungry, tough men who could think and act critically and maturely. I had selected three of them from the lot, a few months back. Their performances during a few morning workouts and small field exercises were all I had to evaluate. They all had the same time in service and experience level, unlike the infantry battalions where typically, at least a few Marines would've had at least a deployment under their belt.

To me, that simplified the process. I didn't have to weigh one man's experience against another's. I was looking for the guys who were able to separate their friendships from their responsibilities and put the squad first. Leading peers is the toughest and unforgiving test for any leader. They were peers with everyone excluding us NCOs, Willis, and our platoon sergeant so they couldn't escape it. They couldn't be scared to tell a friend that he was wrong or be direct. It was their introduction to the infantry adage, "brutal honesty amongst men."

It was a stroke of luck that I ended up with just the right crew. Windall, Nixon, and Elias were hungry. They wanted to excel, and their performance displayed their desire. I took advantage of every opportunity to teach them and spent more time with them than anyone else.

I remembered how we treated FAST Marines in the fleet who couldn't keep up or didn't know how to lead. After experiencing the environments that men like Tyranny and Honeycutt created for them, I understood why many of them weren't ready. They just needed to be led properly.

I learned as much as I taught. Many of the mistakes I had made with Pappy and Andy, I wouldn't fully understand for many years. But what I did know was that I had to be able to guide these guys emotionally, not just professionally. That didn't mean baby them or make life easy for them. It meant that I had to set an example of sky-high expectations, hold them accountable, and understand that they would make mistakes. Then teach them. Just like I had learned in Squad Leader's Course, failure is a much better instructor than success. Blasting them like a drill instructor would be a part of it but it couldn't be the only tool I used if I wanted them to reach their full potential.

The realization that I would have to be more than a blunt instrument landed me at the most important crossroad yet. I had to decide what kind of leader I was going to be, and it set me on a path to understand people and how to interact with them.

I was the only man in the squad with any experience to speak of, so I had to teach them everything, from how to set up their gear to tactics and leadership. For every second I spent instructing or giving orders, I took another to observe the effects. I watched to see how the team leaders handled things. They got to know their guys while I learned about them.

I couldn't completely forsake the "iron fist" method because it would always have its place. I had to become a chameleon of sorts—able to adapt to any situation as a leader. That meant not treating everything and everyone the same. Seeing their progress and how well we worked together, both tactically and in garrison, was enough validation for my new philosophy.

I enlisted to fight, and I had done that. Afghanistan had shown me that there was no place for a protector mentality in the infantry. I remembered how Andy was always on the lookout to help the locals and his frustration at being so close yet so far away. Couple that with the countless instances of child and female suicide bombers in the War on Terror and it was clear that that mentality could have dire consequences. Peace and protection are the farthest concepts away from the infantry's purpose. And these men were infantrymen. It was my responsibility to have them ready for Afghanistan, should they end up there.

The media had kept pushing their narrative, depicting us as protectors and nation builders. No doubt Windall, Nixon, and Elias had seen it, along with the rest of the guys. Hell, some of them may have joined thinking that's what we were doing in Afghanistan.

I thought about the countless patrols that erupted into a torrent of bullets and violent explosions against our capable adversaries. It was all still fresh, and I was just starting to figure out how to carry it with pride. There was no doubt that we spent much more time fighting than building. I would be setting them up to fail if I let them think we were meant to open schools and dig wells instead of kill the enemy and lying wasn't an option.

I had to show them an example of what was going to help them thrive in war. The best way I knew to do that was to show them the type of guy I would want to follow. I'd throw in an accurate picture of the war as I experienced it and hold us all to higher standards that wouldn't just accomplish the mission but would breed a mentality that sought to fulfill potential and push the boundaries of personal growth. Getting the job done was the bare minimum. Discovering a deeper meaning to it all was the real prize, and that's what I wanted for all of us.

With a clearer sense of direction, I decided to invest the most time and effort into the team leaders. Windall was the most direct of the three and took criticism well. He remembered everything and found gratification in development. He reminded me of a young version of Zach because he knew how to balance force with instruction and how to earn the respect of his guys.

Nixon didn't have to convey intensity vocally because it was demonstrated in his extraordinary work ethic. He was smart, as well, and tempered it with humility. He never beat around the bush and wasn't intimidated by rank or experience. If he was asked a question, he gave an honest and tactful answer.

Elias was a combination of the two. He was reliable and tough as hell. I never had to tell him to do anything twice and he picked new things up quickly.

They each had their strengths and weaknesses, and each responded to a different type of instruction. Collectively, they had initiative, brains, and guts—a strong base to build on. When I left 2/6, I expected to get a group of timid kids who needed a babysitter, and I couldn't have been more wrong. I found three cats who wanted to take the opportunity their commitment afforded them, and milk it for everything they could.

When I took a step back to notice how that mentality benefitted the squad, I realized that I had a responsibility to provide them with the challenge and opportunities they were looking for. I couldn't disappoint them. Zach hadn't let me down. They deserved the very best and anything less would be unacceptable. Iron sharpens iron.

The last month we spent in Tropic Bay was February of 2012. Despite the growth we had seen as a platoon, things were getting worse with our commander. Captain Willis seemed to begin a steep personal descent and the effects were clearly visible.

His conduct became erratic. Infractions like drinking on duty and running hours late for platoon hikes were spread among instances of alarming behavior. He grew terse and condescending. He was losing whatever private war he was fighting, and Tyranny's influence pushed him further into isolation and decline.

A few weeks prior, rumors that he had drawn his pistol in anger towards one of the Marines circulated. When we heard, Byrd, Kent and I brought it to the Platoon Sergeant, hoping that he could somehow fix the problem, which was a frivolous notion because he had no power to relieve a commissioned officer. The only other option was to go to Major Tyranny, who was more likely to laugh at us than relieve him.

This would destroy the platoon if left unchecked. It was building into a painful crescendo and I thought there was little that we could do about it. If the rumors were true, then the situation was beyond conduct unbecoming of a commissioned officer and into the realm of unsafe practice. The only thing we knew for sure was that Captain Willis had no business leading a platoon.

The Marines were aware that he was compromised but didn't appear to be too shocked by it. It was just another poor example of officer leadership in FAST and we had the rotten luck of dealing with it. There were other platoons that had good commanders, but they were the exception instead of the rule. It was a stark contrast to my experience in 2/6, for which I was grateful, given the predicament we found ourselves in. At least they had us. Unfortunately for them, I was about to make the biggest mistake of my career.

At the beginning of February, we came off our training week to resume fence line security. Willis made the decision to switch up the shifts and the positions just to try and keep things fresh.

One night, nearing the completion of my twelve-hour shift and having made my final rounds, I went through my end of post routine. Having checked the logbooks and reconciled any discrepancies, I found a nearby lounge in our barracks to clean my M9 pistol and conduct the prescribed reload drills assigned by Willis. With the advanced urban combat course looming in the distance, he encouraged dry fire weapons practice to prepare for the rigorous marksmanship standards.

Drawing the pistol, I went through the motions, sighting in on a television set mounted at chest height before reloading with the empty magazine I had. I got faster and faster, my thoughts trailing to home and my wife or whatever else that came to mind, while my body remained on auto-pilot.

BAM!

Not even twenty-four hours later I was standing at attention before Major Tyranny's desk. I had gotten so used to drilling the reload techniques that I lost focus and fired a shot. And my complacency was about to cost me.

I had no defense. There was no excuse that could vindicate such an act of negligence. All I could do was accept responsibility and then try to figure out how to move forward. It was impossible to contemplate in the moment, given Tyranny's booming fire and brimstone speech.

Outside the door to my right were four of our Marines that had just received maximum non-judicial punishment because two of them fell asleep in the back of a moving vehicle. To Tyranny, the driver and front passenger were just as much at fault, which allowed him to stretch the Uniformed Code of Military Justice to issue maximum punishments for all of them.

I spied the mason jar full of rank insignia on his desk, nearly full of trophies he'd accrued from busting guys down. He enjoyed this. The most sickening part of it all was that I had given the man exactly what he wanted. That's really what burned me up inside.

After it was over and my sergeant's chevrons were resting on the pile in Tyranny's little trophy jar, I exited the building. I wondered if I had had the shortest tenure as a sergeant in the history of the Corps. It was embarrassing more than anything.

The hard part was reconciling how it happened. I'd still be a little pissed at myself if I had gotten drunk and hospitalized a few sailors or gotten caught dipping tobacco on shift, but I could've shrugged that off. This was different though. The only thing I had going for me was the fact that nobody got hurt.

As I got back to my room, the worst part of this humiliating debacle hit like a sledgehammer to the nuts. What were my Marines going to think of me? I wondered if I could stand in front of them again and expect to have their confidence?

This was the most inexcusable mistake that an infantryman can make. Our weapon is more important than our lives and nobody wants to be around someone who can't be trusted with one. I was a decorated combat veteran and the absolute last type of Marine that should be making dumb mistakes like this.

These guys had seen so many examples of garbage leadership since they joined. They didn't have the experience in a top-notch unit like I had back in 2/6 to set things in perspective for them. All they could see, and all I had shown them now, was that the men who were supposed to set the right example for them would inevitably fail them.

I wanted to throw up.

Regardless, I didn't have time to waste licking my self-inflicted wounds. Windall, Nixon, Elias, and the rest of them still needed to be prepared for combat. I had known how this was going play out the second after that shot went off.

A few hours after the incident report was filed I had sent an email to my older brother, seeking his advice. He wasn't angry or judgmental. He simply reminded me that while I had made a grave mistake, I was still the same Marine who had led a squad through Marjah.

My father, who had received my next message, was understanding. As always, he knew exactly what to say, reminding me that there was honor to be found in taking responsibility for my actions and moving forward.

It suddenly dawned on me how inexplicably lucky I was to have the family that I had. Chills went up my spine thinking about how much worse this would be if I didn't have these positive influences in my life. Their words showed me the way forward.

If I was ever going to hold out any hope of earning the respect of my guys again, I'd have to bounce back in the biggest way possible. My performance would have to be damn-near flawless. No doubt, it would be an uphill battle, but Marjah had shown me that nothing was impossible.

Since this would likely destroy any chance I had of reenlisting, I didn't have to worry about career advancement, so that simplified things. What did still matter was being the leader that the squad deserved and proving to myself that I could come back from anything.

I decided to treat it like climbing a mountain in a blizzard. Consistent perfect performance while weathering the storm of condescension and disappointment that I'd inevitably receive from the command back in Virginia when we returned. I wouldn't give them the satisfaction of quitting with what little time I had left to wear the uniform.

And little by little, I'd have to re-earn the trust of every man I was charged with leading.

My punishment entailed living in the barracks in a restricted status for forty-five days with regular check-ins and evening working parties. I'd also receive half pay for two months. I decided to use every ounce of free time buried in books, learning about my trade and hazing myself silly. I wanted to walk out this nightmare looking like a Greek god with a doctorate degree in warfighting knowledge.

I had hit rock bottom for sure. So, the only way to go was up.

After we got back home from three months in Tropic Bay, I measured the progress we had made. We still had a long way to go before any of them would be ready for the Fleet, but they were selfless. They understood that advancement was solely based on merit and that the squad always came first.

Trivial matters such as race, so publicly lauded outside the infantry, never even occurred to us. Everyone accepted that the lethality of the squad and ultimately the platoon was most important. Things like that weren't even on our radar because the infantry demands character over social agendas.

The evidence was in the way they worked together and how they carried themselves with pride. They wanted our squad to be respected and they relished the challenges of hard training. I didn't have to worry about the small things like them wearing their gear properly or cleaning their rooms, because I could see them doing it and correcting each other when needed. They were looking out for each other. Not because they were scared of me but because that was the expectation. We were free to focus on tactics, getting in fighting shape, and developing cohesion because they took ownership of the squad.

We spent every spare second developing combat skills, which left little room for anything else. The training tempo was much higher, which accelerated the process. Very seldom did a full week pass without us in the field.

We learned about each other and pushed every limit that we could. They had started to see that progress wasn't impossible and to understand that all the sacrifices they were making amounted to something that could preserve their lives. There is no substitute for shared hardship and suffering.

The other NCOs and I showed them that our first loyalty was to them, not the command that wanted to fry them or the country that passively appreciated them. That loyalty was returned when we got smart enough, collectively, to handle problems in-house, without involving staff and officers, whenever we could.

Looking forward, we had three months of training after Tropic Bay before we would deploy to Bahrain, and I was confident that we were headed in the right direction. We would have only twenty-one days to spend with family, sprinkled among several field evolutions and evaluations.

On a positive note, we had dedicated countless painful hours to developing an appreciation for infantry values. Discipline and toughness were the foundation that we had laid. Now it was time to build proficiency, lethality, and selflessness. Each of us would craft our example as a combination of those.

If we continued our present trajectory, they would indeed be ready for the battalions. But I wanted more for them. I wanted them to absolutely crush the competition and be the exception for FAST Marines instead of the rule.

They needed to be ruthless and made of iron, more proficient than guys with more experience than them, which would take some doing. They would have a tough time achieving this without a leader who would continue to grow and give them an example to match their commitment. It wasn't just what they deserved; they had grown to expect it. They were watching me, whether I saw it or not. If I lapsed or got sloppy, they'd notice. I would have to continue to evolve.

My tenure in FAST company was the most developmental period of my career. It forced me to work with people instead of hammering them into submission. Teaching them *why* to do something fostered ingenuity and initiative, especially when it came to tactics. We learned doctrinal concepts first, then worked on molding them to different situations. Removing myself from the scenarios forced the team leaders to make uncomfortable decisions.

I wanted them to expect that I would be killed before we found ourselves in a combat situation. They learned my role and each of them taught theirs to a member of their team. It was succession of command, just like Zach had instilled in us, and I was determined to have them well prepared to enact it. I didn't view it as a possibility, but an inevitability.

Our focus shifted during our final training phase before the next deployment. FAST Company's mission was to reinforce sovereign U.S. territory abroad, which meant that we would deploy to the Naval station in Bahrain and serve as a quick reaction force. If an American ambassador to any country in the Middle East called for help, we were going to be it.

We had to train differently. Tactical site security, in this case, is a defensive operation meant to keep an embassy secure so the staff can do their jobs. Up to this point, most of our field exercises drilled team and squad maneuvers with live fire, patrolling, and marksmanship. For the foreseeable future, they would focus on occupying an embassy under duress and maintaining its security.

Camp Allen had no training facilities, so we had to drive a few hours to one of the bigger bases every time we went to the field. We'd arrive at our designated training site aboard Fort Pickett or Quantico and spend days fortifying it.

The initial thirty-six hours, no one ever slept. We would establish a hasty defense around the facility, push out patrols, and build the place up. Triple strand concertina wire had to be staked in around the entire structure with two vehicle checkpoints and hundreds of sandbags had to be filled to reinforce roof top positions and entry points. It was grueling physical labor more akin to that of a Roman legion, thousands of years ago. It didn't matter if we found ourselves in a torrential downpour or being sapped by the humidity and damn near carried off by mosquitos, the work continued until it was done.

As miserable as it was, I had to admire the Marines. Every time we did this, I noticed that the target building started out as a hollow shell and turned into a tactical hotel almost overnight. I had never seen anyone work as hard as our boys.

The requirements set forth by the command and the State Department dictated that we had to be proficient in dealing with a plethora of situations from sniper fire and mortar attacks to chemical warfare, suicide vehicles, and asylum seekers. So, at any point during this initial construction phase, an evaluator could throw a dummy grenade on the ground to simulate incoming artillery and gauge or reaction, which halted everything.

Despite the lack of sleep, adequate nutrition, and constant frustration, the Marines handled themselves with poise and confidence. Windall, Nixon, and Elias controlled their teams and worked themselves beyond the point of exhaustion. Everyone accepted that it was going to suck but that it would suck much more if they complained and grumbled or didn't work as a team.

All except for lance corporal Pink.

Pink was the only one in the squad that hadn't bought in fully. He was smart and capable, but he wanted to be anywhere else rather than sweating it out with us performing this near prison labor. Some of the Marines that I had known in the past with a similar mindset simply performed tasks without any enthusiasm. They did what they had to do to make it through a run or hike or complete a field operation, but they weren't going to put forth an all-star effort. Pink was in a different place mentally. He was bitter. He spent so much time hating the current situation that he neglected his duties. Windall had to personally supervise him to ensure that he had his equipment, paid attention during instructions, showed up to formations, and stayed engaged during tactical operations.

The worst part about it was that he didn't want to be helped. I was harder on him for it. If he didn't want to excel that was his decision. But I had to make sure that he could watch everyone's back and pull the trigger when he had to. If I couldn't get him to that point, then I would be endangering everyone else in the squad if we ended up in a gun fight.

The situation provided a good opportunity for Windall. I was convinced that if he could lead Pink to a better place then he could lead anyone. The squad, however, viewed it very differently. They noticed Pink's mentality and hated him because they had decided to work together and grow into the best versions of themselves while he was too fixated on his own misery to support anyone.

We progressed through the training cycle, moving closer to our deployment to Bahrain. I grew to expect gross tactical errors from Pink before every training event. At times, one of the team leaders would notice him staring out into the woods while everyone else filled sandbags or built concertina wire walls. While on post, he wouldn't bother to make a sketch of his sector of fire or keep his night vision on. When we corrected him, rather harshly, his body language portrayed frustration and resentment. Not at me or whichever team leader had addressed it, but at life in general, it seemed. He just hated being here and fixated on how much he hated it. I knew that he wouldn't be able to focus on anything else until he got over that. But for the time being, he was just going to be miserable.

Pink had put me in a new dilemma as a leader. I had held him to the same standard as everyone else. Crushing him for mistakes that he knew not to make hadn't provided the jolt that I hoped it would. Sitting him down in an office and trying to guide him elicited no change. Listening so I could diagnose his mentality and provide him with a better one didn't help either.

What's more, he had closed himself off. The little insight that he gave when I asked him why he hated everything so much wasn't very revealing. He was homesick and not mentally prepared for the fast pace we were operating at.

I took a moment to curse Sid and Honeycutt back in Training Company. Those two had made it so that all these guys knew was how to be afraid of the UCMJ and memorize academic knowledge. The training didn't develop mental toughness or critical thinking, which would be key to operating under the political microscope inherent with State Department locales. I understood, having completed the course with many of our guys, the kind of disadvantage that placed them at.

But Training Company had been in the rear view for about six months now. Most of the Marines had absorbed the brutal shock that we put them through and adapted to the infantry lifestyle. But not Pink.

It was Spring of 2012 and the platoon still had to attend the

Advanced Urban Combat school plus pass our final field evaluation before deploying to Bahrain.

A hard question confronted me.

I asked myself if it was time to ask captain Willis to remove him from the squad. Part of me thought that he would be better suited in the headquarters group where he could monitor radios and help our platoon sergeant keep track of logistics. It would mean that I wouldn't have to wonder if he was watching his sector on patrol or paying attention on post if we ended up securing an embassy in a hostile country. It would also mean that I would be giving up on him.

Thinking through it all and weighing the consequences, I made my decision. Pink was going to stay with us. Even if I asked Willis to move him, which we had already discussed, there was no guarantee that he would. If Pink could find a way to get over his negative attitude, then the pride and confidence that came with that victory would last the rest of his life.

I thought back to my time with Smithers in Basic Security Guard School. Both men were miserable, but Smithers was willing to compromise his honor by lying and accusing others to get out. Pink had a mental and emotional hurdle to clear. He accepted his shortcomings, angrily, but he never tried to run to the command or blame anyone else, and he didn't quit. That told me that somewhere deep down inside, he had a Savage side waiting to be uncovered. But he would have to be the one to dig it out of himself.

The Advanced Urban Combat course was taught at the same place we had just graduated Basic Security Guard school from. It was ironic that while BSG was my worst experience in the Corps, AUC would turn out to be my favorite.

We were back in Honeycutt's kingdom, but this time, enjoyed a noticeable degree of separation from BSG realm. Our course was taught at the small range complex located over a mile away from everything else and the setup was better than anything I had seen in the Corps. There was a large gravel lot divided into several ranges by ten-foot metal partitions. Behind it, sat a small classroom and two large buildings reinforced for live fire in close quarters.

The school was designed to teach us how to clear rooms and buildings as a team, skills we would need if we were tasked with retaking an embassy. In that scenario, noncombatants would be present which meant that our marksmanship had to be flawless. It would be unacceptable to have our faces plastered all over the news because we stormed a diplomatic post and shot a bunch of State Department workers along with their captors. So, that's where we started.

Everyone in our fifty-man platoon now had a pistol to be used as a secondary weapon to their M4 carbine. The instructor staff was top notch. The level of professionalism and proficiency they displayed was second to none. Every skill that was required with our weapons, they demonstrated first with live fire. Then we would load up seven magazines of M4 ammunition and three of pistol to shoot that skill until we were out. One squad was shooting while another loaded and the last squad was standing by with staplers, new targets, and wooden stands for range repair. As soon as the shooters on the line were done, the next relay moved up and the rotation continued until nightfall.

That was all we did for the first week. The drills became more advanced each day and were timed to add stress and realism. The staff accepted nothing less than the utmost enthusiasm from us and critiqued every shooter constantly. It was impossible to feign proficiency. At the end of every drill, we saw exactly how we performed and were told how to get better. Within seconds, we were firing the next drill.

The physical challenge was exceptional. The instructors adjusted our stances and body position in ways that made shooting seem foreign. We were stretching and torquing muscles in completely new ways. The heat and the weight of a full ammunition load tested the physical and mental toughness of each man.

We engaged from fifty yards and in, moving closer and transitioning from rifle to pistol as needed. The responsibility of always having a weapon ready was placed on each individual shooter. We had to know how many rounds we had and be able to switch weapons, reload, or clear different types of malfunctions with both weapons, instantly. When any of that happened with a shooter to your left or right, you had to shoot the drill and engage his target to cover him. Implicit communication, intensity, and critical thought were required every minute of every day.

The benefits were priceless. The first time I carried a full load of ammunition was on patrol in Marjah. The squad was getting its first taste of that here instead of when it counted most, introducing them to a new element of reality. It's one thing to be able to carry weight in rough terrain but another to be able to actually move and engage with it. The importance placed on marksmanship reinforced lethality as the infantry's top priority.

The timing and accuracy standards to pass the final qualification were tight, incorporating all the skills we had shot for the previous four days. If anyone didn't achieve a passing score, the barrel of their rifle was switched out with a bright blue one that could only fire paint filled rounds for the remainder of the course, which would be another three weeks. There were five in the platoon that failed and had to bear the blue barrels along with hilarious haranguing from their buddies.

Pink surprisingly earned one of the highest marksmanship scores in the platoon. It was good to see him succeed at something and experience a small measure of pride. I hoped that the coming weeks would help break him out of his shell.

I loved the challenge. The fast pace left little time to analyze and get in my own way. I heard the drill called out from a tower to our rear, fired it, and saw the shot placement on the target. Then fired the next drill and the next. When my weapon malfunctioned or ran out, my hands raced to draw the pistol and complete the drill. I had seconds to holster the pistol and reload or clear the malfunction in my carbine before the next drill. It was fast and relentless, focused on killing the enemy as quickly and efficiently as possible, then moving on to any friends he may have.

Perfection was the goal. Half measures and "almosts" counted for nothing. Wild shots got called out by the instructors and I wasn't about to be that guy that couldn't shoot. The target on our silhouette shaped paper adversaries was a six-inch circle drawn where the heart would be. There was a T-shaped box incorporating the soft tissue of the nose and eyes, as well. Anything outside those didn't count. Kill shots were all that mattered.

The staff constantly challenged me and the platoon leadership. They were always over our shoulders when we fired to remind us that our Marines were one shot away from outperforming us. They expected us to shoot better, move faster, and be more intense. Setting the example for proficiency and enthusiasm as a leader was not a request, it was a requirement.

I had been immersed in infantry culture for five years at this point and experienced all these things before. But the instructors at AUC distinguished this experience through the level of importance they placed on everything and the urgency they added. The next phase is where the crucial intangible concepts of teamwork and leadership came into focus for me.

After our week on the gravel ranges, we moved into the shoot houses and began walking through how to clear basic parts of a structure. As a Boot, I had been taught a faster and more general approach to interior movement. Then Zach came along and showed me what we were now, being taught. The way we trained with him gave me an advantage over everyone else and it reminded me just how great a teacher he was. It put me at ease to know that he had been here before and succeeded. I knew what to expect and was able to help the squad understand some of what they struggled with.

Once we started clearing rooms, hallways, and the like we were encouraged to move slow and mentally digest everything. Teamwork and communication were critical. Most schools have a way of overloading students with information, which forced them to mentally dump knowledge instead of retaining it. Here at AUC, special attention was paid to ensuring we translated the skills from the gravel range and continuously built on what we'd learned so far. The whole thing was designed to build consistently on an upward trajectory.

As we moved from different types of rooms and hallways to stairs and ladders, live fire was incorporated which kept us fresh on our weapons handling and worked wonders for our confidence. After the first two days of week two, I had fired more rounds inside a house than the previous five years combined. Guys like Pink and a few others who had been timid and indecisive were forced into situations where they had to direct people. Rank meant nothing inside a house because the cramped confines and angles would leave a team vulnerable if they waited for direction.

We came to view hesitation as a killer just as lethal as an enemy rifle. If a man stopped in a doorway or on a stair well, the flood of Marines behind him would push him forward. It reminded me that this type of fighting required the utmost commitment and focus. We were taught to move in ways that used our bodies to shield everyone else in the squad and dominate the enclosure.

It was a thinking man's game that constantly challenged us to look ahead and negotiate obstacles like opposing doorways and furniture. And it had to be done through methodical fluid movement that protected the team, even at the price of personal safety, and aggressive engagement.

The days were long and nobody in the platoon had anything left at the end. My brain felt like mush trying to learn everything and evaluate the squad. Windall, Elias, and Nixon worked day in and day out despite being drained. At night, they would group together with their teams and study the material trying to retain every ounce of information they could.

The last two weeks of the course added securing the outside of a building and working with other squads. Inside the houses, our instructors waited with paint rounds to critique our mistakes more realistically. The fear factor increased because we had seen their proficiency and knew they weren't going to miss.

After the first time through, we all stumbled out splotched, pink and blue, wondering what the hell went wrong. I looked over at the boys as they stage their gear by the classroom and noticed the same disbelief on their faces.

We had to be better than that. Two instructors had easily destroyed us, and we had ten days left of trading paint rounds with them. Despite the confidence we had built in one another, they showed us just how costly this type of fighting is.

It brought us back down to reality.

I wasn't about to let that ruin all the progress we had made as a squad. We had all learned a little bit more about how everyone thought and dealt with stress. We understood each other a little better and had worked ourselves beyond exhaustion, steadily honing our skills. But if we couldn't keep it together and win when it mattered, it was all for naught.

Thankfully, the squad banded together largely because of the team leaders who wouldn't accept self-pity as a response. They encouraged their guys, corrected mistakes, and accepted responsibility for their actions. I marveled at how differently they each addressed their teams but always seemed to foster a hunger for more. Seeing this type of growth in them and their desire to excel, not merely survive, made me want to take them to war. Together, we were lethal and eager for the challenge.

Noticing this, Willis designated us the assault squad, which we all saw as a supreme honor. It meant that regardless of how bad it looked when we faced the staff, the other squads hadn't outperformed us, and competition drives everything in the infantry.

Later that day, I decided to stay behind and guard the platoon's weapons and gear while they went to get chow. Corporal Byrd decided to stay with me because we had a bone to pick. He was infuriated by Willis' decision. Competitive disappointment and frustration are constants in infantry culture because everything is a competition. And someone has to lose. Usually, both parties accept it without harboring resentment and the rivalry continues.

But Byrd was having trouble letting this one go. He seemed bitter over the fact that we had earned the designation that he and his squad had worked their asses off for, which I could understand. Willis named his squad as our primary support. If we ever had to do this in real life, they would finish securing a building when too many of us were wounded or killed, which expected due to the high cost inherent in urban fighting.

We were trying to air things out because we both agreed that adding animosity between us, on top of what was already felt for Captain Willis, could derail everything. Over the previous months, our relationship had changed. From Byrd's perspective, I was the golden child that could do no wrong. From mine, it was just business as usual. Byrd told me that earlier in the day, Willis informed him that his squad would be the assault and mine would support his. Now that Willis had officially awarded the title to us, Byrd was understandably wondering what the hell happened and why.

I had no clue why Willis, or any commander, would go about making a decision this way. It looked like he was intentionally putting Byrd and I against each other and neither of us appreciated it. Regardless of Willis' intentions, he had inspired distrust and suspicion among his leadership corps which would only spell disaster for the development and performance of the whole platoon.

As we finished AUC and moved through the last remaining weeks before our next deployment, I wondered just how rough this was going to get. It was the last thing that any unit deploying to a powder keg region like the Middle East needed. I had no faith that the command would even notice that Willis' example was toxic- or take any action to mitigate its effects. All I could do was make sure that the boys were ready just in case it all blew up in our faces.

Our main event kicked off in the summer of 2012 when we arrived in the Kingdom of Bahrain for our final deployment. Six to eight months from now, we would rotate back home, and all our guys would be reassigned to different infantry units. What remained for the rest of us, I had no idea. I was too focused on adapting to our new environment and preparing the Marines for that transition. The inevitability of it was always hovering over me, like a specter that shadowed my every move and dominated my subconscious. I was determined to send them off as a proud father would, confident in their skill and integrity, instead of tossing and turning through sleepless nights, wondering if they would get eaten alive by the combat veterans they would have to compete against.

The immediate challenge that confronted us now was just as unnerving. The work up we had just gone through, along with our mini deployment to Tropic Bay, was more fast paced than that of the Fleet. We had done our best to replicate infantry culture and show our guys the way things *should* be. Despite the cumbersome structure and poor command climate of FAST Company, I was confident in the progress we had made. I wasn't going to let anyone use those shortcomings as a crutch.

To my surprise, the commander and 1st Sergeant of FASTCENT, which we now fell under, had things running relatively smoothly. All their Marines, considered permanent personnel, knew their job and what had to be done to get us up in the air with all of our gear and weapons should a distress call come.

Liberty and alcohol consumption were heavily curtailed, which kept most of us on base. It made more sense to spend our off time working out or staying in our barracks rooms instead of going out in town.

Barracks were always shitty in the Corps, regardless of the duty station, so anytime we got a chance to enjoy the larger funding that the other branches received, we relished it. The other NCO's and I were thrilled that we even had a barracks, especially one as nice as this. We had showers, clean sheets, electrical outlets and almost everything was relatively new. We even had a television!

The downside to being with the Navy was that they seemed to abhor anything that remotely resembled hard, realistic training. Base policies required weeks of tedious and cumbersome administrative processes to move anywhere with weapons. The sailors stationed at NSA Bahrain complained to our command frequently about hearing our raised voices during training and correction, which we all found hilarious.

It was the opposite of being at Lejeune or Allen where, throughout every day, the entire base engaged in some form of physical activity. The same can't be said for the entire Navy, of course, but this group in Bahrain seemed allergic to intensity.

Most days were similar to a typical garrison day handling administrative and logistical tasks. Generally, Naval culture values rank and status over example, lethality, and skill. I had seen the same mentality with the sailors on the USS Carter Hall during my first deployment in 2008.

Moving forward, I had to plan a week in advance to schedule weapons draws for reactionary drills, which the Marines weren't privy to. Our success hinged upon being able to assemble instantly, whether they were in the chow hall, at the gym, or asleep in the dead of night. Our chances of responding to diplomatic distress were significantly higher than the other FAST companies around the world because we were responsible for the Middle East.

Despite this, nobody seemed concerned. The feedback I got from the squad echoed the sentiment that everyone else knew it was possible, but they didn't believe that it was probable. I wasn't sure how long the Navy had been in Bahrain, but they appeared to be on vacation instead of forward deployed. It was a pretty slick means for them to earn a "Thank you for your service." and a discounted meal once they got back to the States.

That mentality had infected the Marines of FASTCENT, as well. It was so rare for a platoon like ours to get a mission, that most of them approached their duties with professionalism but without urgency.

Complacency has led many a warrior to an early death and none of us wanted to be added to that list. So, we stayed engaged as best we could, working out twice a day and studying everything relating to our trade. Occasionally, we could get away with drawing our weapons and rehearsing attacks on the base softball field until someone complained. As deadly as the Navy culture could be, it could also be countered with solid small unit leadership, and I had seen that, as a Boot, from men like Badams and Jolo.

The more glaring issue was how to counter Willis. The fear and bitterness that he fostered could lead to a breakdown of command if he lost it in a combat situation, which was my primary concern.

Whatever he was dealing with internally had already won. None of us knew exactly what he was dealing with. We saw him in the FASTCENT office and occasionally ate together in the chow hall, but the interaction was different. He was exhausted. It seemed that he had to try his hardest to present a cordial front that masked the fact that he needed help with something. Once we secured for the day in late afternoon, Willis spent most of his time in his room, alone.

One early September evening, the dam broke. Willis had left the base without authorization to drink away his entire paycheck. His bender lasted a day and a half before he finally showed up at the front gate broke and still drunk. He was confined to his quarters under guard for the next two days until our company executive officer from the States could fly out here and relieve him.

So here we were, forward deployed in the most volatile region on the globe with no officer.

I have to admit that I was shocked-mostly at how royally Willis had fucked up. Even after the drinking on duty and his generally condescending demeanor, his behavior still baffled me. I wondered why anyone with the opportunity to accomplish so many great things could think it was acceptable to go completely overboard. He had infantrymen under his responsibility ready to learn and be led but his audacity to act as he pleased overcame any value he may have placed on impacting them. I didn't understand it.

A new platoon commander was promised by the officer that had flown halfway around the world to collect Willis. In the interim, our platoon sergeant would take his place. It was still a bad situation because none of us were confident with the staff sergeant, but I couldn't help but be glad that nobody had been killed. The last time I saw the succession of command process play out was when Zach and Derek had been killed in Marjah.

But still it took all of that crap that Willis had pulled-months of acting like a jackass- before somebody had the intestinal fortitude to relieve him of command. Why?

This whole situation, along with the overall climate of Security Forces thus far, complicated our efforts with the Marines. They had guys like Brown Bear, Slave, and I pushing them to excel as grunts and setting an example, flawed as it was, of discipline, proficiency, and professionalism in an environment that didn't hold staff and officers accountable unless it was forced to. It was madly confusing for them.

This exact situation never would have developed this far in 2/6. There, if a leader thought himself above the standards of excellence and conduct, he didn't survive long. And that's how it should be for every infantry unit.

Little more than a week later, we were cruising at thirty thousand feet en route to Sana'a, Yemen. I sat in the back right aisle seat of the aircraft, weighing the situation we found ourselves in. The events of the past week replayed in my mind as I observed the body language of the Marines around me. They were tense but not fearful. I thought about the blessing of Willis' absence and turned my gaze to the left, where a mountain of a man with a pristinely bald head sat across the aisle.

A graduate of the Naval Academy and former lineman for their football team, his body seemed cramped in the small seat. Atop his massive, muscular frame his head alternated between resting against the cabin wall with eyes closed and forward leaning to observe, much in the same manner as me. A million thoughts must have been racing through his head and I wondered what it would look like if I could peer inside to view the information traffic jam.

Captain Kowalski was reassigned from Alpha Company to replace Willis. He had flown over from Virginia on short notice to Bahrain and within a week, we had been called on to reinforce the U.S. embassy in Sana'a. We hadn't seen news footage or been given a clear picture of what we were walking into. All we knew was the Ambassador had requested us to respond to the mob of Yemeni people that had stormed the embassy and destroyed everything they could . Shots had been fired and the staff had moved into the safe haven. We didn't know how coordinated the attack was, the extent of the damage, if any casualties had been incurred, or if the mob had dispersed. I would've given anything to know that information as we cruised towards our destination.

I thought about peering inside Captain Kowalski's head again and realized that he had a whole slew of unknowns that I didn't have to worry about. This guy didn't even know us as his squad leaders or the Marines. He was back in Virginia ten days ago then got swept up in the Marine Corps whirlwind. When he arrived in Bahrain, he spent time with each of us NCOs and observed us training and teaching classes. But that was all he had to go off.

His demeanor was markedly different than Willis.' The man stood at well over six feet and weighed about two-hundred and twenty pounds by my estimation. None of it was fat. He seemed well-spoken and confident. In our first conversation, roughly ten days ago, he'd established simple expectations and listened intently to my evaluation of the platoon and the damage that Willis had caused.

We hadn't spent enough time together to earn each other's respect, but the nature of our current situation would accelerate that process. It was inevitable. The nature of infantry work forces everyone's true colors to the surface. It takes more time in garrison environments, but it never fails. Combat and life-threatening situations speed up the process, which meant that very soon Captain Kowalski would see every man in our platoon as he truly was, and we would know him in the same light.

My last thought before we started our initial descent was of Lance Corporal Pink. I looked forward and found him sitting in his seat, head forward just like the others around him. No longer the bitter, homesick boy that couldn't get out of his own way, Pink had started to come into his own. He still struggled physically. He wasn't the fastest, strongest or most skilled but he had begun to break free. Over the past few months in Bahrain, Windall and I had seen him gain a solid understanding of his role as a rifleman. I believed in him now, which is something I would've thought crazy six months ago.

But for all his progress, the events of that morning had rocked him mentally. I flashed back to a scene that took place ten hours ago in the FASTCENT company area. Our Marines were rushing back and forth to finish palletizing our gear. Everything from our individual packs to pelican cases of communication equipment and ammunition was going. It was nearly the same as the countless drills we had conducted since our arrival.

But it was real this time.

That cancerous complacency that had infected the entire base for who knows how long had reared its ugly head. The FASTCENT commander and his team did their part, but their manner let it show. The urgency of the call for aid that they hadn't seriously expected shocked them, and they were near frantic. The cool calm behavior on display prior to that moment was replaced with frustration, which may have contributed to Pink's moment of doubt.

Even so, they coordinated our transport and support to get us what we needed and out the door as quickly as possible.

As the boys finished loading and strapping everything in place with giant cargo nets, I noticed Pink standing near the green pavilion that served as the Company's smoke pit. He was shocked. I spied a small tremble in his hands and his hunched over posture as I closed the ten feet of distance that seemed a like a mile.

The Marines were loading a bus on the other side of the building now. Everything was ready-except for Lance Corporal Pink.

"What's wrong?" I asked.

"I-I don't think I can do this, Corporal."

A small part of me wanted to leave him in Bahrain. But the better part realized that he had come so far, and it would be a shame for him to throw it away based on one moment of doubt. All of us felt it. We just held it inside and went about doing our part, which is easier for most when we look around and see our brothers carrying on.

I looked right at him and read his expression. He wasn't horrified. It was his confidence that was missing. He was implicitly asking how he could muster the courage to come with us, not refusing to perform his duties. This was the next obstacle for him to clear and if he could, then he would have all the evidence he needed to bury the old version of himself and move forward. This was that rare moment where he had the power to alter his own trajectory for good and if I crushed him, it could cripple his spirit. But he would have to choose.

So, I left it up to him.

Looking him square in the eyes, I said, "Pink, sometimes all it takes is that first step. Once we leave here, then you've got the rest of us to lean on." It wasn't as much a question as it was a reminder that he could overcome his fear and that we would be with him every step of the way.

And now here was, a few rows in front of me and Captain Kowalski. I wasn't sure who had convinced who of what, but he took that step. Whether our stay in Yemen was peaceful or violent, long or short, there was no going back now, and he would have the confidence and pride of making the right decision for the rest of his life.

We touched down in Yemen well into the night with a welcome committee from the embassy's security team waiting on us. Captain Kowalski went over to get briefed while the rest of us unloaded the gear and weapons on the runway right next to the plane. The staff sergeant passed out enough ammunition for every man to have a combat load of two-hundred and ten rounds for our M4 carbines and forty-five rounds for our sidearms. I looked around and took in the new environment as I pressed and slid them into the magazines. I could just make out the faint outline of elevation in the darkness. The only hint of civilization was the runway we were on now and the black armored SUVs that waited to take us to the embassy.

We received word from the captain that the riot had dispersed, and a Marine Battalion Landing Team, from the MEU, had the Embassy and nearby Sheraton hotel secured. Relief washed over me followed by disappointment. I was confident in our capabilities as a platoon but retaking an embassy from a hostile force would be tough sledding for anyone. The fact that we weren't first on the scene was infuriating. No other organization in the world prides themselves more on being the first ones into a hostile environment than Marine infantry.

Not more than half an hour later, we loaded up by squads in the bulky Suburbans, and set out towards our destination. We cruised on paved roads for ten minutes before reaching the outskirts of Sana'a. As we sped along the narrow, twisting pavement I tried to soak in everything I could.

Sana'a had similar infrastructure to pictures I had seen of Iraq. Multiple storied buildings crammed together, divided by narrow alleyways and a few two-lane roads like the one we were on now. The place had that same dirty feel to it to it that Marjah had but more buildings. A few half-finished or blown out concrete structures were tucked in between the more modern ones that sported that awkward tan shade that seemed to be the staple of Middle Eastern urban aesthetics.

The engine of our mechanical beast roared as we sped along at over sixty miles an hour. This was my first time in an armored SUV, and I couldn't help but feel "high speed." I imagined it was the same for Windall and Nixon with their teams, crammed in the seats behind us.

The driver's gear was slick: all black and neatly arranged with three single magazine pouches and a communication earpiece that twisted from the top of his plate carrier. I was jealous. We looked like human tanks with our bulky tan carriers that were all beat to shit and dirty.

The massive engine sharply decelerated as we came upon a ten-foot compound wall, nestled in between several tall buildings. We dismounted in the street and moved through a small opening of what was the facility's primary vehicle gate.

Everyone assembled on the inside now, we moved en mass down the paved runway. A few streetlights remained on, allowing us to see some of the aftermath. The place was littered with trash and debris of all sorts.

Continuing down the paved incline, I looked left and noticed several armored vehicles, overturned with cracked windshields and shattered glass seemed to be everywhere. There wasn't a single spot on the main street that wasn't covered with something. I estimated the distance between the main gate and the chancery to be about one hundred meters. The road we were currently traveling continued for another fifty meters and ended at another black gate, lit by a single eerie orange streetlight.

Veering off the path to our left, we arrived at the three-story chancery. In addition to the pale tan paint, it sported multiple black scorch marks and visible damage to the reinforced windows. The security staff brought us up the steps of the building and pointed out the ambassador's residence, about fifty meters further left.

Captain Kowalski ordered first squad to assume the posts that the Marines from the MEU had established.

The scene inside the chancery was odd. Mattresses, trash,

emergency rations, and empty water bottles were haphazardly thrown about, as if the place had turned into a hurricane shelter.

We passed through a door on the left to a staircase that led up to the roof and ascended to where the MEU Marines were. I was heaving by the time I got to the top. We were at seventy-five hundred feet above sea level now and bearing a full combat load for the foreseeable future. Nothing stresses the importance of physical conditioning like elevation.

A squad leader from the MEU Marines met me at the top of the stairs and I had Windall's team scatter to the rooftop positions he had established. For the next hour or so, we moved to each post, and he walked me through the sectors of fire and various reference points, just like the Marines were doing with one another.

The Squad Leader spoke frankly, and I admired his professionalism. I could see that he ran a tight ship. His boys were locked in behind their weapons, making full use of the cover provided by the waist high parapet, surrounding the roof. Helmet mounted PVS 14 night vision devices were flipped down to a man and each post had a hasty range card, generally depicting the terrain and prominent structures per position. No one was smoking or had their gear partially on. And this seemed to be the only place in the entire compound that wasn't covered in trash, scorch marks, or shattered glass.

After he had finished passing his information, the Marines he had come with shuffled down the stairs one by one, transferring the full responsibility of security to us.

There we were. The one thing that nobody in Bahrain believed would happen had happened. I took a moment to marvel at the fact that while this situation was very different from Marjah, both had begun in similar fashion. I replayed the initial flight into COP Kelley just over two years ago and noted how then, as now, I had expected to be in a raging gun fight the second we arrived, only to be disappointed.

Windall, Nixon, and Elias had worked hard to grow into capable and lethal grunts. Their Marines-our Marines- had followed their example and forced the necessary changes on themselves to follow suit. They deserved the opportunity to validate themselves. With a sigh of disappointment, I acknowledged the fact that we didn't get to choose if they would get that chance.

A few hours before sunrise, we were relieved by corporal Byrd's squad and clamored down the flights of stairs to grab a quick nap on the mattresses lining the hallways. When we woke from our three hours of slumber, the full extent of the destruction was on display. Night wasn't concealing shredded sections of turf or hanging trash on the concertina wire that sat atop the ten-foot outer wall. It was surprising to see what an angry crowd was capable of.

We moved from the chancery along the main street collecting what debris we could. Several of the armored vehicles had been irreparably damaged and overturned, even at over eleven thousand pounds per. Five of them lined the street and there wasn't a single one unscathed. Various melee weapons such as pipes, hammers, bricks, and large metal pieces were scattered about, left in place by the assailants.

I stood in place for a moment, looked at the overturned behemoths then back at the crude weapons scattered about and the black scorch marks that splotched nearly everything. Memories from our non-lethal training back at Virginia flashed. If we had been called in a day earlier, we would've been expected to confront the mob, hundreds strong, with bean bag shotgun shells and rubber ball grenades. We were required to employ less than lethal tactics before utilizing deadly force, which was intended to limit unnecessary loss of life.

As comforting as those measures are to politicians, they succeed far more in decreasing our survivability more than anything else.

It seemed ridiculous to me that any unit could reasonably be expected to utilize non-lethal tactics in riot situations when crowds were capable of this kind of destruction. Armed or not, that kind of aggression directed at American troops abroad should warrant deadly force without apology or hesitation.

I shook my head as I moved on.

The ambassador's home, a two-story structure, stood across from the chancery by itself. The double pane windows sported a few marks left by some kind of riot weapon, but it was otherwise undamaged.

I struck out with Brown Bear and Slave to get the lay of the land while we had the daylight. We were responsible for every inch of American soil now, which meant the ten-foot perimeter wall and everything inside.

The main street between the chancery and the ambassador's residence dead ended into a tennis court. Off to the right, there was a nice outdoor pool and an indoor gym, connected by a covered terrace. Passing over the sleek tile surface, I saw a bathroom and we veered left through a tiny outdoor gym area. Out the other side there was a small house where the Marine Security Guard detachment stayed and a covered parking garage to the left, surrounded by chain link fence on the top level.

MSG enjoyed a nice living by our standards. Up until a few days ago they relished a private kitchen, fully stocked bar, and living area with flat screens and couches, in addition to their own private bunks. Talking it over with Brown Bear and Slave, we couldn't figure out why the State Department had them so far away from the chancery. Clearly, the distance could limit their response times.

We talked about the fact that this place looked like a palace compared to what most Americans lived in. If you took away the debris and Molotov scars, it was a small step down from opulence with its palm trees, manicured lawns, and marble tile floors. The pool, tennis courts, and gyms would've resembled a corporate retreat site. On top of that, it was positioned in the city next to people living in poverty.

As we discussed it heading back to the platoon, we decided we really couldn't be mad at the fact that the locals hated us enough to riot. They didn't know that most Americans don't live so lavishly. All they saw was this small palace, filled by different people that wanted to influence their lives, who appeared to laugh at their struggles. To us, it made sense that they hated it enough to try and burn it down.

Our uneventful stay in Sana'a lasted one hundred and eleven days. These Marines had worked themselves beyond exhaustion more times than they could count, beforehand. They'd pulled from history's vast lessons to increase their knowledge base and endured the hardships of training and personal development. I'd have given almost anything to see them in action, but some things just aren't meant to be.

Combating that frustration of boredom and complacency were the constant battles that each squad had to fight. We found ways to make the most of the situation.

In the beginning, there was plenty of time and space to resume preparing the Marines for the Fleet, while we maintained security. The elevation made everything harder, which meant we would be in immaculate fighting shape when we got back to sea level.

Still, the situation could've gone from peaceful to critical in an instant. Despite this, the mood in the platoon was light. My team leaders remained professional and that affected the rest of the squad. Nobody complained about moving our gear from one place to another constantly or checking and rechecking equipment and weapons. They weren't using an abnormal situation as an excuse to cut corners.

Windall, Nixon, and Elias acted like squad leaders and taught their job to their Marines. It was a well-oiled machine and part of me hoped for somebody to give us a reason to fight.

There was an unexpected value that we gleaned from this 111-day experience. Having been on active duty for over five years at this point, I had been fortunate to experience so much. But our time in

Yemen, coexisting with the State Department, shed new light on how different the infantry is and our place in the American hierarchy.

Living conditions improved dramatically. Within a month, each squad had its own indoor, climate-controlled birthing area complete with mattresses and coded entry. We marveled at how quickly the compound had been cleaned. It seemed that in the blink of an eye every double pain window had been replaced, new armored vehicles had been dropped from the sky, and sparkling new flatscreens had mounted themselves to the walls. The small patches of grass, strategically placed throughout, were well maintained and there wasn't a piece of trash to be found anywhere. It galled me to think about how much money was spent to make it all happen. The State Department seemed to have an unlimited budget of taxpayer's dollars to use. It was impressive, really.

Improvements were made to the compound to increase our lethality. We carved a hole through the roof of the chancery overhang so grenades could be dropped onto the steps below if another riot got that far and one of the vehicle entrances was sealed. Between that, the machine guns, and Slave's designated marksmen teams, taking this embassy would've been a costly affair for any attacking force.

We established a training schedule to stay sharp and keep enemy observers from noticing a pattern. During the first six weeks, we could see them, set up in carefully selected windows with cameras and other optics, unabashedly watching us. For the first time, the boys were immersed in a chaotic environment under constant scrutiny from an enemy waiting to highlight every misstep.

We used any place we could find to put in work: the tennis courts became a mock house for room clearing, the garden and outer walkways were used for patrols, and the covered parking lot for full on assault drills. The large, covered garage behind the patio area limited enemy observation, which eased our reservations about them seeing our practices.

I could see a different look on the Marines' faces. It was that curious mix of excitement, aggression, and intensely careful observation peculiar to men in these rare circumstances. I'd had the same look two years before in Marjah. All of them were hyper focused, as any unit typically is at the beginning of an operation. The shock of being thrown in the deep end and the forceful realization that this was not training anymore had that effect, regardless of the location. They responded admirably as true professionals.

The bitter, timid Lance Corporal Pink from before had vanished, replaced by a cautiously enthusiastic better version of himself. He stood his post, worked out with his team, and trained without grumbling to himself or looking like he hated everything in sight. He seemed surprised at how far he had come and appeared to enjoy executing his duties, despite the danger. What's more, the squad had noticed the shift and treated him with more respect.

Pink's transformation was awesome, and I reveled in seeing him enjoy the experience as much as the other Marines did.

About six weeks into our stay at Palace Sana'a, a Marine Law Enforcement platoon was shipped in to assist with some of the security duties outside of the compound. Captain Wendolowski tasked our squad to train them in close quarters tactics. I had never worked directly with LE Marines, or females, so I was interested to take the measure of them.

For the rest of the day and the following morning, we prepared. The team leaders and I planned it out from start to finish and ran through the whole thing multiple times.

The tennis court would be divided in half to run two groups through at a time. The team leaders and I would demonstrate every skill and formation as we highlighted each Marine's responsibility, just like we'd rehearsed. Then the LE Marines would do it as we critiqued and demonstrated further as needed.

The saying, "every Marine a rifleman" has been drilled into every recruit that passes through one of the depots. Every one that earns the title of Marine is proud of their marksmanship skills because we have the hardest qualifications of any service branch. However, nearly every POG that I had encountered seemed to think that their annual qualification badge meant that they were capable of fighting just as effectively as any grunt. We saw this as an opportunity to test that. Having observed Marines from other occupations, I had my doubts. Most Grunts hate the axiom of "every Marine a rifleman" because being a good infantryman requires a plethora of other skills that take a significant amount of time and discipline to master.

The LE Marines' skill level wasn't going to prove anything. Everyone sucks at clearing rooms when they first start, and we were no exception. I wanted to evaluate their intangibles. Did they possess the same ruthlessness, toughness, and fighting spirit that we embodied? That was the critical question, and the answer would prove or disprove the age-old adage.

When they showed up, we put them into two lines on the court and moved from one to the other, evaluating their gear. Many of them had magazine pouches they couldn't reach, flashlights and other accoutrements clipped to their chests, and water bottles in the small dump pouch meant for spent magazines.

As we moved from one Marine to the next, I remembered Zach explaining his gear setup to Captain Brock. Over two years removed at this point, the memory still played fresh in my mind.

About thirty minutes later, the LE Marines had finished adjusting their gear to be at least functional for close quarters work.

Windall, Nixon, and Elias utilized the white lines on the court like a room and walked through the steps of how to clear as I explained what was going on and why. After that we moved forward with the plan.

The first thing that jumped out at all of us was how timid they were. Most Marines are when they learn these skills for the first time, but it usually goes away relatively quickly. Hours into the training, they were still stopping in doorways, unsure of which way to turn, and they hesitated to communicate effectively or loud enough to hear over gunfire. Many of them couldn't shoulder their weapons long enough to move from one simulated room to another, whether because of their gear or lack of strength.

It was obvious that they cared about doing well. They tried hard. But that intense fire that burned so brightly in us just wasn't there. They were Marines. But they didn't have that extra iron in their souls like the men I fought with in 2/6. They reminded me of the MSG Marines that lived on this compound. Both groups were professional, dedicated, and enthusiastic. But neither displayed a demeanor possessed of someone who craves a fight like an infantryman does. Their actions showed us that the force and violence of action that is the cornerstone of infantry culture was foreign to them.

I'm not sure how confident they felt as they departed the compound about eight hours later. I hoped they would never have to use what we showed them. Urban fighting is the costliest type of warfare.

To me, the experienced reinforced what I had learned from the other POGs that I had encountered in my first enlistment and throughout FAST Company: that non-infantry Marines are different. Not lesser, just different. They earned the title the same as we did, but for many of them, that was the most difficult part of their service. For us, it was the easiest. The title of "rifleman" isn't something we seek to hold over other Marine's heads. But it is a title we know, through experience, is earned by far more struggle, learning, and sheer force of will than what it takes to pass an annual rifle qualification- even if it is the best damn course of fire among all the branches. Every Marine is not a rifleman. Our frustration with the issue, as infantrymen, comes from the fact that most people don't know the difference and consequently, that ignorance reinforces the saying that we know to be false in practice.

We had been on site for about five weeks and settled into a general routine. The State Department resumed limited operations shortly after our arrival, but with limited personnel. Now, with more of them out and about the compound, they seemed to be returning to a version of regular living. Government employees buzzed about, and Yemeni workers came and went throughout the day, which provided the illusion of normalcy to everyone except us.

When this happened, it was as if a switch got flipped. Captain Kowalski and the platoon sergeant would return from their morning briefing with the various department heads and issue new mandates from the State Department. One day they'd tell us the tennis courts were now off limits for training. The next day we were told the pool could be used for sunbathing and light recreation but not for swimming laps. A few days later, we were confined to our squad rooms during certain hours so the handful of USAID workers could hold their afternoon meetings by the pool, instead of the offices they were provided. And on and on it went.

Before long, we realized that we couldn't be anywhere in the compound that was considered a public venue unless we were moving to assume the posts or get chow. Even our drills were curtailed to accommodate their whims.

As annoying as it was, we made do by moving the training to more obscure areas or waiting until they left to go back to the Sheraton hotel. We were still visitors on their turf.

The real frustration came when we were told that all fifty of us had only a few hours to workout. Additionally, the State employees didn't want to see our rifles. And that's what made me view the changes in totality.

It was one thing to place silly stipulations on the pool and tennis courts. It was another thing entirely to limit our lethality for the sake of comfort. I'd seen boot Marines get hazed so many times over the years for leaving a weapon unattended; anything from doing pushups until the arms were useless to having the weapon thrown into the chest of the forgetful Marine by an infuriated team leader. These were disciplinary practices that we held dear for one simple and paramount reason: an infantryman's weapon is more important than his life. It's not meant for personal defense. Its purpose is to be used to kill any enemy attempting to harm another Marine in the formation. Much like the purpose of a Greek hoplite's shield being meant for the protection of every other man within the phalanxes of old.

The limits placed on the gym and movement within the compound were just as infuriating because physical and mental toughness is second only to the rifle in infantry culture. The sheer physical force required to move a combat load in a deadly situation for an undetermined amount of time is incomprehensible for anyone who hasn't done it. Adding to this, we were at over seven thousand feet above sea level. Just as with marksmanship, navigation, patrolling, or any other combat skill, toughness is perishable. If we abided by these parameters, it would take maybe two weeks of doing nothing before all the sweat we had forced out of our bodies meant nothing-and we were just like everyone else.

It wasn't that I couldn't understand their reasoning. I simply refused to accept it given the situation and the enemy.

Not more than a six weeks ago over a hundred people had forced their way in here to break everything and try and kill them all. And yet, they were uncomfortable seeing a weapon carried by men who were here to prevent that from happening again. It was petty and decreased our chances of maintaining security in the event of another breach.

I had no way of knowing what they were really thinking but it looked like they didn't want us around anymore. To them, the threat was over, and we were the last thing standing in the way of a complete return to normalcy, even in an environment as volatile as this. Benghazi had exploded just before we were called here, highlighting the precarious global situation for diplomatic outposts. On top of that there were numerous historical examples, such as the bombings of the Marine barracks in Beirut and the embassies in Kenya and Tanzania that were evidence to the contrary. There was always a threat.

I wondered if they just didn't have the balls to tell us thanks and kick us out, so they opted for stupidity instead. But that was just my anger.

The real reason was that other American government institutions are not meant for violence. The State Department's role is to facilitate diplomacy through healthy relationships with other countries. Their mission requires certain appearances to be upheld and host nation comfortability, among other things, to take precedence over security, lethality, and flexibility.

Our role is to locate, close with, and destroy the enemy, which leaves very little room for the values of a diplomatic organization.

War, we were taught, was the last option in the case of diplomatic failure. If that was true, then why did diplomacy and politics matter at all in any situation that we were deployed in? In reality, politics doesn't have a clear stop and war a clear start. It's more gray than black and white. And since we come from a democratic society in which the warrior class submits to the political, the values of the former will always be marginalized by the latter.

Different groups-even ones so culturally distant as we were with State- can still work together and achieve goals. But only if they do so without trying to dilute one other.

They wanted someone to make them feel safe without appearing too menacing. It was similar to Afghanistan where many thought us protectors, liberators, or government project managers. Pairing the two situations, I wondered why our politicians continue to put us in these situations. It was baffling.

If that was what they wanted, they needed to bring in someone else. The infantry is meant to violently eliminate threats to the Constitution and that's it.

The time finally came for us to leave Sana'a. It was just before Christmas in 2012, and Saint Nick had given us an early present in the form of a visit from General James Mattis. Currently the

Commander of U.S. Central Command and a legend to every Marine. Affectionately known as Mad Dog Mattis for his relentless pursuit of enemy in Iraq, he had a reputation for being one of the few men to reach the pinnacle of military rank and maintain a warrior's mindset.

The twelve or so hours before his arrival had been the most excited we had been in weeks.

In a stunning turn of the tables, the State Department vacated the patio and pool area so he could speak to us alone. We formed a small semi-circle just off the path that led down from the chancery and waited briefly before he joined us.

I began sizing him up as soon he came into view, headed towards us. His appearance was striking and not at all what I expected. At average height, he wore a navy-blue tailored suit and a short cut of gray hair sat atop his lightly wrinkled face.

Gathered around him, all fifty of us hung on his every word. He began our short conversation by thanking us and telling us that what we were doing here was meaningful to our country, adding that he wasn't here to do a squad leader's job or micromanage but to answer our questions.

I was taken aback at how at ease he seemed. I darted my eyes around the small formation a noticed several jaws that needed to be picked up off the tile floor. We had half expected a hearty speech, filled with inspiration and stoic wisdom, or a quick photo to be snapped before he vanished. A few days ago, then- Director of the Central Intelligence Agency David Patreus had swung by and done just that. General Mattis, on the other hand, wanted to educate and inform.

Acknowledging our disappointed that the situation hadn't been more kinetic, he explained that our presence was keeping a foothold in the region so we could be prepared to combat the terrorist cells who were tirelessly planning to undermine American efforts. He provided a clear picture of our larger effect in the grand scheme, which none of us had received yet.

A career infantry officer, he had the same intensity in his eyes that we had. His voice steady and firm, he projected the confidence and professionalism of an experienced and humble man.

He departed the embassy after pictures were taken, leaving us to reflect on his words as we went about our business. Through the smoke of a cigarette, I mulled over the measure I had taken of him. His reputation had certainly contributed to my view but there was something more mysterious about the way he carried himself. In the brief ten minutes he was with us, he commanded our attention, not through loud obnoxious speech, but through measured responses and confidence. No doubt a product of his extensive education.

The rarity of the situation wasn't lost on me as I took another deep inhale of the cancerous vapor. The question was: how could I take what he had shown me and use it moving forward?

After our return home and another deployment to Bahrain from July of 2013 to February of 2014, I finally got time to reflect while I was waiting to move out to the west coast. It was healthy to digest the experiences of the previous years and map out the way forward.

Using the time rehash what I learned about why FAST was so different, helped me commit it to memory for later use. I had orders to Second Battalion, Fifth Regiment and anticipated having Security Forces Marines with me. Understanding what hampered them now, I wasn't dreading the prospect of leading them.

Attempting to view my FAST experience through an unbiased and objective lens, difficult as it always is, was productive because it showed me where I was wrong, as well. Every unit in the history of every service branch goes through rough patches. When you change duty stations, your chances that the unit is in top condition with a solid command are a toss-up. Still, most of the time, the ebb and flow move with the deployment cycle. When the command changes, the chances are renewed, like rolling a dice and however it falls, the outcome will be different than the last cycle in some way. FAST may have been garbage during my tenure, but that didn't mean that it was always so or couldn't be great in the future. And the same was true for 2/5, where I was headed.

I had just been through Zach's old stomping grounds and had seen a different side of the Corps. Filtering through the memories of Tropic Bay, Bahrain, and Yemen, I started adding it all up.

The Security Force's regimental structure certainly had a part to play, but the real reason why it was so different was the influence of civilian entities. In 2/6, we were isolated and focused on warfighting, which had a monumental impact on our ability to prepare for Marjah and, consequently, our performance benefitted greatly. I cringed at the thought of how much more costly it would've been if we'd had a commander like Tyranny or Honeycutt.

Normally, when two groups so vastly different coexist closely, conflict and influence are inevitable. The more time they spend together, the more they'll rub off on each other. But in this case, we were secondary to the civilian departments we were embedded with, and they could demand whatever they wanted. FAST had been submerged in Naval and civilian culture for so long that it had simply been absorbed by them.

I learned a bit about our connection with civilian agencies, the vitality of diplomacy, and how the martial component factors into it. It was a paradoxical relationship between politician, warrior, and civilian with complex and competing mentalities.

Another factor to consider was the growing political call for military reform that had gained traction over the last four years. The Obama administration had become enamored with the notion of changing our culture to resemble American society, and part of me could understand why. Our country doesn't see the value in warfare that ancient civilizations did, which explains why there a so few infantrymen in elected positions. But there had to be more to it than that. There was no logical reason behind this demand.

I considered one final thought: there has never been a point in

American history where the service branches embarked on a quest to socially transform civil society. Wars will always affect the country but there has never been a concerted effort of that type. It's always us adapting to them.

I wondered why it was so important for us to change to accommodate a small, progressive portion of America, that isn't in the slightest bit affected by our daily practices. A lot of people who hate the War on Terror still hold us in such high regard. Is it so wrong to simply look at something different and accept it for what it is, if those differences pose no threat and positively affect the outcome for everyone? Isn't that about as American as it gets?

Either way, staying pissed about it certainly wasn't going to change the situation. If a gender rights group or a politician labeled us as barbarians, so be it. By modern standards, we are. If they were going to dictate changes, then I would have only had a few years left to enjoy the culture we had built over the last thirteen years of war. And the last three years with men like Honeycutt and Tierney, plus our stint with the State Department, had given me a preview of what a reformed military was going to look like.

Chapter 7

The Fighting Fifth

Southern California was as beautiful as advertised. Growing up in the southeast, I saw movies and read books about the famous west coast, but I never saw myself actually living there. My wife and I made the cross-country drive from Virginia with her father and our newest addition to the family. Our eldest son, Alexander, had made his debut just six months prior to driving from coast to coast.

I had taken a full 3 weeks of leave to move and physically acclimate to the hills. Forays into nearby Oceanside and the beach broke up the monotony of unpacking boxes and moving furniture. I never believed it before, but there was power and connection in nature that can truly help us appreciate everything we have. The beach, the rugged hills, and the cool ocean breeze helped me take stock of how far I had come and how much my life had changed.

The last time I was here, as a newly married young man, I hadn't even seen combat. Zach was still alive, and I was still enjoying a life lived at Mach ten. Now five years later, I had seen war and was still grappling with the effects of the experience. The violence we inflicted was never a concern to me and I had since visited the resting places for some of our Fallen. But I rarely spoke to any of my squad members from that deployment.

Despite the disconnect I felt from them, I was proud and humbled by how I'd developed. Windall, Nixon, and Elias were all nearing the end of their enlistments and they'd proven more than ready to confront the challenges of their battalions. I'd kept in touch with them as they continued their journeys and it felt good to see them go on and become great squad leaders.

I was excited about this next chapter. I looked forward to having another squad of Marines to mentor and lead and craved the challenge of earning their respect. I'd been a squad leader for nearly half a decade at this point and if Uncle Sam gave me the option to do it forever, I'd jump at the chance. The prospect of being promoted and becoming a platoon sergeant seemed so depressing and so far, removed from the interpersonal connection of a squad.

On top of it all, I was a father now, and I had no idea what I was doing. Jenn and I were young and in love and just laughing our way through the experience, learning how to adjust as best we could. So, we enjoyed the time we had knowing that soon I'd be gone again.

West coast Marines prided themselves on their physical toughness and I swore that I wasn't going to be one of the Marines that couldn't handle the transition. Coming from the East coast, we heard horror stories of 2nd Marine Division grunts moving across country, only to be broken on the hills out here. Apparently, it was a trend, so I didn't expect a warm welcome.

Despite the stereotypes, I was going to be ready. I was used to this kind of performance pressure at this point. It was normal. I felt it every time there was a change in leadership at my previous units and when I moved from 2/6 to FAST. It's a natural part of existence in a highly competitive culture like the infantry.

Being a squad leader in 2/5 was going to be my kind of challenge. I showed up midway through the pre-deployment training cycle and after a few personnel shifts, I was assigned to Golf Company, First Platoon as the first squad leader. It was a mixed bag of disgruntled, salty Lance Corporals led by a few green team leaders from the Security Forces Regiment. My experiences in Marjah with corporal Andy would prove invaluable working with them.

I felt confident. I knew how to play this game because I had just come from the same Regiment. I knew what kind of disadvantage these two were dealing with. Neither of them had been led by competent grunts who prepared them for the infantry battalions. From what they told me, their experience had been centered around fixed security operations and trying their best to not get busted down in rank. As a result, they were behind physically and tactically, which is exactly what I expected, coming from a different part of the same regiment.

The other Marines had been led by a crop of seniors not unlike mine from 2/6. They had fought in the battle of Sangin at the same time we were slugging it out in Marjah. Afterwards, they came home to finish their contracts training these Marines, before returning to civilian life. They'd passed on their expectations concerning the treatment of Boot Marines and the conduct of training, to this group that was mine now.

On top of it all, the Corps overall was in a transitional social situation. The civilian leadership had grown increasingly mettlesome in military affairs over the last several years, which placed everything we did under a microscope. The politicians had knee jerk reactions to "barbaric" practices and forced many of the changes I'd anticipated in FAST company. They had already repealed the ban on homosexuals openly serving in 2010 and since then hazing had become a high priority.

The pressure was pushed down onto general officers and all the way through to our level. Having a new Marine do pushups for dropping a rifle, harsh verbal corrections for infractions great or small, blood striping new Corporals, and even the tradition of shaving a Boot's head prior to his first deployment were declared sacrilege. The terms "Boot" and "POG" were labeled derogatory.

NCOs and billet leaders that had distinguished themselves on the battlefield were cut down in rank and forced out of the service for teaching their Marines using the same methods they had been taught with. The Honeycutts and Tyrannys had to be in heaven. In a way it did feel as if their FAST environments were being spread to the battalions, which didn't bode well for us in the next war.

The whole thing gave us a tase of how politicians view the American military institution. Washington simply refused to see the value of our culture, opting instead to remake it into an armed extension of American society. Seeing it all from start to finish, I came to the very unsettling conclusion that we had almost nothing in common with them.

While this was ongoing, the political elite worked to open all occupational specialties to women. I didn't think that any one of these impositions alone was going to amount to much change. But grouped all together in the immediate years leading up to an election, I saw it as a declaration of cultural war. One in which our politicians would abuse our trust, faith, and confidence to advance their party goals even if it meant more Americans killed in the next war.

What's more, if the generals didn't pass it down and have it enforced, they'd be relieved, and a more compliant replacement would be installed. Or so it seemed to us down at the bottom of the food chain. The same thing filtered down to us. So, we had to be more careful about how we went about enforcing discipline and training for war. It didn't make anything impossible, but it was frustrating as hell.

From my vantage point, example and accountability were the keys to existing in this newly established gray area. Preparing men for war and showing them how to build themselves into lethal, confident, proficient warfighters was still the goal. The methods had to be slightly adjusted but the end state wasn't going to change. The trick would be doing it in a manner that still maximized intensity and preserved the values of our culture, while not getting busted down.

So, this was the current state of the Corps when I showed up to 2/5 to lead this squad of Marines. The one thing we all had in common was the general disdain for all of these newly implemented policies. The disgruntled group had only known the more hard-nosed leadership approach shown to them by the Sangin veterans on the last cycle. They were disappointed with their experience because they felt they missed the war and joined up just in time for politics to water everything down. Plus, they were pissed off about being led by two Security Forces corporals- and now a Security Forces Sergeant. It was that same contempt for the Regiment that I was introduced to all those years ago and I marveled at how little some things changed and how radically others did.

Thinking back to my early days in my first unit, I empathized with their frustrations between how they had been brought up versus how protected the incoming Boots were. I also knew that having this kind of rift in a squad could prove fatal and foster further division. If left unchecked, it would paralyze the group and even the simplest of tasks wouldn't get accomplished.

The only medicine for it is to show them what right looks like. The inherent physical and mental demands of infantry life have a way of showing everyone who belongs and who doesn't all on their own. So, I decided we were going to train ourselves silly. On top of that, I was going to focus on getting these two team leaders up to standard. They needed someone to show them the true value that the warrior lifestyle holds for them, regardless of all the outside noise and things beyond our control.

Each one of them would have to decide to either let those aspects of it make them miserable or make the best out of what was in front of them. I had resolved to show them how to live this life to the fullest and hold them to an uncomfortably higher standard. The rest was up to them.

Fortunately for all of us, the company commander was a man by the name of Captain Hill, who had just completed instructor duty at the famed Infantry Officer's Course in Quantico, Virginia. While it was never officially confirmed, that meant that he would be able to attract the best graduates from that course to be our platoon commanders.

He was a well-spoken and professional man with a confidence that was based on expertise. His tall lanky build made him stand out in a sea of desert MARPAT uniforms and he had a way of transferring his confidence to all of us during tactical operations. The calm professional tone he struck starkly contrasted with his short crop of hair and hardened facial features.

What really separated him from my past commanders was the way he built the company to function. He expected the platoon commanders and squad leaders to run the show while he supported our efforts to accomplish any assigned task. "Conditions set" was his favorite term to use and he said it like a mantra. It was infused in every operation and weekend or holiday liberty brief. From his perspective, his purpose was to plan and position us to succeed under any circumstance and give us the tools we needed to win. It was never about him. Once he had put all the pieces in their proper place, he let us loose to execute and flowed to where the points of friction were.

His philosophy of "condition set leadership," as I called it, translated down to the platoon commander we received. Lieutenant Glenn was a history major from Yale University and the honor graduate from his IOC class. Built like a lean freight train, he played football for the Ivy League institution and carried himself well. He had sandy brown hair and a finely cut look about him. His physical and mental stamina were unmatched in the platoon and the proficiency he displayed in tactical operations was superior to that of the other entry level Lieutenants I had worked with previously. Clearly, IOC was putting out a much better product than it had when I had first joined, which was very encouraging.

Glenn was humble. He had a vision for the type of lethal platoon he wanted to lead, and he constantly relied on our experience as squad leaders to shape it. Physical and mental toughness were to be the foundation that supported brilliance in the basics. The relationship he and I developed was built on trust and mutual respect. This was by far the best approach to leadership I had seen by someone in his position, and it paid off.

We were free to train our squads as we saw fit and communicated directly behind closed doors. When deficiencies were identified, such as the two team leaders under my charge, he didn't micromanage the situation. It appeared to me that as I worked with those two, Glenn spent a lot of time in the background observing and learning about how to communicate with enlisted men.

The first three hours of every day in garrison were reserved for physical training, which was expected to be unreasonable by normal standards. Telephone poles were carried up the steep hills and simulated casualties were hauled about on the dirt trails. Ground fighting, gas mask runs in kit, and hikes were common practice.

Tactically, my focus was on teaching the team leaders how to lead their Marines. Their physical stamina began improving when we took to the hills daily to train in full kit. Before long, they knew where to place themselves in the formation to communicate and control critical events. They understood how to apply the concepts of suppression, movement, and mutual support.

I could see the extra hint of confidence in how they walked and heard it when they addressed their teams. They were growing and every time I saw them lead their guys in a live fire assault or at the head of the formation during a brutal workout, I felt pride beyond measure. Individual accomplishment paled in comparison to seeing them excel on their own. It was the same pride that I felt with Windall, Nixon, and Elias back in FAST company and it constantly reminded me of why I stayed in the uniform.

We deployed on the 31st Marine Expeditionary Unit in May of 2015, in good shape as a unit. The deployment itself was unremarkable from an action standpoint. It was difficult to secure training areas in

Okinawa, Japan so most of our time was spent training on softball fields and in barracks or working out for three or four hours a day. Just like being back in the states except we didn't get to see our families and enjoyed a slight bump in pay.

I grappled with decisions about my future. Watching my wife and one year old through a computer monitor forced me to question if this was worth it. Afghanistan was over for the infantry and there was no prospect of war that I could see on the horizon.

I started wondering if I really wanted to be away from them so I could drink sake and see new places. Sitting in my barracks room with my customary twelve pack of local beer, I started to add up all the time I had missed with my wife. We had been married for over 5 years and I had been away for more than half of it. I had missed her terribly on every deployment, but adding a young son to the mix made the absence sting so much more.

The positive was that I loved the infantry, even if it seemed that the larger Marine Corps was headed for dark days. I felt the challenge of true purpose every time I dropped my worn battle rig onto my shoulders and carried my weapon. Then there was the prospect of seeing young men grow into better versions of themselves and developing alongside them. Nothing compared to knowing that I was a part of that.

But as I drank my way through that line of thinking, I asked myself the fatal question: "Doesn't my son deserve that opportunity as well?"

Chapter 8

Reforming The Force

December of 2015 brought a slight chill to beautiful southern California. The air was crisp, and I had grown quite fond of the Marine layer that occasionally rolled in from the Pacific. One morning, I sat down for a quick breakfast in the Fifth Marines chow hall at Camp San Mateo.

The 31st Marine Expeditionary Unit that we had just returned from would be my final deployment. We were undergoing the typical command shake up and were about to begin the next work up for the unit to return to the Pacific for repeat tour. My good luck had held and the deployment with 2/5 was as fulfilling as any I had had.

Captain Hill had the right idea about training and the standards were set as high as they could be. To top it off, Lieutenant Glenn had fostered an environment where leaders were given the freedom they needed to train effectively, provided we played by the rules. He and I had developed a friendship founded on respect and trust that I valued before he rotated to Weapons Company, assuming command of his next platoon.

LIFE WAS SIMPLE AND BEAUTIFUL.

I shuffled through the chow line with everyone else and made small talk with a few Marines I knew before settling into a seat in front of a large flat screen. We were awaiting an important announcement from Secretary of Defense Ash Carter. I knew what was coming but still held out hope that I was wrong.

The political efforts to reshape the armed forces into a mirror image of civilian society had been kicked into overdrive during the preceding months. With all of the talk centering around the shifting policies, it seemed that the Obama administration was dead set on making any change they could, even if it came at the price of unnecessary deaths in future conflicts. The whole thing had been twisted into a morally just crusade.

Reducing the number of sexual assaults and hazing incidents had been harped on for years just like the repeal of the "Don't Ask, Don't Tell" policy prior to. The exclusion of women from combat arms specialties had been the hot topic afterwards.

Media outlets and activists worked with politicians and collectively labeled the rule as an unfair and archaic practice of a primitive institution fueled by "toxic masculinity." One of former Secretary Carter's predecessors, Leon Panetta, was the first to announce the change in early January of 2013 before handing over the reins the following month to Chuck Hagel, which positioned Carter to be the one to make it official.

Since then, the Marine Corps had assembled the Ground Combat Element Integrated Task Force, which constructed a unit modeled after the Battalion Landing Team traditionally employed on Marine Expeditionary Units. From July of 2014 to July of 2015, the ad hoc force performed various individual and unit training tasks common to several combat arms specialties.

Within the task force, there was an all-male infantry element and a mixed gender unit performing the same live fire ranges, the same movements under the same loads and time constraints, and so on.

The intent was to produce comparative data to present to the powers that be prior to a decision being made.

The importance of this experiment and its data highlighted the different approaches taken by the Obama administration and top military leadership. The former viewed the whole endeavor through a narrow lens of political capital and social reconciliation. The latter was bound by duty to offer their best military advice, then carry out the decision, personal feelings aside.

The study was a far-from-complete examination of the duties performed by the occupations that were selected, including the infantry. High attrition rates due to injuries or voluntary exit from the unit contributed to unpredictable and volatile personnel availability, which limited the conduct and repetition of certain events. The tasks themselves were selected based on a number of factors including, "those that were of a limited duration (maximum of several hours to complete) due to the requirement that tasks be repeatable in the form of experimental trials."[2]

So, the study included intermittent breaks that allowed the Marines to recover physically and psychologically. That's not always feasible in combat due to its unpredictable nature. No matter how hard the previous patrol was, how difficult the terrain, how vicious the fire fight, who was killed or wounded, or whatever family issues arise back home, the next fight is right around the corner.

The reality of infantry operations in our war was that in between patrols our outposts were attacked, we stood hours and hours of post, were called up as a quick reaction force, or any combination thereof. Stack on top of all that the relentless tempo that limited most of us to a mere four hours of sleep at best, and it's clear that breaks, both mental and physical, were very rare and largely dependent on unpredictable enemy action.

During the study's phase of squad level attacks, conducted by mixed gender and all male groups comparatively, the results revealed that women were outperformed. They were slower in covering distance and negotiating obstacles with a 35-pound load and less accurate than males with the M4, M27, and M16 with mounted M203 grenade launcher by margins of 2 percent to 20 percent, depending on the weapon system. The gap in movement speeds between males and females increased in the mixed gender machine gun and mortar groups that carried more weight.

All this was conducted in a simulated combat environment free of sleep deprivation, malnutrition, or cumulative fatigue from previous operations- all of which are significant factors in combat. On top of that the average load carried by most Grunts in combat will at least double, if not triple in weight compared to the task force's 35 pounds. This specific scenario was more ideal than realistic and even in that environment, mixed gender squads failed to shoot and move as effectively as all male squads.[3]

Whether it's by 99 percent or 0.01 percent, or a speed of one second versus one hour, less lethal is just that and accepting this decrease in combat power as "marginal" or "manageable" is arrogant.

The experiment concluded that:

"The female Marines integrated into the closed MOS units demonstrated that they are capable of performing the physically demanding tasks, but not necessarily at the same level as their male counterparts in terms of performance, fatigue, workload, or cohesion.

"Integrated units, compared with all-male units, showed degradations in the time to complete tasks, move under load, and achieve timely effects on target. The size of the differences observed between units and tasks varied widely. The more telling aspect of the comparisons is the cumulative impacts. The pace, timing, and accuracy of any singular task is not necessarily important, but taken together, and in the context of actual combat operations, the cumulative differences can lead to substantial effects on the unit, and the unit's ability to accomplish the mission.

"Gender and MOS type are the best predictors of occupational injuries. In particular, we found that females are more likely to incur occupational injuries, resulting in reduced readiness compared to their male counterparts. Males, on the other hand, are more likely to incur non-occupational injuries. Additionally, Marines in vehicle MOSs tended to have lower injury rates than those in MOSs that march (i.e., foot mobile) or Artillery MOSs.[4"]

Another important factor in this whole debacle is that the majority of notable people who promoted gender integration in the first place, such as former SECDEFs Leon Panetta and Ash Carter or President Barak Obama have either never seen combat or spent any amount of time wearing a uniform, much less in the infantry. They don't know our capabilities or understand our cultural values and how that impacts battlefield performance.

It appeared to me that the biggest barriers between civil society and us are a lack of understanding for one another and acceptance of the differences, once understood.

A few minutes after I had salted the spongy powdered eggs and taken a few bites, the Secretary began his statement by offering condolences to the victims of the San Bernardino shooting and proceeded to announce that he was ordering the services to open all occupational specialties to females. I listened intently, struggling to control my bearing as this man reduced the last decade and a half of tactical warfighting success to a massive equal opportunity statement in a matter of fifteen minutes, before opening the floor to questions. The facility buzzed with whispered conversations that drowned out the reporter's inquiries.

I had lost my appetite. I stowed my tray full of food and proceeded to the exit, exchanging a mix of disheartened and enraged glances with the few combat veterans who had just seen and understood the gravity of what had happened.

As I stepped back out into the California sun and felt the cool air rush over me, my stomach turned cold, and I wondered why this had happened. I asked myself, "Had we really failed so miserably that this is what the country thought was necessary for us to win? Was this all the last near-decade of my life was going to amount to? What about those that had done so much more than I had? What about our Fallen and their families?"

If history is truly written by the victor, then our identity as a fighting force was in danger of being overwritten. A vague image came into thought of museums that displayed a timeline of our war ending in this announcement. The implication being that this was what we had fought for. It wouldn't be the culture founded on discipline, toughness, selflessness, proficiency, lethality, and example that we built and developed in.

They would replace that with a label of the generation that fostered diversity and inclusion. Sure, it would take years for that to come to fruition but eventually, maybe even in our lifetime, it was more than likely going to happen.

I proceeded down the sidewalk towards the Company office for the daily platoon sergeant's meeting and thought back to my time in places like Marjah, living without basic hygiene and privacy, constantly patrolling and fighting. I remembered what it was like to try and scarf down a meal next to one of my squad mates defecating in an ammo can and the dysentery that plagued us all.

The memories of pushing my body beyond the normal expectation of extremes came next. I relived the burning in my heaving lungs and the intimate feeling of the weight on my shoulders while enemy rifle rounds ripped past my face.

Finally, the training operations in truly desolate places like Australia and Saudi Arabia came to mind. How could *anyone* in their right mind think that that putting women in that type of environment was a good idea?

I stopped for a moment beneath the ladder well of the Golf company's office building and looked behind me to First Sergeant's Hill, one of the most humbling and sacred places in the world to us. I wondered what those men memorialized atop would think about all this.

The hill bears a six-foot tall cross for every Marine killed in the War on Terror that belonged to Fifth Marine Regiment and 1st Combat Engineer Battalion. The first time I made the treacherous climb to the top, the breath left my lungs. Never had I seen such an awesome sight. The simple crosses adorned with an inscription for the Marines they commemorated looked down on us as a reminder of our legacy and those who had come before.

I thought of the culture I had been a part of, and that was now part of me, for the past eight years; the way we conducted ourselves as professionals and confronted our weaknesses, and how we defined a man's worth based on his contribution to the team. We prioritized the infantry values over comfort and emotions.

Before I stepped inside, I recognized the fact that the political vision of the Armed Forces of the future and the culture that we had built and fought for were irreconcilable. They wanted an institution that valued diversity, inclusion, and individual gratification over lethality and the internal development that our culture fostered.

The next day there wasn't a single combat veteran around who didn't have a hangover. The previous night was one of those rare occasions when we realized that all our accomplishments and progress were but small droplets of water in a very large ocean and a certain amount of futility forever accompanied them. We could secure every Afghan or Iraqi village, give a pack of crayons and a coloring book to every child, kill every terrorist, and install democracy the world over, but if people on the outside wanted more, whether they knew what they were demanding or not, they would simply take it.

We had pledged our honor as men to submit to civilian authority when we signed the contract in keeping with tradition of the American military institution, whether we liked it or not. And that was it. It was clear that the current class of politician had no qualms with abusing the trust we placed in them and our willing submission to civilian authority.

There was a small consolation in that General Joe Dunford, serving as the Chairman of the Joint Chiefs of Staff, requested that the Infantry and a few other specialties be exempt. At least he did *something*, in stark contrast to the other service heads.

I had made my decision about what to do in this situation, long before it came to pass. All that was left was to follow through. So, I denied orders to become a combat instructor at the School of Infantry and declined to reenlist the following day, which was the easy part.

The last, and most important part was to help prepare the Marines to carry the torch, which was now more crucial than ever. It was a challenge I relished and pursued relentlessly. Now that I had an expiration date, everything took on a more critical meaning. Even the simplest of tasks were accompanied by a heightened sense of urgency.

Taking all the reforms into account, I realized that there wasn't a damn thing I could do about it. Enlisted men enforce policy while officers- or in this case, politicians- make it. It was completely beyond my control, and I had to accept that as a condition of my honor, affirmed when I took the oath of enlistment.

The debate over whether or not any of the reforms should be implemented, or how it should be done was over. Railing against the inevitable would accomplish nothing. The real question now was could we maintain tactical dominance on the battlefield with all these policies in place? And only the results of the next war were going to provide those answers.

My last big adventure in the Corps came in January of 2016, and I was determined to be proud of how I left the service. I wasn't going to shirk responsibility just because I had chosen to move on to the next chapter of my life. I had seen that from others over the years and it always set the precedent for a poor attitude in some of the Marines that still had time on contract. I wanted this last group to be committed to preserving our culture amidst all the changes that were inevitably coming. Crying and bitching about it wouldn't accomplish anything and I reminded myself that feelings meant nothing. It was time to go to work.

In hindsight, this last stretch of my career may have been the most fun that I ever had. We got a platoon sergeant, Staff Sergeant Dash, who understood the infantry. A veteran of the Ramadi fight in Iraq, he possessed intimate knowledge of night operations that highlighted his experience. The appreciation for patrolling and fighting in the dark, and using the technology that aids it, is one of the generational quirks that makes the Iraq veterans differ slightly from those of us who only fought in Afghanistan.

He was tough as nails and he matched the shared I placed on hard, realistic training, brutal honesty among men, professionalism, proficiency, and lethality before all else. My sole purpose in life until I left Camp Pendleton for the last time was to pass on every bit of knowledge and experience that I had. And together, Dash and I were going to milk everything we could out of this opportunity.

The Company was still undergoing the usual personnel shuffle and we hadn't been assigned an officer. That meant that Dash would be the acting platoon commander and I would stand in as platoon sergeant. We designated the squad and team leaders based on experience and who was going to deploy with the unit.

With the organization set, we took to the hills to train, ramping up the intensity significantly. There wasn't any time to ease into it because our thirty-man platoon, comprised entirely of enlisted men and one corpsman, was going north for mountain warfare training in a matter of weeks.

Bridgeport, California displayed an opposing type of beauty to the beaches and palm trees of the southern half of the state. As we drove north, the hills grew into the snowcapped Sierra Nevada mountains, covered with pine trees. It was breathtaking and intimidating.

Over the years, I heard mixed reviews about the Marine Corps Mountain Warfare Training Center. Some lauded it as the best training experience they'd had while others told stories of how the rugged terrain and thin air broke men's wills.

The anticipation was palpable on the charter bus as we made our way towards the infamous training site.

The first week was filled with cookie cutter training in typical Marine Corps fashion. Each morning we hiked out, every time to a slightly more distant area, to receive survival classes and acclimate to the elevation. It didn't take long for the stragglers to identify themselves. There were only a handful of them but once the first one fell behind on that first morning hike, the rest followed quickly. Within the first three days, the ones who didn't have the right mindset feigned injury or simply accepted whatever administrative punishment to avoid embarking on the real journey with the rest of us.

In the frozen squad bays, they stood there looking on in shocked horror as we tore into their gear, stripping everything useful with laughter and excitement. Based on our jovial expressions of good fortune, a casual bystander may have thought that we'd just won the lottery. The second that a Marine called it quits, a swarm of others would gleefully descend on the pile of tactical treasures to claim a pair of snowshoes, boots, or survival rations to keep handy during the next phase.

It wasn't personal. There wasn't any deep animosity or Machiavellian conspiracy to make Marines want to quit. It was much more practical. Approaching training as critical preparation for war, we preferred to trim the fat here instead of overseas where casualties would be inevitable.

With each of them, a conversation was always had to remind

them of how they could contribute and develop. It was made very clear that once they made their decision, they'd have to live with it. Everyone felt the invisible force of excitement mixed with anxiety. These few simply didn't make the decision to accept it as a natural human reaction and resolve to move forward despite it.

The sad truth was that while they had let themselves and us down, the Corps' personnel policies wouldn't allow us to kick them out of the infantry for refusing to train. They'd stay here in the comfort and safety of lower base camp while the rest of us braved the mountains and approaching winter storm. Sure, they'd receive negative paperwork in their service record, but ultimately, they'd be allowed to deploy where any number of unforeseen circumstances could put lives in their hands. It was ludicrous. Situations like this made me envy the special operations community for their staunch will to maintain their forces internally, free of the bureaucracy that hampered the larger Marine Corps. In their world, if a man couldn't pull his weight, he went somewhere else where he couldn't potentially endanger the safety and effectiveness of the team.

The mountains were truly a grand sight to behold. We marched at a slow pace in tactical column on the sides of an unimproved road, elevating with every step as lower base camp disappeared behind us.

Our standard MARPAT utilities and boots were substituted for uniforms tailored to the terrain. We wore the issued water-resistant shell top and bottom, light chest rigs with no armor plates, and Kevlar helmets. Over top, we sported light white camouflage coverings and gigantic, poorly fitted snowshoes known as "mickey mouse boots." They were heavy and awkward but durable enough to endure the rocks and keep moisture out. The trouble with them was they had no ventilation, so socks had to be changed more frequently and recycled without washing. All said, with kit, weapons, water, and cross-country skis attached to our packs, each man was carrying around sixty to seventy pounds.

During the marches I took the traditional post for Platoon Sergeants towards the rear of the formation to catch any stragglers. Dash led from up front and the squad leaders moved freely monitoring their Marines as we climbed higher and higher.

Mountain training was a very different experience all together. Not just because of how much the terrain dictated movement, but just in terms of general hygiene. Nothing could be left behind, meaning that trash from rations and fecal matter had to be packed, too. We each carried four white and silver "wag bags" that looked like they belonged on a space shuttle mission to defecate in. Once Nature's call had been heeded, they were strapped to the outside of the ruck until the Company Gunnery Sergeant could collect them all from every man and haul them down to lower base camp.

Chap stick and sunglasses were as valuable as gold to prevent burns from the sunlight's reflection off the snow. There was about three feet on the ground, which had rolled in the night before we left camp for this last three-week phase of training. Enough continued to fall periodically to keep the mountains blanketed for the entire evolution, which would culminate in a force-on-force exercise, pitting us against a platoon of Army Rangers.

Dash and I relished the opportunity. Live fire training is invaluable, but it's inherently limited in terms of human simulation. Paper targets don't shoot back or think. Force-on-force meant we got to maneuver against a living, trained, reasoning element that was just as unpredictable as us. Going head-to-head with a worthy adversary in the Rangers heightened the adventurous nature of the whole operation.

As we progressed through the first two weeks, I could see the accelerated development of our young platoon. There were only a handful of us who had deployed at all, and only three of us were combat veterans. Ninety percent of the platoon had graduated from Infantry School not even six months ago and a few of them had come to the Company the week before we left Pendleton. This was their first legitimate field operation in the Marine Corps, which was a hell of a way to start things off. I didn't envy them.

The emotional roller coaster that comes with being a Boot Marine was challenging enough for any young man. But being thrown right into brutal mountain warfare training heightened everything for them. It was like asking a middle school athlete to compete on the collegiate level, but with mortal consequence.

I could see the nervousness on their shivering, reddened faces as we trudged up the steep inclines. Every one of them struggled but only a few made the poor decision to focus on their pain and fall behind the formation, which surprised me. Back at lower base camp I anticipated a high number of stragglers, but they had surprised me.

Each time we moved along a narrow cut in the mountains, their expressions turned fearful. A wrong step could end in a very long and violent tumble with permanent repercussions and their demeanor conveyed the sense that every one of them understood the stakes as we negotiated the natural obstacles with caution.

Heat casualties grew as we hiked from one training area to another. A great deal had been made about it before we left the camp, and I had thought it odd that overheating was such a concern. We were climbing in and out of snow every day and the elevation was over 6,500 feet above sea level. Until now, I didn't know how much harder the human body had to work simply to exist in a cold environment. The elevation complicated it. Every basic human function from walking, breathing, and taking a shit was more taxing. Adding to all that, we were hiking up mountains, cross country skiing, and negotiating sheer face ledges with weapons and gear day in and day out.

For the Marines that had just showed up to the unit, the mental toll was heavy. To them, this is what the infantry had in store for them for the next four years. They didn't realize that Bridgeport wasn't a novice level exercise. Dash and I loved the scenario because we knew that the ones who didn't quit would be hardened steel at the end of it all. It was a way to trim the fat as we climbed, slid, and patrolled in the most challenging and painfully beautiful environment I'd ever seen.

I thought about Hannibal, the famous Carthaginian general who invaded Rome through the Alps in the Autumn of 218 B.C. Every time I doubted whether our young Marines could last, the example of Hannibal's army reminded me that grunts had been performing incredible feats for thousands of years. We were carrying the torch of martial development.

One Marine particularly stood out. Corporal Wick, now a squad leader, had deployed with us on the last MEU. He was a product of the savvy hard-nosed Sangin veterans that preceded my arrival to 2/5. During the last deployment, I saw in him a young man that was deeply disappointed in the fact that he hadn't gone to war. Acknowledging the fact that he had no control over it didn't help. He was impressionable and seemed bitter.

But after we got home and many of his friends processed out of the Marine Corps, something changed in him. He would've given anything to move on to civilian life, like his buddies, but his core values kept him going. Quitting simply wasn't a part of his identity. So, begrudgingly, he accepted his responsibilities as a squad leader and resolved to do his best.

Wick's journey is a testament to his character and to the personal development that infantry culture drives in young men. Our Boot Marines, many still being field broken, drew the necessary motivation to power through the snow and endure the cold discomfort of the mountains because of his example. His desire to return to civilian life was no secret, yet he was always leading from the front and holding himself to a higher standard.

In our private conversations I encouraged him to remain focused on the prize at the end of his time in uniform. I wanted him to know that I was proud of his progress, but more importantly, that he could be proud of it for the rest of his life if he finished the race with honor.

As we progressed through the training, the terminal mood of the platoon gave way to quite confidence. Moving past the basic training of the first two weeks, the instructor staff started running us through tactical exercises in between the long marches. We had hiked roughly thirty kilometers and were poised to kick off our little three-day war against the Rangers.

The company held up in a defensive position for a day so we could construct a terrain model and receive an operations order from the staff. From this point on, the environment was strictly tactical, meaning we could be attacked at any time.

Rehearsals and planning complete, we stepped off from the site under cover of darkness heading to another defensive position.

The terrain became more treacherous, and we found ourselves moving tactically against the snow and ice that blanketed the rocks. Several times, we had to slide down steep slopes. Kneeling at the top of each one, I counted the Marines as they went by, falling back on their rucks to speed down the slopes on their backsides like a stream of overturned tactical penguins. Following them down, the rush that came over me was exhilarating. It reminded me of some of the action movies I'd seen as a kid.

We settled into our defensive posture a few hours before sunrise. The falling snow had ceased, and the moonlight provided excellent illumination through our night vision goggles. It hadn't been easy going but the Marines had held up well.

Dash and I moved to each position after the squad leaders had done their checks and verified the sectors of fire. The guns were interlocked, and everyone was alert. The company position was established with third platoon to our right and second on our left flank, their lines wrapping back behind ours to tie together. From the air, it would've resembled a bold U shape with a less severe curve.

Just before sunrise, the action kicked off. From my position on the far left of our lines I heard the frantic alarm sounded by one of our Lieutenants. It was too late for that. The Rangers had infiltrated.

Looking over my right shoulder to where the headquarters element was stationed, three of them emerged, spitting blank fire from raised rifles beneath the two green circles that illuminated their faces from their night vision.

They had achieved surprise and what's more, they were sporting the same loose white camouflage that we wore, making it difficult to distinguish them from our own troops. As they advanced, third platoon adjusted a machinegun and laid down a hail of fire to simulate the killing that ended the affair. The guns fell silent, and Marines went through the process of verifying the dead and sweeping them for intelligence.

The enemy had done well infiltrating and inflicting heavy casualties. Had it been a real engagement, our company would have quite a few widows to console. As the bodies were searched, one of the "dead" Rangers looked up and sarcastically reminded us that soon we would be doing the same thing to them. I chuckled at the nonchalance of the man laying in the snow. It was just the nature of force-on-force training, and we all accepted it with a sense of futility and dark humor.

The instructors furnished the next destination to our command and less than an hour later, we were on the move again, zigzagging our way up the steep surfaces amidst sporadic contact with our enemy. Several hours into it, they opened fire from an adjacent mountain. A steep draw between us and them prevented maneuver, prompting us to respond with machineguns to simulate suppression and close air support or artillery.

I exchanged dark chuckles with Dash and the squad leaders every time the guns fired. A member of the staff, clad in his signature orange interceptor vest, called a halt to the action to let us know we had "killed" them all. This time it would've been the Rangers' turn to comfort the grieving.

The hours passed and the action ebbed and flowed.

The constructed scenario came to a head on day three, with our platoon atop a very dangerous peak, overlooking the rest of the company in a defensive position. The snow had resumed with a vengeance hours before we separated from the company.

The climb up had been hard. I was more worried about one of our Marines slipping and bouncing off the jagged rocks to end up as a giant, mangled red stain at the bottom. The incline was steep, almost a sheer face with craggy rocks jutting up every which way like angry frozen stalagmites. Visibility had been reduced to about ten yards due to the falling snow and the temperature was so low that we didn't care about being cold anymore.

We were serving as overwatch for the rest of the company below. This was the most prominent piece of terrain nearby, and we suspected our new Company Commander wanted to further evaluate his young officers, hence the reason for our deportation to what we now called "The Lonely Mountain." We appreciated the task, even with the especially arduous climb. Being the only enlisted-led platoon, we accepted it with our typical dark humor as a band of misfits being exiled. Once high atop our new perch, I checked the GPS strapped to my wrist and chuckled at the elevation reading of just under 9,000 feet.

The Marines had done well, mostly. I saw the contempt for discomfort and pain on their reddened faces, covered with frozen snot or sweat stained balaclavas. The brand-new gear they had received weeks before was now held together with cord and tape.

We were a ragged bunch but hardened. They were learning what they were truly capable of and that was the invaluable part of the whole experience.

I took just a moment to myself while traversing the maze of rocks and crevices to appreciate the moment. The snowfall had lessened, and the clouds had risen slightly to reveal the most beautiful sunrise I'd ever seen. The distant star, too low to shine on the company below, painted the sky orange and yellow beneath the dark clouds. Cradling my rifle, I took a seat in the snow and drew in a deep breath with only the sound of the howling wind to accompany my thoughts. I was entranced by the beauty of it all; not just the promising sunrise before me, but by the internal triumph for our boys.

I looked left to the small four-man tent housing corporal Wick and turned my gaze back to the morning light, beaming with pride of my own at seeing him grow into such a mature young man. It was all the evidence I needed to know that everything had been worth it. What we had built, during our nation's longest war, wasn't toxic and oppressive like some outsiders had made it out to be. And it wasn't founded on arrogance or sentimentality.

It was a culture that held the values of discipline and toughness in such high regard that it facilitated the development of lethality and proficiency. The sacrifice and challenge of the infantry lifestyle brought out selflessness from within and afforded us the opportunity to craft our own examples. This was the path to true development and there was a special magnetism that attracted each of us to it and to each other. I marveled at it all and I knew that I was forever changed for the better.

After we returned to Pendleton, my time was split between completing the multitude of administrative tasks required for me to leave the service and training with the Marines. I knew that I had put the process off as long as I could, and now it was going to take time away from everything else.

When Easter rolled around, my wife and I set up an egg hunt in our small front yard. Laughing and marveling at our son, still figuring out how to walk, we enjoyed one of the fondest memories we would make in this stage of our life together. The last egg, which my wife suspiciously encouraged me to pick up, contained a small strip of paper in her handwriting that read "Blackwell baby #2 November 2016."

We were so happy, even with all the uncertainty ahead.

I strode up to company formation the following morning to deliver the good word only to find that Dash had beat me to the punch. His wife was also expecting, he had just learned. After handshakes and well wishes were extended it was back to business.

They had a deployment to prepare for and I would be back in Tennessee before the end of the year.

I loved teaching Grunts. From my early days as a team leader onward it was the most rewarding aspect of this lifestyle. Every opportunity to give them something out of my toolbox also provided me with a chance to learn from them and I was reminded of the old saying, iron sharpens iron.

I focused on the squad leaders because I'd accrued three-quarters of my experience in that role and for the next seven months, the only time I wasn't with them was when some arbitrary administrative obligation of the separation process pulled me away.

In the final phase, all exiting service members are required to attend a weeklong event called the Transition Readiness Seminar. Very early on, it seemed that the whole thing was a liability program so "important" people could say they prepared us for reintegration into normal society. It reaffirmed the fact that we were such opposites to our civilian counterparts, and other service members. The mere existence of the course was confirmation of a culture gap.

There were a small handful of us from the infantry and I noticed just how easily and enthusiastically everyone else chugged the Kool-Aid. It seemed that they were returning from an unnecessarily long vacation, while we were being shot into space like monkeys in a beat-up tin can.

Aside from the single job fair and resume preparation workshops, it was a full week wasted on telling us how to dress, how not to swear, how to conduct an interview, and how to not commit suicide. The implied message was that we needed to overwrite the warriors we had become, as a matter of survival in the real world. Listening to the instructors, I thought that everyone would've been much better off if we all just accepted that we would never be normal again and that there was absolutely nothing wrong with that. The frustrating part was that I was losing time I could've spent with the platoon.

Shortly thereafter, and seemingly all too soon, the day finally came for me to leave what I believed to be the best part of America to the men who would carry our legacy forward. I could not have been prouder of them. We had trained, bled, suffered, worked, played and bonded together. The only thing I could've asked for was the opportunity to go to war with them. We would have destroyed any enemy in front of us.

This last group gave me hope because they were tough, hungry, and held close the infantry values, understanding full well that, while combat wasn't on the table, they still had a worthy and challenging endeavor in front of them. A new war would be fought for the preservation of our culture. Real and fabricated information would replace bullets and bombs and the example that they set would be their means of defense. It wasn't the fight we wanted but we rarely got to choose that.

I hoped that our countrymen could learn from us to remember that emotions can be put aside to work together for something better, instead of angrily demanding change just because something was different. I believed that we could still learn from one another and understand each other if we demonstrate the maturity and will to do so.

As time passes, our generation of warriors will be studied, judged, and packaged neatly to be placed on a shelf in history's library next to our predecessors. As future generations look back at us and those that came before, will they revere our commitment, dedication, performance, and our identity? Will they see us as an example of what America stands for instead of what it was or has become? Will they accept the implicit challenge of our culture and battlefield performance to *earn* something that is greater than a college degree, wealth, or social status?

When push comes to shove, Americans will need a force of lethal savages to remind our enemies that while they may observe strife and discord from afar, when it comes down to the close fight, they will not be facing the politicians, activists, or virtue signalers. It is the fighting man who will locate, close with, and destroy them without hesitation or apology. And they will relish the preparation for it within a culture that has been validated by over two hundred and forty-five years of warfighting success.

For this part of American history, we were the men in the arena. We craved more than an average life and found it in the infantry. Meeting that challenge and the development that came from it showed us who we were and what we are capable of. We earned that critical knowledge, suffering in the mud under the combat load and fighting abroad. That is our example and our legacy.

For all the blood that the Infantrymen has shed from Baghdad to Fallujah and Ramadi, from Marjah to Sangin and everywhere we have fought in the Global War on Terror, remember us for who we are, not as liberators and protectors or champions of equality and inclusion, but as Savages.

Epilogue

2016 marked the beginning of a very critical phase in my life. I was drowning in the unfulfilling corporate job described in the opening chapter and developed an impulsive drinking habit. I let it go on for two years until eventually I noticed the negative effects on my attitude. Fueled by the alcohol, I had become bitter and entitled, thinking that I deserved more out of life because of what I had done in the Corps.

The excessive weight gained as a result starkly contrasted with my self-image of the warrior I had been. Over time, I resented my situation and directed that towards my family until it became unbearable for all of us.

I got back in shape and secured contract work in Kabul, Afghanistan which required sobriety, and finished the first draft of this book. After a year, I realized that watching my family through screens wasn't how I wanted to spend my life and returned home months prior to the disastrous withdrawal of American forces.

Despite my sobriety, I slowly slipped into a state of depression and misery, working sixty-five hours a week at another job that didn't align with who I was meant to be. The fact is, I hadn't even dedicated time explore who that man was. And that's where I had gone wrong.

It wasn't until 2022, when I reached a low point of depression, anger, and futile frustration, that I acknowledged the fact that I needed to make deep, life-altering changes. I looked at the previous years of self-loathing and poor decisions and noticed that I had followed the path that others had laid out for me. I jumped at the first job I could get my hands on, stopped working out, got fat, and relied on alcohol to numb the effects of my unhappiness. Internally, I justified it by telling myself that this is what was expected of veterans after we became civilians again. I had sold myself the lie that it was okay to be that guy because I'd seen other combat veterans do it. On top of that, I barely slept, choosing instead to burn my meager off time on social media surfing and ingesting the victimhood narrative from outside influences.

I had surrendered my free will to people I didn't know and subconsciously allowed them to direct my thoughts.

Once I realized this, and the fact that it would destroy my family if left unchecked, I decided to sacrifice whatever was necessary to change my life. My wife and kids deserved better and so did I. What I needed now was direction, I was missing the "how" of it all. So, I traded the influences that dominated my time and thoughts for a small tribe of others who were committed to development.

That started the snowball of revelations that led me to a completely different perspective. And for the first time in six years, I felt the same spark and fire that I had known as an infantryman. Discipline and determination became my foundational core values.

As I shed pounds in the gym and devoted my time to personal study, my demeanor reflected a change in attitude. The visible lean physique that I began crafting was an outward result of the internal development that I had been craving but had denied myself for those six years.

I realized that I never needed to overwrite the warrior that I had become. I wasn't meant to be a cog in the giant wheel of corporate

America or to have my thinking and direction dictated to me. It was my responsibility to become the best version of myself and that is what I committed myself to.

It has been nearly a year since I began this extraordinary course correction and what I've learned is that the foundation of who I am was established by my parents and then refined in the infantry. The values of discipline, toughness, lethality, selflessness, proficiency, and example are what helped me claw my way out of the prison that I'd created to become something more.

In less than a year, I had restructured my entire life. Instead of accepting that it was okay to be a drunken, dependent, bitter combat veteran I have accepted the reality that my life and my happiness are my responsibility alone. Instead of justifying a lazy pleasure-centric lifestyle based on the media or popular sentiment, I chose a path of discipline, perseverance, and challenge.

These decisions, and the daily work they translate into, are the true exercise of free will and the pursuit of the American dream. I have a responsibility and a deep desire to share this knowledge with as many people as I can.

Because of all this, the learning from the lows and highs of my experience, I have finished this book and found true fulfillment in development, my family, and coaching. A life spent constantly striving for self-mastery and helping others develop is the life that I have chosen to live on my own terms. And the best part is that it only ends in death. I will live every moment of that journey to the fullest.

Discipline
Toughness
Selflessness
Lethality
Proficiency
Example

Acknowledgments

As with any great endeavor, this work would not be possible without the help and support of a few wonderful people. My wife's love and spirit have reminded me to celebrate the small victories and enjoy the journey. Our two boys, who inherited her curiosity, have always had a way of asking the questions that I needed to answer throughout this process. The happiness and challenge that they have given me is inspiring and I am beyond fortunate to be able to share my life with them.

My parents, who spent many sleepless nights concerned for my safety, have moved me with their unwavering support. Their unconditional love, care, and sacrifice built the foundation of the man I am today.

As I wrote this, over a decade after the events described, it dawned on me just how fortunate I am to have been surrounded by such great people. The men that I fought with are some of the best that I have ever known. To them, I extend my deepest gratitude and respect for delivering me safely back home, a much better man than the one that left.

Throughout the many drafts, I had the meeting new people and reconnecting with old friends who volunteered their time and energy to help. My sincere thanks to Adam and Lucas for this.

Cliff Foreman, Chris Nelson, David Snipes, and Sam Coffee have been guiding influences that, on many occasions, had the courage to challenge my points and kept me moving forward with integrity. These friendships were developed in the infantry, and I am grateful to them for their example.

My editor, Nora Gaskin Esthimer provided the type of necessary insight and deep examination that facilitated its completion. Her skill and understanding are truly amazing.

Lastly, during a very critical time in my life- after my service- I crossed paths with Nick, Josh, and a wonderful tribe of people committed to becoming the best versions of themselves. Most of them have never served. And yet they stoked the fire within me that propelled me to discover my purpose in life and complete this labor. To them, I am forever grateful and inspired.

Thank you.

Notes

Afghanistan

1. McChrystal, Stanley A. My Share of the Task: a Memoir. Portfolio/Penguin, 2014.

Reforming the Force

1. Ground Combat Element Integrated Task Force, USMC. "Experimental Assessment Report." Line of Effort 3 GCEITF, 14 Aug. 2015, dod.defense.gov/Portals/1/Documents/wisr-studies/USMC%20-%20Line%20Of%20Effort%203%20GCEITF%20Experimental%20Assessment%20Report2.pdf.
2. Ground Combat Element Integrated Task Force. Limitations. 6.
3. Ground Combat Element Integrated Task Force. 54.
4. Ground Combat Element Integrated Task Force. 75.

About the Author

Stew Blackwell enlisted in the US Marine Corps right out of high school and deployed six times, including a combat tour to Marjah, Afghanistan, a rapid response mission to Sana'a, Yemen, Guantanamo Bay, and multiple Marine Expeditionary Units. He retired from active duty in 2016, after just under ten years of service. After returning to civilian life, Stew sought out contract employment overseas at the US Embassy and the international airport in Kabul, Afghanistan. He currently lives in Mississippi with his wife and two sons.

In his debut book, *Savages*, Blackwell examines the culture of the small unit warfighter during the Global War on Terror's *Enduring Freedom* Campaign. His mission was to elevate the understanding of the armed forces for readers by presenting a view of military culture which is based on his years of experience and extensive research. Blackwell presents the legacy of the small unit warrior from his own experience in hopes that it will help aid in understanding this culture.

Blackwell started at the beginning and defined the infantry as it is to those within it, complete with its own value system that directly contributes to the success of the force where it matters most—the battlefield. By describing key events in training and in Afghanistan, he immerses the reader in a vastly different society that values hardship, suffering, and deep, life-altering personal development over comfort and self-preservation. He brings to light the monumental differences between the roles of grunts and everyone else, as well as how the two groups were employed throughout the war, which can contrast starkly with how many civilians view them.

About the Publisher
TACTICAL 16

Tactical 16 Publishing is an unconventional publisher that understands the therapeutic value inherent in writing. We help veterans, first responders, and their families and friends to tell their stories using their words.

We are on a mission to capture the history of America's heroes: stories about sacrifices during chaos, humor amid tragedy, and victories learned from experiences not readily recreated — real stories from real people.

Tactical 16 has published books in leadership, business, fiction, and children's genres. We produce all types of works, from self-help to memoirs that preserve unique stories not yet told.

You don't have to be a polished author to join our ranks. If you can write with passion and be unapologetic, we want to talk. Go to Tactical16.com to contact us and to learn more.

All of Tactical 16's books are available on our online bookstore, T16Books.com. Visit it today to see more books from our selection of authors and to find a new adventure to read!

HOP ON HOP OFF

A Collection of Life Lessons &
Trade Secrets for Aspiring Leaders

A journey through the creative
chaos of manufacturing

V. MURALI

notionpress
.com

INDIA · SINGAPORE · MALAYSIA

ISBN 979-8-88783-530-3